Arthur Young, William Strahan

The Farmer's Tour Through The East Of England

Arthur Young, William Strahan

The Farmer's Tour Through The East Of England

ISBN/EAN: 9783741118319

Manufactured in Europe, USA, Canada, Australia, Japa

Cover: Foto ©Andreas Hilbeck / pixelio.de

Manufactured and distributed by brebook publishing software (www.brebook.com)

Arthur Young, William Strahan

The Farmer's Tour Through The East Of England

THE
FARMER's TOUR
THROUGH THE
EAST of ENGLAND.

BEING

The Register of a Journey through various Counties of this Kingdom, to enquire into the State of AGRICULTURE, &c.

CONTAINING,

I. The particular Methods of cultivating the Soil.
II. The Conduct of live Stock, and the modern System of Breeding.
III. The State of Population, the Poor, Labour, Provisions, &c.
IV. The Rental and Value of the Soil, and its Division into Farms, with various Circumstances attending their Size and State.
V. The Minutes of above five hundred original Experiments, communicated by several of the Nobility, Gentry, &c.

WITH

Other Subjects that tend to explain the present State of ENGLISH HUSBANDRY.

By the Author of the FARMER'S LETTERS, and the TOURS through the North and South of England.

VOL. IV.

LONDON:

Printed for W. STRAHAN; W. NICOLL, No. 51, St. Paul's Church-Yard; B. COLLINS, at Salisbury; and J. BALFOUR, at Edinburgh.

MDCCLXXI.

CONTENTS

OF THE

FOURTH VOLUME.

Letter
XXX. *FROM* Taunton *to* Bath. — *Mr.* Bampfield's, *at* Hestercomb. — *Sir* Charles Tynt's, *at* Halswell. — *Lord* Egmont's, *at* Enmore, Page 1 *to* 25.

XXXI. *From* Bath *to* Barnet. — *Sheep Husbandry of* Wiltshire. — *Mr.* Andrews's, *at the* Grove. — *Mr.* Cowslade's *Experiments.* — *Peat.* — *Mr.* Clayton's *Experiments.* — *Sir* John Hoby Mill's. — *Mr.* Burke's. — *The Earl of* Holderness's, - 26 *to* 92.

XXXII. *Review of the Intelligence concerning Carrots,* - - 93 *to* 112.

XXXIII. *Ditto of Potatoes,* - 113 *to* 123.

XXXIV. *Ditto of Madder,* 124 *to* 130.

XXXV. *Ditto of Burnet,* - 131 *to* 140.

XXXVI. *Ditto of Sainfoine,* 141 *to* 147.

XXXVII. *Ditto of Lucerne,* 148 *to* 162.

XXXVIII. *Ditto of Clover,* - 163 *to* 169.

XXXIX. *Ditto of Cabbages,* - 170 *to* 190.

XL. *Ditto of Turnips,* = 191 *to* 194.

XLI. *Ditto of Hops,* = 195 *to* 196.

CONTENTS.

Letter
XLII. *Ditto of Drilled Crops,* 197 to 217.
XLIII. *Ditto of Rental,* - 218 to 229.
XLIV. *Ditto of Products of Corn,* 230 to 237.
XLV. *Ditto Products of Pulse,* 238 to 242.
XLVI. *Ditto Quantities of Seed,* 243 to 252.
XLVII. *Ditto of Tillage,* - 253 to 273.
XLVIII. *Ditto of Sheep,* - 274 to 291.
XLIX. *Ditto of Cows,* - 292 to 300.
L. *Ditto of the Price of Provisions,* 301 to 307.
LI. *Ditto of Firing, Tools, &c.* 308 to 310.
LII. *Ditto the Price of Labour,* 311 to 317.
LIII. *Comparison of Labour and Provisions,* 318 to 334.
LIV. *Ditto with Rates and Rise of Labour,* 335 to 366.
LV. *Review of the Particulars of Farms,* 367 to 384.
LVI. *Ditto of stocking Farms,* 385 to 388.
LVII. *Ditto of Tythe,* - 388 to 389.
LVIII. *Ditto of the Value of the Soil,* 390 to 393.
LIX. *Ditto of Manuring,* - 394 to 454.
LX. *State of the Soil in* England, *proportioned to this Tour,* - - 455.

APPENDIX, - 470 to 506.

ADDENDA; *Criticisms answered,* 507.

THE FARMER's TOUR THROUGH ENGLAND.

LETTER XXX.

MATTHEW COOMBS, of *Taunton* * *St. James*, has practised the drilling of peafe three years: he makes his rows equally diftant, 20 inches afunder, ufes ten pecks, or three bufhels of feed *per* acre, and cleans them by two, three, or four horfe-hoeings, and alfo hand-hoes and weeds them. He likewife draws down the

---

* In the way from *Henlade* to *Bridgewater*, I went out of the direct road for the pleafure of feeing three places, which I had heard of before

the rows of peafe to the fun with rakes, when twelve inches high. This operation he thinks effential to the welfare of the crop. The produce rifes from 20 to 40 bufhels *per* acre. Eight acres laft year yielded him 40*l.* for kids fold at market, and 140 bufhels of dry peafe. The expences of the culture are,

    Hand-hoeing and weeding, 1 *s.*
    Drawing the peafe, 1 *s.*
    Horfe-hoeing, 3 *s.*   His

---

before I came into *Somerfetfhire:* thefe are *Heftercomb*, the feat of ——— *Bampfield*, Efq. *Halfwell*, Sir *Charles Tynte*'s, and *Enmore-Caftle*, the earl of *Egmont*'s.

    The gardens at *Heftercomb* are the object: a rural fequeftered vale with wood; much of the ground wild and romantic: Mr. *Bampfield* has filled this canvafs in a manner that does honour to his tafte. A walk winds around the whole in fome places along the fides of the hills, at others it dips into retired bottoms, and rifes again over the eminences, commanding views of the diftant country. Here was no water, but it was brought from the higher lands, and is exhibited in various forms. The grounds are finely thickened with wood, which is fo artfully managed, as to make the extent appear vaftly larger than it really is.

                                      The

His course of crops is,
1. Wheat and eddish turnips.
2. Drilled pease, and turnips after.
3. Wheat sown in *February*.
4. Barley.
5. Clover one year.

This honest farmer rises much above the practice of his neighbours, and deserves commendation for so doing: he is a sensible intelligent man.

The walk first leads from the house, behind some thick wood, on the side of a fine falling valley, to a bench, which is elegantly situated: at the bottom of a bold declivity is a lake, quite environed with an amphitheatre of hanging wood; the varied, waving slopes of green, break into the dark grove in the most beautiful manner: an urn on a rising knole is excellently situated, half obscured by the shade of the trees: a small fall of water from out a mossy bank, thickly tufted with wood, enlivens this most agreeable scene. Above the whole a hermitage is seen, situated on a projecting point of the hill; from whence it looks down on all the objects beneath. The parts of this view are extremely well connected, though various. The lake at your feet, the shelving lawn, and the thick woods, unite most happily with the water-fall; from thence your eye feels no pain in passing

About *Halfwell*, the courſe is,

1. Wheat
2. Barley or oats
3. Clover and ray-graſs 2 years.

Alſo,

1. Wheat
2. Barley
3. Clover
4. Wheat
5. Peaſe or beans.

Wheat yields on an average 15 buſhels, barley 18, oats 25, beans 20, peaſe 14. They have ſome turnips, but none

---

to the urn, which is in the very ſhade of the woods, that thicken quite to the hermitage.

Riſing the hill you come to a winding terraſs, from which you look down to the right, on the hollow, with the water at the bottom: the effect fine. Between the hills you catch the diſtant country, which is compoſed of rich incloſures. From hence the ſcene changes totally, to a cool, ſequeſtered vale, almoſt wholly ſhaded by the thick woods, that hang on the ſides of the hills: no building or diſtant proſpect is ſeen, but a tranſparent ſpring guſhes out of a little ſpot of rock, moſs and wood, and trickles over a pebble courſe through the lawn: the path then leads through a dark wood, and comes out at a ruſtic ſeat, from which you look at once on a caſcade that will rivet you to the ſpot with admiration.

A bold ſtream ruſhes from out a rock, and falls in the moſt natural manner imaginable about

none hoed. Their tillage they perform chiefly with oxen, 6 or 8 in a plough and one horse: an acre a day good work.

Sir *Charles Tynte* uses them in harness (a practice I before thought had been peculiar to Mr. *Cooke* of *Derbyshire*) one before another, or abreast at pleasure; and never puts more than four in a plough: they move much quicker than in yoaks, and draw heavier weights. Four doing the work of 6 or 8 and one horse, is an amazing

---

about 40 feet, nearly perpendicular over a bank of rock-work, moss, ivy and weeds. Never was nature so admirably imitated. The back ground is a wood quite impervious, and as steep as the fall of the stream: the whole spot is a little opening in a thick wood, and no object to be seen but that which engrosses your attention. The accompanyment is as happy as the principal: a gloomy wood, whose branches bend about with all the ease of nature, and exclude every thing but the sun beams, which sparkle on the falling water: the floor of this sequestered dell is a small lawn, in which the water is lost. So complete a scene, in which every thing is complete, and nothing to offend, will not be often seen.

amazing saving; and yet it is certainly a fact, that 4 in Sir *Charles*'s team are equal to 6 and an horse in the farmers, and sometimes to 8. A comparison so extremely decisive, that it is amazing they do not imitate it : I suppose the expence of harness, added to the loss of laying aside the yoaks, is what deters them; for one farmer I talked with, who had all his life been used to oxen, allowed

---

Leaving this most agreeable spot, the walk leads through a piece of wild ground, which contrasts the more interesting scenes we have passed ; but the shrubby grass, scattered with single trees, whose tops unite with the woods that spread over the hills, form a retirement that will not allow you to drop your attention.

The path winds from hence up the hill, through a dark wood, from which it breaks suddenly into an alcove bench, opening at once on a fine prospect over the vale of *Taunton*. Crossing the pasture, and again entering the woods, you come to a small bench, from which you have a very pretty birds-eye landscape through the branches of the trees, on a part of the vale of *Taunton*, with the steeples of the town: it is managed with taste. Rising the hill again, we next came to the hermitage or witch house, from the figure of an old witch painted

allowed that his landlord's were faster walking beasts than his, though he did not put so many in a plough.

There is much rich grazing land around *Bridgwater*, that lets from 20 to 40 *s.* an acre. It is chiefly used for fatting *Devonshire* heifers, which they buy in at *Candlemas* from 3 *l.* to 6 *l.* each, and keep them at hay till the grass springs; then they allot a beast to every acre, which pays on an

---

painted in the center pannel: the occasion of a very genteel compliment to the grounds from Dr. *Langhorne:*

    O'er *Bampfield*'s woods, by various nature grac'd,
    A *witch* presides!—but then that witch is TASTE.

The view from hence is very striking; the spot is the top of a hill, which projects boldly over the vale, and being lofty, the declivity is steep; the hollow vale, with the lake at the bottom, deep sunk in the hanging woods, has a great effect; the union of lawn, hill, wood and water, romantic. The distant country above opens to the eye, and renders the whole complete.

From hence, the walk leads to a seat, which looks full into a fine hollow, totally surrounded with impervious woods; not one intruding object; but an enchanter seems to have torn up a cascade, and flung it into the dark bosom of these noble groves. A scene more perfectly picturesque

8 THE FARMER's TOUR

an average 40 s. profit. Besides this every acre will fatten from one and a half to two wethers in the winter, to 8 s. a head profit: this grass land must be incomparably good. There is a vast tract of rich grazing marsh from *Bridgewater* towards *Bristol*, and quite to *Axbridge*. It lets from 25 s. to 30 s. an acre: 20 of these acres will fatten 16 oxen of 50 score in the summer, and 40 wethers in the winter. The profit on the oxen

---

picturesque I have not viewed: never was a falling water more happily united with the various shades of retiring woods; not an edging, or flat bank of trees, or mere back ground, but this is seen deep in the recesses of a woody hollow, and beneath the eye, with the peculiarity of looking *down* on a water-fall, with a greater effect than eyeing it *upwards:* a circumstance I remember no where besides. It is a scene, which sets the pencil at defiance.

From this spot, the path carries you to many natural openings in the wood, which let in a great variety of prospects, excellently managed to set off the preceding scenes by contrast: *they* are in general sequestered, and borrow half their charms from the gloomy shades, in which they are viewed: *these* are more open and gay; in some places you look down on the vale, with the opposite hills varied with woods and scattered trees; in others, over the home fields and catch, through

oxen is from 4*l.* to 5*l.* and 8*s.* a head on the sheep.

Hearing there was a great cattle fair kept annually in an arable field at *Bridgewater*, I was desirous of knowing its products; supposing that they must be very considerable from so rich a fold; the course of crops regular on it is,

1. Wheat, manured for with 20 loads an acre.
2. Pease or beans.
3. Clover one year.

Which

---

through the plantations, distant objects, with the rich vale of *Taunton* opening in various breaks. The whole admirably contrived for the introduction of uncommon variety in a small space of ground.

Mr. *Bampfield* has ornamented his house with several paintings of his own performance. His copy of *Vandyke*'s king *Charles* on horseback is executed with all the fire and freedom of the original. The landscape over the chimney in the dining-room, a composition of his own, is beautiful: the brilliancy and warmth of the tints are very pleasing. In the drawing-room is a piece of birds in needle-work by Mrs. *Bampfield*, in which the colours are astonishingly fine; the hen's back is nature itself, and the relief uncommonly bold. Some smaller pieces in the same

Which is a better courfe than many in *Somerfetfhire*: part of this field (it is an open one) is,

   1. Wheat, 2. Peafe,

conftantly. As to crops they give no reafon to fuppofe the land the better for the fair.

Wheat, 20 bufhels,

Barley, 30 ditto.

Peafe, 25 ditto.

Beans, 30 ditto.

Clover, 2 loads of hay, and then a crop of feed.

In

---

fame room, of other birds, &c. are touched with a fpirit and livelinefs, that do honour to the lady's genius.

  *   *   *   *

From *Heftercombe* to *Enmore-Caftle*, I took the road by *Cutherftone* lodge, a very high ground, which commands a moft extenfive view over the *Briftol* channel, acrofs *Glamorganfhire*, to the mountains of *Brecknock*. The channel, with the *Holmes*, is a fine object, and the waving hills and vales around the lodge, cut into inclofures, are pleafing; but the whole is not equal in beauty to feveral profpects I have elfewhere feen. The objects are too indiftinct: you look over a country twelve miles to the channel, that is 21 miles over, then the whole county of

Glamorgan,

In all this country they manure as much as they can for wheat: some few for beans; but no hand-hoeing, and sow the wheat after the beans.

Throughout the vale of *Taunton* and here also, they are very attentive to getting their wheat lands into good husband-like order: I think they mind this point more than any other. They plough much of their land on to narrow beds from 4 to 10 feet over,

---

Glamorgan, and far into *Brecknockshire*: this is too great: the eye receives no pleasure from being told, that it sees fourscore miles. A channel five miles wide, at the bottom of the declivity, and winding round a cultivated country, with the *Welch* mountains rising immediately from the opposite shore, would be ten times more striking than *Cutherston*. The view of the *Isle of Wight* channel, from the hill above *Cowes*, much exceeds this in real beauty.

Excuse this digression, which I should have avoided, had I not been told, that this view was the noblest in *England*.

Enmore-Castle is situated on a gradually rising hill, in the midst of a fine rich country, about four miles from *Bridgwater*. It is one of the most peculiar buildings in the kingdom: it is a large quadrangular castle, built of a dark-coloured stone, round a court. It is surrounded by a dry

over, and break all the clods that are left by the harrows, drawing at the same time the loose earth from the furrows on to the beds; this they call clodding and hacking, and when finished, the fields have a very neat appearance; but what is very astonishing, with all this attention to their wheat lands, they do not (as I before observed about *Henlade*) know what a water-furrow is! On wet clayey soils, and flat ones too, they have no contrivance to carry

---

a dry fosse, 40 feet wide and 16 deep. This opens all round into the offices under the castle, and likewise (which is the peculiarity) into a whole range of others under the lawn, which surrounds it; and among the rest to the stables, which are all under ground: an excellent contrivance to have them conveniently near the house: how it agrees with the constitutions of the horses I know not. The principal way into the stables is at a distance from the castle, where the entrance is at the side of the hill. The following is a list of the rooms.

The hall 40 by 28, and 27 high; a gallery round it, but it is too dark.

The armoury, 36 by 22.

The anti-chamber, 25 by 18.

Bed-chamber, 22 by 18.

Dressing-room, 22 by 14. Here are several good portraits.

The rest offices.

carry off the water, which lodges in the furrows of the beds, and which muſt half poiſon no flight portion of their crops.

Leaving *Bridgewater*, I took the road to *Bath*, paſſing within ſight of a very remarkable tract of country, called *King's Sedgmoor*: it is on an average nine miles long and two broad; it is a flat black peat bog, but ſo very rich, that ſome ſenſible farmers

---

In the principal ſtory are,
 The gallery 66 by 22, and 19 high.
 The dining-room 41 by 22, and 19 high.
 The library 46 by 19.
 Lord *Egmont*'s dreſſing-room, 19 by 17.
 Bed-chamber 29 by 16.
 Lady *Egmont*'s dreſſing-room 19 by 17. Over the chimney the taking down from the croſs, in the ſtile of *Albert Durer*. There are many figures, and moſt minute, though unmeaning expreſſion. There is neither compoſition, nor any knowledge of the clear obſcure.
 Lady's wardrobe, 15 by 11.
 Lady's woman's room, 19 by 13.
 Another room, 20 by 19.
 The cabinet, 18 by 17. So called, but it is a mere waiting room.
 Dreſſing room, 22 by 14. Here are ſeveral pictures, landſcapes; ſtill life, &c.

Bed-

farmers assured me, it wanted nothing but draining to be made well worth from 20 s. to 25 s. an acre, on an average. But at present it is so encompassed by higher lands, that the water has no way to get off, bu by evaporation; in winter it is a sea, and yields scarce any food, except in very dry summers. What a disgrace to the whole nation is it, to have 11,520 such acres lie waste in a kingdom that is quarrelling about high

---

Bed-chamber, 22 by 20. Crimson velvet, hung with tapestry.

Anti-chamber, 25 by 19. Hung with tapestry; some of it fine.

Saloon, 44 by 30, and 20 high. The windows of this room are so low and small, that it is rather dark. Over the chimney a very good portrait. It is hung with fine tapestry.

Drawing-room, 25 by 19. Here are four admirable portraits, of fine colouring and excellent expression.

*   *   *

Halswell, the seat of Sir *Charles Tynte*, Bart. is beautifully situated in the middle of an ornamented park, about two miles from *Enmore* castle. What chiefly attracts the attention of strangers, are the decorated grounds. The riding which leads to the principal points of view, crosses the park from the house; commanding a fine view of the rich vale of *Bridgwater*. It then

high prices of provisions! The present use made of this moor is not of the value of 2 *s*. 6 *d*. an acre.

Quantoc hills are an other very extensive tract of waste land; the soil part rocky; and what is called in this country *a stone rush*; which I take to be excellent land for sainfoine; but much of this space is of a better quality; I was informed that it would let inclosed, and without further improvement,

---

then runs by the side of a woody precipice, and up through some new plantations; from a dark part of which you enter through a door into a temple dedicated to *Robin Hood*; upon which a most noble prospect breaks at once on the beholder; which acts not a little by the surprize of the entrance. The ground shelves from it in front, and to the right gradually; but to the left in bolder slopes; where the dips are beautifully grouped with wood; and the hills above them rise in waving inclosures.

About the house the groves thicken; and a vast vale of rich inclosures, spotted in a beautiful manner, with white objects stretch beyond it to the distance of 12 miles; then you command the channel, which is here 9 miles over; the *Holm* rising in the midst of it very boldly; and beyond the whole, the mountains of *Wales* rise one

ment, at 4*s.* an acre; at prefent it does not yield as many farthings. It is 14 miles long by 2 broad, on an average; fo here are 17,920 acres more that want only inclofing to be advanced from nothing to 4*s.*

Hunsfield moors are another wafte that wants inclofing alone, to be made worth 20*s.* an acre; rich meadow.

About *Glaftonbury* there are very extenfive tracts of fine meadows that let from 20*s.*

---

one behind another. This view, I think, much excells that from *Cutherfton* lodge.

From hence the riding leads up the hills, commanding all the way a moft extenfive profpect. After which it turns down through a plantation to a fingle fmall oak, with a few pales about it, and a bench. Here the grounds finking from the eye, form a moft fweet landfcape. The lawns undulate in the fineft manner, and the groves of oak feem to drop into the hollows. The clumps and fcattered trees have an uncommon elegance, and unite the fore ground of the fcene with *Robin Hood*'s temple, which is here feen to great advantage. Beyond the whole you have the diftant extenfive profpect.

From hence the riding leads down the hill to a wood of noble oaks, which fhade a wild fequeftered fpot; where a limpid fpring rifes at

the

20*s.* to 40*s.* an acre. It is applied to keeping many cows and fatting beasts. Here likewise is a vast moor called the turfery, in which they dig turf for burning: it is a flat bog, and might all be made very good meadow. There is a full view of all these lands from the *Tor* and *Windmill* hills. The latter hill consists of a fine rich sandy loam; the principal part of which is let to potatoe men, at 40*s.* an acre. Their method of cultivating

---

the foot of a rock, over-hung in a fine bold manner by wood which grows from its clefts. The water winds away through the grove in a proper manner.

Here is a tablet with these lines.

When *Israel's* wand'ring sons the desart trod,
The melting rock obey'd the prophet's rod;
Forth gush'd the stream, the tribes their thirst allay'd,
Forgetful of their *God* they rose and play'd.
Ye happy swains for whom these waters flow,
Oh! may your hearts with grateful ardors glow;
Lo, here a fountain streams at his command,
Not o'er a barren, but a fruitful land;
Where Nature's choicest gifts the vallies fill,
And smiling Plenty gladdens ev'ry hill.

Turning the corner you catch a bridge, under a thick shade, and then come to the *Druid*'s temple, built in a just stile of bark, &c. the view quite gloomy and confined; the water winds silently along, except a little gushing fall, which hurts

ing them is to dig the land into beds, 9 feet over; they dung all but the new land on first breaking up, at the rate of about 3 *C. wt.* of dung *per* lug, of 20 feet by 9 wide: 10 bushels of sets, which are chiefly small ones, plant an acre; they keep them clean by hand-weeding, and cover the beds with earth out of furrows; dig up the crop with spades; it amounts to from 6 pecks to 3 bushels *per* lug, average 9 pecks;

per

---

hurts not the emotions raised by so sequestered a scene.

Following the path towards the bridge, you catch, just before you come at it, a little landscape through the trees, of distant water finely united with wood.—From the bridge the river appears to great advantage; nobly embanked on one side with tall spreading trees; and on the other with green slopes scattered with single ones.

From these retired and gloomy spots, you leave the dark groves, and open into a more chearful ground; the river is bounded only on one side by thick wood, and on the other by waving lawns open to the fields, and scattered thinly with trees. From a bench on the banks you view a flight fall of water well shaded.

Advancing, the character of the ground again changes most happily; the woods open on
both

per acre 544 bushels, which is very considerable. They plant them two or three years running on the same land; but the two first crops are generally the best. They often sow wheat for the third crop, and sometimes get at the rate of 40 bushels *per* acre.

All the way to *Wells* the country is chiefly grass, which lets from 18*s*. to 30*s*. an acre.

Near both sides the water; waving lawns of the most lively verdure—trees thinly scattered—brighter streams—touches of distant prospect—and elegant buildings—all unite to raise the most chearful ideas, which were prepared for, by gradually leaving the gloom of the more sequestered woods. A break through the trees to the right, lets in a view of the rotunda.

Passing to the *Ionic* portico, which is excellently placed, the scenery in view is truly enchanting: the lawn is gently waved, and spotted with trees and shrubs in the happiest taste. The water seems to wind naturally through a falling vale; and a swelling hill, crowned by the rotunda, forms a complete picture. The whole scene is really elegant; every part is riant, and bears the stamp of pleasure.

As you cross the bridge, you look to the right on a very beautiful cascade, which makes five or six slight falls over a moss and ivy bank, under a dark shade of wood. The slopes, wood

Near that town are very large tracts of flat marshy land, half poisoned with wet; it wants nothing but draining to be rendered the best meadow in the country.

There is very little manufacturing of consequence here besides some stockings; they have a little in the silk way, which employs some children.

About *Compton*, within 12 miles of *Bath*, their course is,

---

and water, unite to render the scene striking. But the point of view being the bridge, and standing on another cascade, is not agreeable; it somewhat weakens the effect.

Turning down by the water the lawn continues very beautiful, and you gain a fine view of the *Ionic* portico on a rising slope, which here appears to great advantage; but the middle cascade, which you here command, should be totally hid; it is an inferior repetition of the principal one.

Rising the hill by the side of the water, you have from a bench under a spreading wood an agreeable view of a bridge; and a little further, another commands the same object, and has also a very pleasing opening through the trees to the portico. The view to the left *up* to the water, is a confirmation of *Shenstone*'s observation.

The riding which follows on the bank of the river under the gloomy shade of numerous most venerable trees, is a fit residence for Contempla-

1. Fallow 3. Barley
2. Wheat 4. Oats.

The crops of wheat 30 bushels; of barley 30; and of oats 40. The land is rich; lets from 16 s. to 40 s. an acre; average 25 s. Farms rise from small ones to 200 l. a year.

At *Stone Easton* the road crosses a common of good dry sound land, that is visibly very improveable; the spontaneous growth, grass, furze, or fern: I made some enquiries

tion to dwell in. The openings across the water on the opposite lawn, are just sufficient to heighten by contrast. The awful shade—the solemn stillness of the scene, broken by nothing but the fall of distant waters; have altogether a great effect, and impress upon the mind a melancholy scarcely effaced by the chearful view of a rich vale with the water winding through it, which is seen on crossing the park towards the house.

Halfwell, upon the whole, has received rich gifts from nature, and very pleasing ones from art. The riding is of large extent, and commands a great variety of distant prospect, and rich landscapes; the home scenes are elegant, and set off by the shade of such noble wood, that every impression they make is rendered forcible. The buildings are in a light and pleasing stile.

ries concerning it, and found that Mr. *Cox* has inclofed 500 acres of it that was overrun with trumpery; he has ploughed and manured it richly with lime, and laid it down to grafs, which is now 20 *s.* an acre. Such fpirit is highly commendable; and many are the tracts of wafte open land, at prefent of ufe to nobody, which would pay equally well for improvement.

About *Compton* there are great tracts of rich inclofed land that let at 30*s.* an acre. Refpecting the management of a confiderable part of their land, it is fo curious as to deferve particular attention; firft they marle, 30 loads an acre; and on the credit of that, the following is their courfe;

1. Wheat	7. Barley
2. Wheat	8. Oats
3. Wheat	9. Wheat
4. Oats	10. Barley
5. Barley	11. Oats
6. Wheat	12. Wheat.

Bravo! my *Somerfetfhire* lads! And what then? Why then, Sir, we lime on a fallow, and take feven crops more. Incomparable!

They

They lay 20 quarters of lime *per* acre, at 10*d.* a quarter.—Their products are as follow.

Wheat, 3 quarters.
Barley, 4.
Oats, 5.
Peafe, 2.

Very few turnips, and none hoed. No beans. Thefe crops are a ftrong proof (if any was wanting) of their vile hufbandry. Land at 30*s.* an acre, marled and limed, to yield no better products than the worft foils in the kingdom under good management. I will not venture a pofitive aflertion, but I do not, at prefent, think there is any country very well cultivated, whatever the foil, but what yields equal products: foil, rent, lime and marle confidered, their courfes of crops ought to be fome of thefe;

1. Beans	3. Clover
2. Barley	4. Wheat.
1. Beans	2. Wheat.
1. Beans	4. Barley
2. Wheat	5. Clover
3. Peafe	6. Wheat

But

But above all;

1. Cabbages
2. Barley
3. Clover
4. Wheat
5. Beans
6. Barley
7. Peafe
8. Oats
9. Clover
10. Wheat.

The beans and peafe all drilled, and horfe and hand-hoed; the crops certainly would not be lefs than, Wheat, 4 quarters; Barley, 6; Oats, 8; Beans, 6; Peafe, 4; a fyftem that would pay them infinitely better than their prefent one.

Nine miles from *Bath* I obferved the wheat land well water-furrowed, for the firft time fince I had been in *Somerfetfhire*. Againft the feventh mile ftone is a field of fine fainfoine on a hill; from which I conclude that it would do on the pooreft hills in this country. A few miles before I came to *Bath*, it was with pleafure that I obferved moft of the grafs fields, on the fides of fteep hills, cut acrofs with fmall trenches for conveying water over them out of the ditches which receive all that come from the higher lands. This is excellent management, and deferves univerfal imitation.

In

In all this courſe of country the hay is chiefly ſtacked about the fields.—Their tillage is performed with four or ſix oxen and a horſe. Rents are generally high; I found none under 20 s.

LETTER XXXI.

I DO not expect much information in crossing *Wiltshire*, except concerning sheep: about that part of their management I shall be particular in my enquiries. Near *Bath**, the lands, as may be supposed, are artificially very rich, and let at high rents. Four miles from thence, I came to *King's Down*. Rent of land in that neighbourhood rises from 10*s*. to 40*s*. an acre. The sheep here are all *Wiltshires*:
they

---

* The additions every day making to this city are uncommon, and greatly is it to the honour of all those concerned in raising the new streets, that they build on a regular plan; so that every side is a complete front. Besides the Circus, which is now finished, and is an area no where equalled in the kingdom, there is a street leads from it to a set of buildings now raising, to be in the form of a crescent, which will have a very noble effect; yet the architecture is not faultless: the ground-floor being plain walls instead of rustics is an experiment
not

they fold the ewes moſt part of the winter, with no more hurt to them than to wethers. The profit they reckon,

    Lamb, 10s. to 15s.

    Wool, 2s.

Two hundred will fold an acre in a week.

Farms are in general from 100l. to 300l. a year. Their courſes of crops,

1. Fallow   3. Barley
2. Wheat   4. Clover.

And ſome, not all, add,

5. Wheat   6. Barley.

Alſo,

1. Fallow   3. Barley.
2. Wheat

---

not perfectly ſuccefsful. Againſt the principal floor and attic is a regular range of *Ionic* pillars; but the windows of the attic are crowded quite into the capitals of the pillars, which offends the eye. Beſides this pile, there are ſeveral others, whoſe magnitude ſhews how flouriſhing this city is: *Paragon Buildings*, a concave range, *York Buildings*, *Edgar Buildings*, &c. amazing edifices for a town ſupported by pleaſure and diſeaſe! The ſeat neither of government nor commerce.

There are some turnips, and most of them hoed; the value from 40 s. to 3 l. an acre.

From *Melksham* to the *Devizes*, nine tenths of the country is grass, and lets from 20 s. to 40 s. an acre; average 25 s. It is mostly applied to dairies, which rise to 60 cows; many are let; the price used to be 3 l. but now it is 4 l. They give four, five or six gallons of milk a day.

About *Rundevey* the country is chiefly open field, and the course,

1. Fallow
2. Wheat
3. Barley
4. Oats.

Wheat yields three quarters and a half *per* acre; barley and oats not more on an average. Land lets from 15 s. to 18 s. an acre: the farms large. In their ploughs they use six oxen, sometimes four; and three or four horses.

They fold their ewes as well as wethers all winter long on the land for barley; while they are lambing they pen them in the farm yard, and after that fold them with the wethers. They hand-hoe their turnips twice; an acre is worth from 40 s. to 50 s.

At

At *Bishops-Cannons* I made fresh enquiries concerning sheep: they here fold the ewes quite through the year upon the cold hills, lambs and all; nor do they ever find any inconvenience from the practice. They lamb in the fold, and the lambs find out their dams without any difficulty. Ewes they reckon make more water than wethers; but the latter dung most. The balance of value for folding they think even. They leave them in the fold till nine or ten o'clock in the morning: 200 sheep will fold an acre in 10 nights.

Rents here run at 15 s. an acre. The course of crops,

1. Fallow
2. Wheat
3. Barley
4. Oats.

Wheat yields four quarters an acre; and barley and oats the same.

LABOUR.

Ten-pence a day all the year round.
Reaping, 5 s.
Mowing corn, 10 d.
———— grass, 1 s. 6 d. to 20 d.
Head-man's wages, 6 l. to 7 l.
Next ditto, 3 l. to 4 l.

PROVISIONS.

Bread,		2 *d. per lb.*
Butter,	-	7 for 18 *oz.*
Cheese,	-	3 ¼ *per lb.*
Beef,	-	2 ½
Mutton,	-	3 ¼
Pork,	-	3
Milk,	-	½ *d. per* pint.
Potatoes,	-	6 a peck.

Labourer's house-rent, 30 *s.* to 40 *s.*

———— Firing, 30 *s.* The farmers sell all their pea and bean straw to the labourers for burning: as vile a piece of husbandry as can well be supposed.

In a few miles more, repeating my enquiries about sheep, I again found that they penned them in the farm yards, littered warmly with straw, and feed them with hay in racks till the lambs get strength, when they fold them as usual. A flock of 300 will annually sell 100 old ones, at 20 *s.* to 23 *s.* and 100 lambs at 10 *s.* or 12 *s.*

I observed in several places in the way to *Marlborough*, that they had a very neat way of getting gravel: they open a hole, and

and sifting the gravel that arises, take out the stones, and leaving the earth, &c. in it, lay down the turf again, so that the grass is not at all damaged: this is a practice which much deserves imitation.

Land lets about *Overton*, the inclosure at 20*s*. an acre, and the open fields at 12*s*. The course is,

1. Fallow
2. Wheat
3. Barley.

Wheat yields 3 ½ quarters an acre, barley 4 quarters; but few turnips: their flocks of sheep are about 1000: they fold them all the year through, except at lambing, and then pen in the yard: they use no lime or marle in this country in manuring, only the fold and yard dung.

No oxen in tillage; four horses in a plough.

From *Marlborough* to *Hungerford*, the average rent is about 15*s*. or 16*s*. an acre: there are tracts of exceeding rich watered meadows here, particularly some belonging to Mr. *Popham*, that let from 40*s*. to 4*l*. an acre: they very often mow them twice, and get two ton of hay the first cutting, and from one to one and a half the

the second; the after-grass of some meadows alone let for 40 s. an acre. These are immense rates, and much exceed the grass in the neighbourhood of great cities; and shews strongly the uncommon importance of having a command of water to throw at pleasure over grass lands.

It was here I first met with peat ashes. They bring them from *Newbury*; but many farmers buy the peat itself there, and burn it here; if bought at *Newbury*, they cost 5 d.; burnt here it comes to 6 d. but this extra penny they think well laid out, because the *Newbury* burners mix dross with the peat; so that the quality is more than a penny worse. They lay them chiefly on clover from 10 to 20 bushels an acre. It does great good to this crop, and some to the following wheat; but on the clover in a wet year the effect is to be seen to an inch. Peat ashes are sometimes sown on the green wheat in spring. They here fold their ewes through the winter, as well as the wethers: here and there a farmer, who pens them while lambing on straw in the farm yard. Lambs

sell

fell up to 15 s. wool 3 s. The course of crops here is,

1. Fallow   3. Barley
2. Wheat   4. Oats.
   Also,
1. Fallow   3. Barley
2. Wheat   4. Clover.
   Also,
1. Turnips   4. Clover
2. Barley   5. Wheat
3. Barley   6. Barley.

Wheat yields 2 quarters an acre, barley 3, oats 4.

Of husbandry in the neighbourhood of *Newbury*, particularly about *Donnington*, I am enabled to give a more minute account through the obliging attention of *Petty Andrews*, and *Frederick Cowslade*, Esqrs.

Farms rise from 30 *l*. to 300 *l*. a year; but are in general about 100 *l*. a year. The soil is a strong loam on clay, chalk, and gravel; not much that is light enough for turnips. It lets from 10 s. to 40 s. a year; average, 15 s.

To *Reading*, 17 s.
To *Hungerford*, 13 s.
The *Vale of White Horse*, 20 s.

The courses of crops most common are,

1. Turnips
2. Barley
3. Clover one year
4. Wheat.

1. Turnips
2. Wheat
3. Barley
4. Clover one year
5. Oats.

1. Turnips
2. Barley
3. Clover
4. Summer fallow
5. Pease and beans mixed
6. Wheat.

And this last is one of the strangest courses I ever heard of.

For wheat on clover land they plough but once; otherwise from three to five times; sow two bushels and a peck of seed, and reckon three quarters the average produce. They have an uncommon high opinion of changing seed; have large quantities from *Surry*, the *Isle of Thanet*, &c. They plough thrice for barley, sow three bushels an acre, and get four quarters in return. For oats they give but one earth, sow four bushels an acre; the average crop five quarters; they rise to ten quarters. They stir thrice for pease, drill

four

four bushels an acre, in rows equally distant 15 inches; they hand-hoe them twice; and a few farmers horse-hoe them with the *Berkshire* shim; the crop four quarters an acre. They give but one earth for beans, plant three bushels an acre in rows 18 inches asunder, and drop them in holes nine or ten inches asunder, and four or five beans in a hole, so that they come up in bunches. I should apprehend this crouding the roots together must prevent the tillering, and answer no good purpose, especially in rich land: they hand-hoe them twice, and reap about four quarters and a half *per* acre.

In the *Vale of White Horse*, the crops rise to,

Wheat, 4 to 8 quarters.
Oats, 6 quarters.
Beans, 5 quarters.
Pease, 5 quarters.
Very little barley.

No rape or cole-seed is cultivated here; for turnips they plough from thrice to six times, hand-hoe twice, and feed them on the land with sheep; the average value 1*l.* 11*s.* 6*d. per* acre. Clover they mow once

once for hay, and get from two to three tons an acre, at 30 *s.* a ton, and feed the second growth. Refpecting the goodnefs of the wheat crop that follows, they do not reckon that there is any difference between mowing and feeding.

Both fummer and winter tares are cultivated for feeding fheep, and alfo for foiling horfes in the ftable: one acre will keep fix horfes a month; this, at 2 *s.* 6 *d.* a week, comes to 3 *l.* an acre: a good return, confidering the ameliorating quality of the tares, and the plenty of dung raifed in foiling.

They have a great deal of fainfoine, fow it on all poor lands, without regarding the under ftrata of the earth; it does without a chalk rock: lafts 15 years, and mown every year. A good acre will give three tons of hay, at 30 *s.* and an after-grafs worth 20 *s.*; in all, 5 *l.* 10 *s.*: a vaft produce, and on their poor lands too! I will engage, that it much exceeds their richeft arable.

In regard to manuring, they are excellent farmers in their attention to that part of hufbandry; and here it is neceffary to begin

begin with peat, for which they are moſt famous.

Peat is a very regular ſtratum, under another of common earth, but generally under a black meadow mold, from 1 to 3 feet deep; it is itſelf generally from 7 to 10 feet deep; but in one peat earth I was in, it is not more than 4 feet thick: under it is a body, which they call *marne*, a whitiſh, ſtiff, ſticking clay. The peat looks and feels very much like black butter; there is no roughneſs in it, nor any roots; ſo that it differs materially from the peat common in moſt parts of the kingdom, which is a net-work of roots, a ſpunge of them. The common conjecture is, that peat was formed by the deſtruction of a whole foreſt, and is compoſed of the rotten timber; acorns, leaves, moſs, branches, and whole trees, are ſometimes found in it perfectly ſound. The peat moors about *Thorne* in *Yorkſhire*, are five or ſix feet deep, very flat and regular, and under them much ſuch a clay as at *Newbury*. In them they alſo find whole trees, and many of them quite ſound: they are chiefly firs, and the whole country are very deſirous of getting these firs, to make pales of; for by long experience it has been found, that they are almost incorruptible, no instance scarcely being known of their decaying. But this peat is all a fibrous mass of little roots, and yields very few ashes. The quality they both possess of preserving timber, seems rather an objection to the real peat being composed of rotten wood, especially as the trees are found so deep in the peat, as to make it reasonable to think they must have been among those which composed the mass; however, this is only a conjecture.

Most of the peat in digging is under water, and the peat-spoon, with which it is dug, should always be in the water, from the ease thereby acquired of cutting and throwing it off the spoon; it is after drying burnt, not as some people have imagined in heaps, merely for the ashes, but in houses, like all other peat, and then the ashes are collected. The price at the pit is 9*s.* for a waggon load of 40 bushels, and the ashes are worth half the money; the price 6*d.* a bushel. They burn in the peat grounds an inferior sort for the mere ashes, mixing the upper stratum of black earth

earth with it; and thefe afhes they fell at 3*d.* a bufhel. An acre of peat ground is worth 200*l.*

Many farmers come from 15 to 16 miles for it.

The general quantity fpread on an acre is ten bufhels: they ufe it only on clover in *March.* The red afh is the moft efteemed: it lafts only the clover crop; but that is encreafed by it, as 3 to 2.

Larger quantities have been tried *per* acre, but without greater effects. They have a ftory, common here, of a man who fowed forty or fifty bufhels *per* acre, and the wind blowing a fmall quantity over the hedge on to his neighbour's clover, he was furprifed afterwards to find, that the wind had judged much better than himfelf; for his neighbour's clover was more improved than his own.

But the farmers here do not confine themfelves to peat; rags they have from *London,* and find them very ferviceable to their lighter lands. Soot they fow on their green wheat in the fpring, 12 bufhels an acre, at 8*d.*; and they ufe malt duft on their barley lands. Chalk they ufe by way of mellowing the land, and making it plough the easier.

They do not chop their stubbles; but their hay they stack at home.

In their fences they follow the plashing method.

Their best grass land is the watered meadow, which lets at 40 *s.* an acre. They water it all the year, except two months while the crop is growing: they mow twice, and get four tons an acre, worth 25 *s.* a ton; and the spring and after grass food is worth about 10 *s.* more. All these meadows rot sheep, turn them in when you will; except ewes with lamb. This is directly opposite to the practice of the whole county of *Dorset:* and if both are right, the rot does not arise from the *water*, but the *soil*. But there is no point so disputed as this of the rot.

The breed of cattle here is the long-horned *Derbyshire*; cows give 4 or 5 *lb.* of butter a week, from two gallons of milk a day; the total produce 4 or 5 *l.* They do not keep the more swine on account of cows. The winter food is wholly hay and straw.

straw. In rearing calves, they do not fuck at all.

Swine fatten in general from ten to fifty fcore.

In my *Six Months Tour through the North of England*, I mentioned a hog being fattened by Mr. *Selwood* to 57 fcore, which is 81 ftone 6 *lb.* at 14 *lb.* to the ftone. I have been much ridiculed for offering to pretend to think of fuch a thing. Mr. *Andrews* did not recollect the exact particulars, but wrote to Col. *Sellwood*; and fince I left the *Grove*, I had a letter from him, in which he writes as follows:— " Lieut. Col. *Sellwood* has fent me the following well-attefted particulars.

" Pigs fatted by *Richard Sellwood*, Efq. of *Bright Walton, Berks*.

" *March*, 1752, a hog killed, that weighed, exclufive of the blood, fixty-one fcore twelve pounds; when opened and cut out, it weighed fifty-feven fcore eleven pounds.

" *February*, 1770, killed another, which, when cut out, weighed forty-four fcore fourteen pounds. Signed by *R. Sellwood*."

I think thefe particulars are a fufficient
anfwer

answer to those, who before made themselves so merry at my expence.

Flocks of sheep rise to 3 or 400: they are chiefly stock sheep of the *Wiltshire* breed; the profit,

			£.	s.	d.
Lamb,	-	-	0	10	0
Wool,	-	-	0	2	6
Total,	-	-	0	12	6

The winter food turnips, and a little hay. They value the fold at 4*d. per* night *per* score. Relative to the rot, besides the above fact of their meadows effecting it, they observe that no sheep will ever rot, while it has a lamb by the side. Springs they think have nothing to do with the disease, nor will all wet places rot, but all watered meadows will. This is consonant with a part of Mr. *Bakewell*'s opinion, mentioned in the first volume, that no water rots but what *flows*.

In their tillage they reckon five horses necessary for 100 acres of arable land, use four in a plough, and do an acre a day, five inches deep; the price 6*s.* an acre. Cutting straw into chaff is practised.

There

There are some oxen used; but they do not answer so well as horses.

The time of breaking up stubbles is after the wheat sowing. They use wheel ploughs, with the beam resting on very high gallows, something like the *Norfolk* ones, but not near so light.

In hiring farms, they reckon five rents necessary to stock.

Land sells at 30 years purchase; land tax at 4*s.* is 2*s.* 6*d.*

Tythes both gathered and compounded; the composition 3*s.* an acre round.

Poor rates 4*s.* in the pound; 20 years ago only 6*d.* In the town of *Newbury* 7*s.* but not to the full amount of real rents. The employment of the women and children spinning. They all drink tea twice a day.

The following are the particulars of a farm;

150 Acres in all	40 Acres wheat
20 Grass	40 Barley
130 Arable	15 Oats
100*l.* Rent	15 Turnips
8 Horses	20 Clover
6 Cows	3 Men
8 Young cattle	2 Boys
150 Sheep	1 Maid
30 Swine	2 Labourers.

Mr. *Cowslade*, of the *Priory* at *Donnington*, has tried some experiments which well deserve being known.

Experiment, No. 1.

To discover the importance of brining wheat seed, he has tried it for several years drying with lime; and on comparison with the seed unbrined, he observes, that it is a preservative from the smut; for corn will be smutty, that comes from seed unbrined, while that brined is quite free, and the soil the same.

Experiment, No. 2.

Three acres were in 1763 drilled with wheat, in equally distant rows, 18 inches asunder, one and a half bushel seed *per* acre; it was carefully hand-hoed: the crop three quarters and a half *per* acre; which is a produce considerable enough to prove the merit of the culture.

Experiment, No. 3.

Two acres, in 1764, were drilled with wheat in equally distant rows, one foot asunder; a bushel and half of seed *per* acre; it was hand-hoed once; the crop three quarters and a half *per* acre. Adjoining was a piece of broad-cast wheat; soil, tillage,

lage, &c. the same, sown with 2 bushels and a quarter *per* acre; the crop five quarters *per* acre: this great superiority of the broad-cast, induced Mr. *Cowslade* to give up drilling wheat, as the common method was so evidently better.

But he drills all his pease and beans, and seldom gets less than four or five quarters *per* acre.

Experiment, No. 4.

Sainfoine this gentleman finds a most profitable crop; he has got at one cutting 5 tons of hay *per* acre, which is the greatest crop (well authenticated) that I have heard of.

Experiment, No. 5.

Mr. *Cowslade* planted one *Batavia* potatoe which weighed 2 *oz*. and it produced 10 *lb*.—This trial should be pursued, for the sort is not generally known; it may turn out more productive than the common ones.*

---

* Mr. *Andrews* has built a house at the grove near *Newbury*, in the *Gothic* stile; and ornamented the grounds about it with much taste. The situation is on a rising ground, backed by a hill crowned with wood; out of which rises *Donnington* castle. A lawn spreads around the house, and falls to a very fine water; a stream enlarged

Near *Reading* the foil is a good rich loam on gravel, which lets at 20 s. an acre. The courfe of crops here ufed is,

1. Fallow   4. Clover 1 or 2 years
2. Wheat   5. Wheat
3. Barley   6. Barley

There are not many turnips; when they are fown, it is now and then inftead of a fallow. Wheat yields 3, or 3 ½ quarters *per* acre; Barley, 5; Oats, 6; Peafe they drill

---

enlarged into a river, which takes a winding eafy courfe near a mile long, and of a confiderable breadth; there are three or four iflands in it, one of which is thickly planted, and affords fhelter to many fwans and wild fowl which frequent the water, at the fame time that they add to the beauty of the place. Over the river the country confifts of corn fields which rife agreeably. The lawn is very neat; the trees and clumps well managed, and the wood, in which the water terminates at each end, finifhes the fcene in a pleafing manner. There is a winding gravel walk through both the groves on the banks of the river, which opens to feveral retired and pleafing fcenes; at one fpot is a pretty ruftic *Gothic* temple, built of flint, near a cafcade, which the river forms by falling over a natural ridge of ftone. The whole place is laid out with great tafte.

Plate XXIX. is a plate of Mr. *Andrews's*, taken from a drawing of his own; the point of view the grove by the river to the right of the houfe.

PL. XVIII. Vol. 4. p. 11. 36.

drill in equally distant rows, 18 inches asunder; hand-hoe them once; the crop 3¼ quarters *per* acre.

Farms here are in general from 100*l.* to 200*l.* a year.

In their tillage they generally use 4 horses and a driver, but sometimes, after several ploughings, only 2 horses, but a driver always.

The house is a good one; the stair-case peculiar, but agreeable; and the library a large, handsome, and well proportioned room. Mr. *Andrews* has several pictures by some of the principal masters.

Rembrandt. An old man's head. Very strong: the expression of the hands and face fine.

Corn. Johnson. Portrait of a duke of *Austria.* The head in a noble stile of expression.

Its companion. A lady. The colouring and minute expression great.

Hall. A copy from a laughing boy: well done.

M. Angelo Carravaggio. Fruit: well executed.

Unknown. A small portrait of king *James.* Good.

Swaine. A moonlight piece of shipping. The effects of the light agreeable.

De Neff. A piece of architecture in perspective. Natural.

Baptist. Two flower pieces.

Berghem. Cattle.

Fluens. Two small pieces of scripture history. Pleasing.

There are many variations around *Marlow* and *Harleyford*, the seat of *William Clayton*, Esq. for the particulars of the following account, I am obliged to that gentleman.

Farms rise from 40 *l.* to 300 *l.* a year; but are in general about 100 *l.* The soils are various, gravel, loam, chalk, and clay; the hills let at 10 *s.* or 12 *s.* an acre; the whole in general, meadows included, at 15 *s.*

To

Carlo Dolci. A small head of Christ.
Swaine. A piece of shipping.
Vel. Brughle. Two landscapes.
Collet. Small landscapes with figures and buildings. There is a warmth and mellowness in the colours that are pleasing.
Old Frank. A city taken by storm. Singular and very strong expression.

Sir *Joseph Andrews* has a seat in this neighbourhood, where are, among other pictures, a boy by *Amiconi*, which is executed with a pleasing tenderness of tints. Also six views of *Rome* by *Occhiali*, of which the colouring is fine; the perspective good, and well finished. Here also is a Wake by *Rubens*, with many figures of capital expression; there are various attitudes spirited, and some men's heads in a great stile. His wife in one corner; a better figure than common with *Rubens*; and the back of another woman in the front ground in fine relief. Likewise a repast; the master unknown; the group agreeable. There are also six pieces by *Canaletti*.

To *Henley*, it runs at 15 s.
To *Reading*, 15 s.
To *Beconsfield*, 7 s. 6 d.
The courfe of crops common here, is,

1. Turnips   5. Peafe.
2. Barley   And fometimes add
3. Clover, 1 year   6. Wheat.
4. Wheat

Alfo,

1. Fallow   3. Barley
2. Wheat   4. Peafe.

They plough but once for wheat on clover; 3, 4, or 5 times in a fallow; fow 3 bufhels an acre; the crop 3 quarters. For barley they plough three times; fow 3 ½ bufhels; the crop 4 ½ quarters. They give but one ftirring for oats; fow 4 bufhels an acre; the crop 4 ½ or 5 quarters an acre. They give two earths for peafe; fow 3 bufhels an acre; many are drilled in equally diftant rows, and twice horfe-hoed with the fhim; the crop 3 ½ quarters.

For turnips they plough from three to fix times; hand-hoe them twice at the expence of 5 s. and 3 s. 6 d.; and feed them all on the land with fheep. Clover they mow twice for hay, and get 3 loads an acre. Winter vetches they cultivate for foiling horfes; 1 acre will keep 4 or 5 a month. They fow much fainfoine on the hills; mow it for hay, and get from 1 to 2 loads of hay an acre; but manure it with afhes once in two years.

In manuring they depend moft on purchafed dreffings. Peat afhes they have from *Newbury*; and fome afhes, foot, &c. are bought at different towns. But few of their flocks are large enough for folding. No ftubbles here are chopt; and they fell all their hay; fo the farm-yard fyftem may be gueffed. On their ftrong lands they fow buck-wheat, and plough it in.

The breed of cattle here, is the *Derbyfhire* long-horned cows for dairies, but they are not of confequence. Mr. *Clayton* has a *Holdernefs* cow that has given 12 *lb.* of butter a week; fhe gave 18 quarts of milk at a meal. Lord *Granville* had one that gave 20 quarts.

Swine fatten up to 30 ftone.

In their tillage they reckon 6 horfes neceffary for 100 acres of arable land; ufe 4

in

in a plough, and do an acre a day; they ſtir 6 or 7 inches deep; the price 9 s. an acre. Cutting ſtraw into chaff is well known. The time of breaking ſtubbles for a fallow, is between *Michaelmas* and *Chriſtmas*. Wheel ploughs chiefly uſed.

Land ſells at 30 years purchaſe. Tythes are gathered. Land-tax, at 4 s. in the pound, is 2 s. 8 d. Poor rates were 4 s. 9 d. in the pound; now only 2 s. 6 d.; and at the ſame time that this deduction has been made, they have almoſt paid off the debt they contracted for building a poor-houſe; and this meaſure is what has ſunk the rates. They allow no tea in the houſe; but they have had much trouble to effect it.

The employment is lace making; it is very difficult to get women, &c. to work in the fields.—All drink tea.

There are many vaſt woods of beech in this country; moſt of which are in the hands of the landlords themſelves. The management of them is peculiar. They do not take regular fells, as of underwood, but let them grow up in ſingle ſtems till they are young trees: they pick them every 6 or 7 years; cutting down from the 12th to the 20th part, at 32 or 33 years growth; and the whole product is rived into billets for firing, and all goes to *London:* this pays about 10*s. per* acre *per ann.* rent. Most of these woods have 30*l.* or 35*l.* an acre in wood on them, are consequently more valuable in that, than in the fee-simple of the land.

LABOUR.

In harvest, 35*s.* a month and board.
In hay-time and winter, 1*s.* 2*d.* a day.
Reaping, 5*s.*
Mowing corn, 1*s.* 6*d.*
——— grass, 2*s.*
The rates of labour not risen in 20 years.

PROVISIONS.

Bread,	-	2*d. per lb.*
Cheese,	-	4
Butter,	-	7½
Beef,	-	4
Mutton,	-	4
Veal,	-	5
Pork,	-	4
Bacon,	-	6

Labourer's house-rent, 30*s.* to 40*s.*
————— firing, the labour of digging roots.

BUILDING.

Bricks *per* thousand, 16 s.
Tiles, 18 s.
Oak timber *per* foot, 1 s. to 2 s.
Ash ditto, 1 s.
Elm ditto, 10 d.
Beech ditto, 6 d.

The trials and observations made by Mr. *Clayton*, are highly deserving the attention of the public; that he practises husbandry on no small scale, will appear from the particulars of his farm.

550 Acres in all	20 Turnips
360 Wood	14 Horses
80 Grass	10 Cows
120 Arable	6 Young cattle
400 *l*. Rent	300 Sheep
40 Wheat	16 Swine
40 Barley	8 Labourers
20 Clover	3 Boys.

Experiment, No. 1.

Sainfoine Mr. *Clayton* tried comparatively in three pieces of ground on the hills, six years ago.

No. 1. A stoney surface 2 feet deep on chalk.

No. 2.   A loamy soil on clay, on the side of a hill, 5 or 6 feet deep, on chalk.

No. 3.   Very shallow soil, but a few inches deep, on chalk.

The event;

No. 1. has yielded annually 2 loads of hay an acre, worth 30 s. a load; the after-grass 8 s. 6 d.

No. 2.   The same.

No. 3.   Has produced only 1 load an acre. But it is very observable that this field has a sharp declivity on both sides into a bottom; so that there the soil is 6 feet deep of the washings from the hills; in this part, the crop has always been so great, that it could scarcely stand on the ground; but on all the rest of the field not more than 1 load an acre.

From this experiment, which is a valuable one, it is very evident that the stratum of chalk being near the surface, is not at all necessary for the crop; for the product is better from 6 feet than from 6 inches. Which shews that the idea, common, of sainfoine thriving only on very shallow soils, is a false one.

Experiment, No. 2.

In preparing a ſtrong clay field for laying down to graſs; the ſoil proved ſo tough, that it could not be got into order by the common tools: Mr. *Clayton* made a ſpiky roller for it, which effected the buſineſs completely. He accordingly ſowed it with very fine hay ſeeds; and deſigns it as a nurſery to gather from by hand; the ſorts ſo gained he purpoſes to ſow in drills. This trial ſhews how important a ſpiky roller is in many caſes; the loſing a ſeaſon, or, what is worſe, ſowing land when not in proper order, are often conſequences of wanting this machine.

Experiment, No. 3.

An acre and half of ſtoney loam on clay, and under that chalk, was cleaned by a ſummer fallow, and ſown with lucerne (no corn) in 1765, part broad-caſt, and part in drills equally diſtant, 18 inches aſunder. It was kept clean by hand-hoeing; and mown once, beſides a ſlight feeding; but the produce inconſiderable.

In 1766 it was mown thrice for horſes: The broad-caſt was harrowed; but that operation

operation being ineffective from the hardness of the soil, this induced him to plough it with a round share, and left it like a fallow; but still that part of it was not to be kept clean. The broad-cast maintained at the rate of 5 horses, from the middle of *May* till *Michaelmas*; the drilled 4; the value 2*s. per* horse *per* week.

1767.

This year the drilled was cleaned by horse and hand-hoeing; and the broad-cast by ploughing and harrowing; the produce of both the same as last year.

And thus it has continued ever since. Mr. *Clayton* tried also transplanting in rows equally distant, 18 inches asunder; but there was no difference between that and the drilled.

Soiling horses with lucerne he has for three years observed to be an infallible cure for botts.

5 Horses, at 28 *s*.	£.9 0 0
4, At ditto,	7 4 0

Experiment, No. 4.

In 1767 fourteen acres were laid to grass after a very clean fallow without corn; the following feeds *per* acre.

Cow grafs,	-	3 *lb.*
Dutch clover,	-	6
Three poa's	-	3
Two trefoiles	-	2
		14 *lb.*

The 11th of *July*, in two years, he mowed 2 ton an acre of excellent hay, befides having a very valuable after-grafs. — That the land was in great heart may eafily be conceived from fo very fmall a quantity of feeds anfwering fo well. But Mr. *Clayton* from this trial thinks that there are no better forts to be recommended than thefe.

Experiment, No. 5.

Twenty five acres of land were laid down to grafs, after a clean fallow, with corn; nothing fown but a plenty of common hay feeds. The refult was very unfavourable; it turned out fower bad grafs, and came to no good turf. In four years he manured it well, and fowed white clover; this was of great fervice to it—fince then it has been a good pafture.

Thefe

These two experiments prove that land should be laid *without* corn; and also that a very few good grafs feeds are far preferable to the greateſt quantity of that rubbiſh commonly called hay feeds.

Experiment, No. 6.

Peat Mr. *Clayton* has found in one of his meadows; it is black, but full of roots; burns to a red aſh, and ſells at 6 *d.* a buſhel on the ſpot; a burner from *Newbury* preferred it to *Newbury* aſhes. He has tried it on clover; 10 buſhels *per* acre; and the effect is as great as the *Newbury:* the clover, not peated, did not produce ſo much, as that manured, by half. He alſo tried it on ſainfoine, but it did not ſo much good as ſea-coal aſhes; for the latter he gives 6 *d.* a buſhel at *Marlow*; they are brought from *London*; and he lays from 12 to 20 buſhels *per* acre—the effect always very great on both clover and ſainfoine.

Experiment, No. 7.

The worſt weed with which Mr. *Clayton* is troubled in his grafs-land, is mofs; and he has tried various methods to deſtroy it without

without effect: At laſt he manured it with ſoot, and that totally killed it.

Experiment, No. 8.

Among other manures, this gentleman has tried woollen rags; that they are a beneficial dreſſing, cannot be doubted, but I was deſirous of knowing on what ſoils they do beſt. Common huſbandmen lay them chiefly on wet ſtiff ſoils, with a view to keep them open and mellow; but it is aſſerted by ſome, that their attracting ſo much moiſture from the air, renders them proper only for hot dry ſoils. Mr. *Clayton* has uſed them on both; his expreſſion was, " that he finds them more beneficial on wet cold land, than on hot, dry, gravelly ſoils."—This is, as far as it extends, deciſive; and I need not add that theory, in theſe points, muſt give way to practice.

Experiment, No. 9.

Two contiguous fields of wheat, ſown on a fallow, were, for a compariſon, manured differently; one with lime, 80 buſhels an acre, after the corn was ſown; the other was part dunged from the yard, and
part

part dreffed with woollen rags. The product of the latter field was moft confiderable, but it was much blighted; whereas the limed one was nearly free from that diftemper.

Experiment, No. 10.

Mud from the river *Thames*, Mr. *Clayton* has tried on both grafs and arable land, frefh from the river, and alfo kept fome time, and turned over. The principal effect he has obferved from it is the production of an amazing quantity of weeds, though lefs on grafs than arable: this has deterred him from ufing more of it; but I fhould apprehend, if it was kept two years, turned over feveral times, and well mixed with lime, that it would prove a rich manure. As to the producing weeds, if it then had that effect, I would lay it on for a hoeing crop, when the effect would not matter. It certainly is probable, that the mud brings feeds, but not clear: it may be its excellence as a manure, that forces all thofe in the land to vegetate.

Experiment, No. 11.

In 1769, four acres well fallowed were planted with turnip cabbages, and fed off with sheep in *April* and *May*, 1770: they kept 60 ewes, 60 lambs, and 30 fat wethers five weeks and a half, which Mr. *Clayton* reckons at 4*d. per* week: this amounts to 8*l.* 5*s.* or *per* acre 2*l.* 1*s.* which, upon the whole, is a result favourable to the plant; as they last through the season, that is the most critical in the whole year. In a snow, Mr. *Clayton* has observed some of them eaten down by the hares, and afterwards grown over with a coat, and been quite secure from the weather. This year he has a crop of *Reynolds*'s cabbage turnip, which promises to be good sheep feed.

Experiment, No. 12.

Mr. *Clayton* had a crop of wheat, drilled in equally-distant rows, five inches asunder; it was kept clean hand-hoed, proved a good crop, but not equal to the broad-cast.

Experiment, No. 13.

Burnet was tried in laying down a field of 28 acres, part of it with sainfoine, part white

white *Dutch* clover, part bird grafs, and part burnet, and the field has at various feafons been fed with fheep, cows, horfes, &c. and they all eat the burnet quite as clofe as any of the other graffes; and the cattle of all forts are generally on the burnet part once or twice a day. This is a very fair trial, and fhews that burnet is by no means fo defpicable a plant as many would have us imagine.

Experiment, No. 14.

Sixteen acres were laid down with *Rocque*'s bird grafs. Mr. *Clayton* thinks it a valuable grafs; it is as early in the fpring as ray grafs; it thickens very much on the ground. All cattle are fond of it, and fheep remarkably fo.

Experiment, No. 15.

In planting, Mr. *Clayton* has alfo been attentive. *Weymouth* pines, fpruce, *Scotch* filver, balm of *Gilead*, the larch, cedar of *Lebanon*, and the *Virginia* cedar, all at ten feet fquare, of 13 years growth: they are worth 1 *s.* a tree now: the larch is beft, next the *Weymouth* pine and fpruce; the balm of *Gilead* does not thrive at all.

Mr.

Mr. *Clayton* plants all sorts of trees, ever-greens as well as others, in *November* and *December*, if not frosty, and has had better success than with spring planting.

A pinaster of an hundred years old was blown down, and being sawn out, it proved a red deal, but very coarse: it contained a load and a half of timber. Some *Scotch* also, of the same age, were blown down: they were red deals, and much harder and better than the foreign. The soil a thin sharp loam near the chalk *.

Sir

---

* Mr. *Clayton* has built one of the most agreeable houses I know, in a most elegant situation, and has disposed the grounds in a manner that does great honour to his taste. A fine swelling knole rises from the bank of the river *Thames*, on which the house is built, and has (from the offices being quite hid behind wood) the exact appearance of a large temple: an effect, which is never completely gained without being uncommonly agreeable. An extensive lawn waves around it, bounded on one side by the river, and on the other by a fine hanging grove, which spreads over the sides of the hill. A finer union of wood, water and lawn, can hardly be imagined.

The

Sir *John Hoby Mill*, Bart. of *Bisham-abbey* near *Marlow*, has this year a very important experiment on cabbages, carrots, and turnips; the particulars of which he was so kind as to give me.

A small field was this year cropped with these vegetables. The soil is a rich, deep, black loam, worth 3*l.* an acre: it was ploughed in *October* very deep; and twice more in the spring; the latter of these spring ploughings was given while the land was quite wet, which was very prejudicial to the crop, and also occasioned such delay, that

---

The wood is of a dark shade; in some places it projects down to the level of the lawn; in others it retires from it, and admits the livelier green among its deeper tints. It crowns the brows of some of the declivities, boldly hanging on their edges; while, on other spots, it thickens over the whole hill, to form a dark, unvaried back ground to the house, and contrasts the resplendent stream, which glides through the vale below.

The principal floor of the house is exceedingly well disposed into a dining-room, 27 by 21, with an ellipsis bow, through the windows of which the river is commanded in a most striking manner. In this room is a small antique bust of *Venus*,

that the carrots could not be sown till *April*. They were kept clean by hand-hoeing. All the expences of tillage, cleaning, &c. &c. came to 4*l.* 4*s. per* acre; and the drawing, cleaning the roots, carting home, came to 1*l.* 10*s. per* acre; the distance to which they were carted 300 yards.

The turnips were sown in *June*; and hand-hoed twice.

The cabbages were planted at the same time, in rows, 3 feet by 2; and kept clean by hand-hoeing.

Early in *November* I marked a square perch

Venus, and several portraits by Sir *Peter Lely*. On one side it opens into a drawing-room, 27 by 18; and on the other, into a noble library, of 36 by 18, with a bow of 18 by 7. The chimney-piece *Doric*, the entablature supported by columns of variegated marble. On the staircase is a very good piece by *Snyders*.

The offices, though near the house, are quite hid by the wood. Lady *Louisa Clayton* has a neat little rustic temple in the grove, which opens into her dairy. The whole building agreeable and in taste. From hence, on the brow of the hill, there is a fine winding terras, which commands various beautiful views of the river.

perch of each, and cutting off the tops of the turnips and carrots, and the roots of the cabbages; the produce was as follows.

CARROTS.

	Carrots.	lb.
No. 1. A bushel basket,	70	57
2. ——	66	59
3. ——	50	51
4. ——	78	67
5. ——	10	13
	274	247

From hence it appears that the carrots weighed above ¼ *lb.* each.

A perch yielding 4 bushel baskets and 1-6th, is in the proportion of 667 *per* acre, each 66 *lb.*

247 *lb. per* perch, are 17 tons, 12 C. 96 *lb. per* acre.

But this produce would have been much more confiderable, had the tillage been given while the land was dry and in good order.

Respecting the application of the crop, one porker was fattened quite on carrots; two others were confined 10 days to carrots, and eat 1 bushel a day; after this, 10 days
more

more at carrots, 9 pecks a day, and barley-meal 2 bushels in the ten days; when killed they weighed 64 *lb.* and 56 *lb.*

Had barley-meal only been used, they would have eat 6 bushels, the carrots therefore saved 4 bushels. They eat 15 bushels of carrots; which are therefore tantamount in value to 4 bushels of barley-meal, or 12 *s.*: this is 9 *d.* ⅕ *per* bushel of 66 *lb.* Suppose 56 *lb.* the average bushel of carrots, this is 8 *d. per* bushel; and the crop in such bushels amounts to 700.

At the same time 8 bacon hogs, that will be 10 score each, were put to carrots, and fed one month on them, to the saving 32 bushels of barley meal; after which they will have 4 bushels of barley each, but must otherwise have had 8.

		£	s.	d.
The crop is 667 bushels *per* acre; this, at 9 *d.* ⅕ *per* bushel, amounts to		25	0	0
Expences,	£.4 4 0			
Cleaning and carting,	1 10 0			
Rent,	3 0 0			
		8	14	0
Clear profit,		16	6	0

A square perch of the cabbages was as follows.

		Cabbages.	Wt.
No. 1. Bushel.		6 —	31
2.	———	5 —	31
3.	———	6 —	33
4.	———	7 —	31
5.	———	8 —	47
6.	———	8 —	44
7.	———	11 —	49
		51	266

This is rather better than 5 *lb.* each.
266 *lb.* on a perch, are 19 tons *per* acre.

The turnips were;

		Turnips.	*lb.*
No. 1. Bushel.		43 —	55
2.	———	103 —	57
3.	———	57 —	56
4.	———	54 —	55
5.	———	40 —	51
6.	———	47 —	51
7.	———	12 —	14
		356	339

This is not one pound each.

339 *lb. per* perch, are 24 tons and 4 C. *wt. per* acre.

Here it appears that the turnips exceed the cabbages in weight, but then I should observe that the latter are not the great *Scotch*, but a much inferior sort. However, the carrots much exceed in value both the turnips and cabbages.*

From *Marlow* I crossed the country to *Beconsfield*; for the following particulars of husbandry around that place, I am indebted to the very obliging attention of *Edmund Burke*, Esq.

Farms rise from 20*l*. to 200*l*. a year, but are in general about 80*l*. The soil is various; clays, loam on chalk, and gravelly clay, and much stoney loam. The arable lets from 7*s*. to 11*s*. an acre; the grass from 15*s*. to 20*s*. an acre.

The courses of crops are,

1. Turnips
2. Barley
3. Clover and ray-grass one or two years
4. Wheat
5. Barley
6. Clover
7. Oats.

---

* *Bisham Abbey*, the seat of Sir *John Hoby Mill*, is very well situated on the banks of the *Thames*; a range of wood that partly surrounds it, crowns the hills in a very noble manner.

There is nothing objectable in this courſe, but the barley of the fifth year following the wheat, which occaſions three crops of corn in the laſt four years, and the fourth clover, ſown with a ſecond corn crop. This muſt exhauſt the ſoil, and fill it with weeds. Alſo,

1. Fallow   3. Oats.
2. Wheat

Another:

1. Fallow   3. Peaſe
2. Wheat   4. Wheat.

For wheat on clover they plough but once, but three times in fallowing; ſow nine pecks of ſeed on the latter, and ten on the former, and reckon the average produce at two quarters. They ſtir three times for barley, ſow three or four buſhels an acre; the crop three quarters. For oats they ſtir but once, ſow three buſhels an acre, and gain on a medium not more than three quarters. They give one or two ſtirrings for peaſe, uſe three or four buſhels of ſeed, never hand-hoe them; the crop two quarters and a half. They plough but once for beans, ſow four buſhels an acre broad-caſt, never hoe them; the crop the ſame as of peaſe.

For

For turnips three earths are given; they are hand-hoed once or twice; all are fed with sheep; the average value 35 s. an acre.

Clover they mow twice for hay, and get four loads an acre at the two; and they reckon that the wheat sown on this grass, *mown*, is better than that which follows it when *fed*.

Both winter and summer tares are used for soiling horses; an acre of summer ones will keep four horses a month.

There is much sainfoine on their white chalky land; they sow four bushels an acre, and it lasts twenty years; always mow it once for hay: some farmers have mown it twice in a year, without finding their crops damaged by so doing: the product at once cutting rises to three loads an acre; but in general not exceeding two.

Buck-wheat is sometimes cultivated on their poorest lands; they sow two pecks an acre, and get three quarters in return.

In respect to manuring, there is not much to commend in their practice: they do not chop their stubble; and though they stack their hay at home, yet as much is fold as they can difpofe of; nor do they fold any fheep but wethers.

Chalk they lay on their ftrong foils, 15 or 20 loads an acre, in order to mellow, and make it plough the better. After grubbing up a wood, they reckon the land muft be chalked, in order to fweeten it. Compofts of dung, earth and chalk, they think extremely beneficial.

Coal afhes they fow on clover, 40 bufhels an acre, and find that they anfwer better than any other manure; they give at *London* 6*s.* the load of 50 bufhels, and they reckon the carriage, by the time they are on the land, at 14*s.* more.

Soot they fow in *March* on the green wheat, 30 or 40 bufhels an acre, at 5*d.* or 6*d.* a bufhel. They reckon that it forces the ftraw much, but is apt to caufe a blight. Both foot and afhes they alfo ufe for fainfoine, 40 bufhels an acre, in *March*.

Some few farmers ufe rabbit's dung for turnips; alfo malt duft for the fame roots, 30 bufhels an acre, at 5*d.*; but the effect is not fo good as rabbit dung.

They

They know nothing of draining in this country.

Plashing hedges is commonly practised.

The meadows are the richest grass lands here; they let from 20 *s.* to 40 *s.* an acre; all are mown for hay. The breed of cattle most common is the long-horned *Derbyshire:* a good cow they reckon will give 7 *lb.* of butter a week, from three gallons of milk a day, but most are applied to suckling: the product about 5 *l.* 5 *s.* a cow. The winter food chiefly hay, no turnips; which is very strange, where suckling is practised; to give cows, so applied, hay, while turnips are to be had, is a most unprofitable conduct.

It is a common practice to put many beasts of all sorts to fatten in the vale of *Aylesbury*, during 20 weeks, at 1 *s.* 6 *d.* a week; if the beast fattens sooner, another is sent instead of it; but if it takes a longer time, no more is paid than the 30 *s.*

Swine they fatten from eight to twenty five score.

Flocks rise to 3 or 400; but not so many the whole year, not more than half. They buy in every year, either *Dorset* or *Wiltshire* ewes:

ewes: the former reckoned best, because they lamb earlier; the price 18 s. for the *Dorset*, and 15 s. for the *Wiltshire*; they fatten them; and sell the lambs at 16 s. to 20 s.

Average,	-	-	£. 0	18	0
The ewe at,	-	-	0	18	0
The wool,	-	-	0	2	0
Total,	-	-	1	18	0
First cost,	-		0	18	0
Profit,	-	-	1	0	0

This the *Dorsets*; but the wool of the *Wiltshires* are not worth more than 1 s. 6 d. They buy in in *March*, and sell at that time twelvemonth; but the most profitable time would be at *Weyhill* fair in *October*.

In their tillage, they reckon six horses necessary for 100 acres of arable land; they use from four to six in a plough, do an acre a day, from four to six inches deep, the price 7 s. or 8 s. an acre. They allow their horses a peck of oats a day, and some more: cutting straw into chaff is commonly practised. They break up their stubbles for a fallow about *Christmas*.

Single-

Single-wheel ploughs chiefly ufed.

In the hiring and ftocking farms, they reckon that three rents will do.

Land fells at from 25 to 30 years purchafe.

Tythes chiefly gathered.

Poor rates 2 s. 6 d. in the pound. The employment, lace-making. All drink tea.

There are fome leafes; but on many eftates none.

LABOUR.

In harveft, 2 s. and beer.
In hay-time, 1 s. 4 d. and ditto.
In winter, 1 s. 2 d.
Reaping, 6 s. to 7 s.
Mowing corn, 1 s. 3 d. to 1 s. 4 d.
——— grafs, 2 s. to 2 s. 6 d.
Hoeing turnips, 5 s.
Head-man's wages, 8 l.
Next ditto, 6 l.
Lad's, 4 l.
Dairy-maid's, 3 l. to 4 l.
Women a day in harveft, 10 d. and beer.
In hay-time, ditto.

PROVISIONS.

Bread,	1 $d.\frac{1}{4}$ *per lb.* (9 *lb.* for 11 $d.\frac{1}{2}$.)
Cheese,	$4\frac{1}{4}$
Butter,	$7\frac{1}{4}$
Beef,	3
Mutton,	4
Veal,	5
Pork,	4
Bacon,	7
Milk,	$\frac{1}{2}$ *per* pint; but very little to be had.
Potatoes,	8 *per* peck.

Labourer's house-rent, 40 *s.* to 50 *s.*
——————— firing, 30 *s.*

There are many beech woods in this country, managed pretty much in the same manner as those about *Menlow*. They thin them here once in nine years, and pick the best trees, to the amount of from 4 *l.* to 10 *l.* an acre.

Mr. *Burke* has been an arable farmer but a short time; he has however made so good a use of it, as to have formed several experiments, which will speak sufficiently for themselves; but let me first insert the particulars of his farm, which will shew that the scale of his husbandry is not small,

410 Acres in all	2 Carrots
160 Grafs	1 Cabbages
160 Arable	2 Potatoes
90 Wood	8 Vetches
250 *l.* Rent	6 Horses
40 Acres wheat	14 Cows
25 Barley	6 Young cattle
16 Oats	40 Swine
16 Peafe	1 Man
25 Turnips	2 Boys
25 Clover	6 Labourers.

CARROTS.

Experiment, No. 1.

Two acres of good rich deep wheat loam, more inclinable to gravel than fand, and rather wet, were fallowed in 1769, receiving three common ploughings; in the winter manured with 30 loads of yard dung thoroughly rotten, ploughed 16 inches deep in *January*, with four horfes in a plough, going twice in a furrow: the middle of *February* harrowed in 4 *lb. per* acre of carrot feed. It came up very well, and the plants were twice hand-hoed, at the expence of 30*s.* an acre; being fet out, at the diftance of eight inches from each

each other. In *October*, &c. they were taken up as wanted; the expence of digging up and cleaning, is 7 *s.* 6 *d.* a load of 50 bushels.

The carrots are not so straight and fair as those which grow in sand, but are of an higher and finer colour, and most aromatic smell; firm, and admirably tasted. In the application of the crop, Mr. *Burke* tried the boiling them for fattening hogs; he put up several porkers of about 20 *lb.* the quarter, some to barley meal, and others to boiled carrots, with which they were supplied very plentifully; 3 weeks elapsed without their making the smallest progress. Mr. *Burke* had made a similar trial the year before, and the result was the same. This result is unfortunate; but he intends next year to renew the trials, until success attends them; or a clear knowledge is gained, why it cannot be expected. I am not sorry to find some experiments, in which carrots for this application turn out inferior, because I hope it will animate the farming part of my readers to give their attention minutely to this point; that it may be fully and clearly known in what degree this root given alone will fatten:

whether

whether porkers or hogs for bacon—whether compleatly, or only getting them in better flesh—whether they must be longer confined to them, than to the more usual sorts of food? All these are points of consequence, but in which we are by no means clear.

DEEP PLOUGHING.

Mr. *Burke* ploughs in common from 10 to 12 inches deep: this being double what the farmers ever attempt, surprized his bailiff, who declared that his crops would be utterly ruined; but a regular and unbroken success in every one has convinced him, that deep ploughing is not so pernicious a practice as he apprehended. The products have been better than those of the neighbouring farmers. Now this is a most material point, for if he has such crops at first, he most undoubtedly will have great ones afterwards; for by keeping to that depth in the successive tillage, the whole soil so deep will become one uniform mass; and there cannot remain a doubt, but all sorts of vegetables will come to greater perfection in such a stratum, than in one of only four or five inches deep; for the roots even of
white

white corn will presently strike a foot deep, and it is idle to suppose that such a power is given them for nothing: wherever they go, they certainly draw nourishment.

DRAINING.

Experiment, No. 2.

Ten acres of land were so very wet, that the crops produced by it were trifling. Mr. *Burke* cut hollow drains across it, 18 inches deep, and three wide at bottom; some of them three feet deep, varying with the fall of the land; they were filled with chalk stones, and some with bushes· the latter the cheapest: the drains answered extremely well, for the land has since been quite dry.

DRILLED BEANS.

Experiment, No. 3.

A field of a strong loamy soil very foul, that came in course to be fallowed, was drilled with beans in equally-distant rows, 18 inches asunder, as a trial of this husbandry, for cleaning land when out of order, instead of a fallow: they were hand-hoed twice; the crop turned out indifferent, but the field was perfectly cleaned by them.

POTATOES.
Experiment, No. 4.

Two acres, contiguous to the carrots of *Experiment*, No. 1, were planted with potatoes in *March*, 1770, in rows equally-distant, one foot asunder; they were manured for with 15 loads an acre of rotten yard dung; they were twice hand-hoed, and as often weeded.

LUCERNE.
Experiment, No. 5.

A rood of land, a good stoney loam, was manured with a common dressing of yard dung, and drilled with lucerne, in equally-distant rows, 18 inches asunder. In 1769, it was cut three times; and kept perfectly free from weeds by hoeing. This year it has been cut four times, and kept clean as before: the produce has in general been, each cutting, keeping two horses eight days: this is an acre keeping two horses four weeks and half, and the three cuttings of 1769, consequently kept them thirteen weeks and a half, which, at 2 s. 6 d. *per* horse *per* week, amounts to 3 l. 7 s. 6 d,

3*l*. 7*s*. 6*d*. The four of 1769, to 4*l*. 10*s*. but the plantation is not near arrived at perfection.

MANURES.

Experiment, No. 6.

Lime was tried on pasture, the soil a gravelly loam, 100 bushels *per* acre; but it proved of no service.

Experiment, No. 7.

A comparison was made between pigeon's dung, rabbit's dung, and yard dung, proportioned to their respective values. The pigeon's dung was the best; then the rabbit's dung, and lastly the yard dung.

OXEN.

Oxen this gentleman uses in his tillage with great success; he works them in harness in the manner already mentioned to be practised by Mr. *Cooke* and Sir *Charles Tynte*; he uses three and one horse in a plough, or four oxen, and they do an acre a day; whereas the farmers plough no more land with from four to six horses: it is from hence very evident, that the practice must answer very greatly; it reduces the price of tillage more than half.

SHEEP.

It is the custom of this country to fold only the wethers; but Mr. *Burke* has regularly practised the folding his ewes as well as wethers, and without the least inconvenience to his flock.

CABBAGES.
Experiment, No. 8.

In the same field, as the carrots of *Experiment,* No. 2. half an acre was winter-fallowed, trench-ploughed, and manured with yard dung; it was then thrown on to the four-feet ridge, and at *Midsummer* planted with cabbages (the seed sown for the great *Scotch)* in single rows on each ridge, two feet asunder. They turned out a *Scotch* kale; very strong, branching and luxuriant in growth; the leaves were stripping in *November* for cattle, and the stalks left for producing a spring crop of shoots; and I doubt not, but the quantity will then also be very considerable.

These experiments are valuable, and cannot but be attended with very good effects to the husbandry of the neighbourhood; but the introducing the culture of carrots, the folding ewes, the use of oxen, and the practice of hollow draining can scarcely fail of proving highly important: these articles of management continued with the spirit, with which Mr. *Burke* will prosecute them, will by degrees bring his tenants into the same conduct: the advantages which must result from such an imitation are many and striking. His country is much indebted to him for giving so laudable an attention to the improvement of her husbandry *.

From

---

* This gentleman's seat, near *Beconsfield*, is a large, regular, and convenient house, extremely well situated in the midst of an agreeable park, which commands various views of the adjacent country, rendered fine by the uncommon number of woods, which spread over the sides of the hills. The north front of the house looks over a large extent of country, wholly surrounded with distant woods, which have so magnificent an appearance, that one would think every tree planted with design to ornament it.

In the house is a very fine collection of antique busts and statues, likewise several pictures by the greatest hands: among others,

Guido. *Europa:* her figure is not agreeable, but the picture very well executed; the colouring is chaste.

From *Beconsfield*, I took the road through *Uxbridge* to *Brentford*, where I turned off to *Sion-Hill*.

The Earl of *Holderneſſe*, at his elegant villa, *Sion-Hill*, has laid down much arable land to graſs, and with great ſucceſs. His farm was all wet arable land and unprofitable; this determined him to throw the whole to graſs; and in executing it, his lordſhip,

---

Morellio.   *Venus* riſing from the bath; a very large picture; fine.
Carlo Marratt.   Holy family.
Pouſſin.   A dance of boy angels; ſtrong relief, and very good colouring.
Titian.   Exceeding fine; the colouring ſtriking.
Gaſ. Pouſſin.   A landſcape: the keeping and colours fine; but the figures admirable: the attitude of the virgin turning to the boy preſenting fruit, is inimitable, and the child in her arms, reaching out its hand to the figure on the pedeſtal, natural: the whole group complete and elegant.
Carlo Marratt.   The *Virgin* teaching a boy, *Jeſus*, to read: her head is well done, the fall of the countenance eaſy.
Unknown.   Holy family, the *Virgin*, *Chriſt*, and *St. John*, elegantly grouped: the *Virgin's* countenance and attention pleaſing,

lordship, instead of the slovenly custom of many of his neighbours, of sowing only ray grass and clover, with such a design, he used nothing but clean dressed hay seeds, white clover and trefoile; the lands were all laid by the previous tillage, perfectly level, were clean, fine and in good heart. The seeds were all sown *without* corn, a method which lord *Holderness* has practised on all his estates, and with such success, that he

---

pleasing, and extremely well coloured; the boy fine.

Unknown. The marriage of *St. Catharine*, a pleasing group; the countenance very attentive, the boy excellent; the colours lively, but tender.

Ditto. *Jupiter*, and two bold and well-executed figures; the outlines strong and expressive, and the colouring good.

Gas. Poussin. Landscape: were it not for the buildings, the piece would be a total gloom; but it is finely done: the composition and colouring are good.

Ditto. Its companion, a more chearful subject, very fine.

Titian. A sleeping *Cupid*, exceedingly beautiful.

Unknown. A sea-piece; fine.

Ditto. A small figure of a saint, most highly finished; the drapery good, and the colouring very brilliant.

he has determined never to purfue any other. The fields are all well turfed, and of a good herbage.

Cabbages his lordfhip has cultivated fome years at *Sion*. The fort a large flat-headed winter cabbage, which he procured from *Newbury* in *Berkfhire*; the method ufed was to draw furrows at four feet, acrofs the fields both ways; and where they interfect the plants are fet, confe_quently

---

Unknown. *Venus*: a fmall picture, finely finifhed; her attitude is pleafing, and the flow of the drapery elegant.
Ditto. Mars and *Venus*; in fmall.
Ditto. A flower-piece, finifhed in the higheft manner.
Carlo Maratt. The *Aurora* after *Guido*; exceeding fine; the grace and elegance of the original happily preferved.
Titian. A group of female figures; good.
Guido. An old man's head.
Raphael Mengs. Two heads in a peculiar but pleafing ftile.
Borgognone. Two battle-pieces.
Gaf. Pouffin. Five landfcapes, admirably fine.
Velafque. A revelling fcene; a ftrong dark expreffion, the light and fhade quite blotches.
Luca Giordano. Two pieces; fine.
Scarlatti. A fick man's dreams; ftrangely wild, but

quently they are lower than the surface of the field: this his lordship thinks is an advantage, as they enjoy more moisture, the earth is easier drawn to their shanks; and what is of very great consequence, standing in squares, the horse-hoeing is given *both* ways, crossing each other, which saves much expence of hand-hoeing, at the same time that the land is so much better tilled.

This method has turned out very advantageous, many of the cabbages rising from 25 to 30 *lb*. The use they are applied to is fattening oxen. His lordship grazes many large beasts on his new-laid fields, and he finishes them with cabbages; gives them on a dry grass field, with hay in a small house constantly for them: turnips he sometimes uses in the same manner.

His lordship's dairy of cows is a very fine one, of the *Holderness* breed; but the cow-house

---

	but fanciful: it is in the same stile as a madman's brains at *Kiplin*; and Lord *Spencer* has one of witchcraft.
Unknown.	*Susanna* and the Elders; a copy: her attitude, the eagerness of the old men, the light and shade, and keeping, are well done.

house is extremely well contrived; there is a space before their heads, wide enough to walk with the hay; and what I have not before seen, a trench is cut in the pavement just at their heels, and so close to them, that all the dung falls into it: there is no drain from it, so all the dung, urine, and the refuse hay, is mixed up together, and barrowed on to the dunghill; all the urine is preserved thus, and without any trouble: the dunghill is close to the pigsties (which are also very well contrived) so the different dungs are regularly mixed together, which is certainly an advantage *.

From *Sion* I returned to *Uxbridge*, and took the road home through *Stanmore* and

---

* *Sion-Hill* is not a large house, but the apartments excellently disposed: a dining-room 22 by 18, where is a large fine portrait of the Duke of *Chandois*. A drawing-room, 50 by 20, with a bow; the chimney-piece is of white marble, the cornice projecting beyond the center, and resting on *Ionic* pillars of *Siena* marble. The view from the bow is pleasing, the grounds wave and fall agreeably. Besides these rooms, there is a breakfast-room, and a handsome library. In the *Attic* story are three bed-chambers, and three dressing-rooms. Lady *Holdernesse*'s

and *Edgware*. In the way to the former place, there is some meadow that lets at 25*s*. to 40*s*. an acre: but many open fields at 12*s*. and 13*s*. which are cultivated in the following course.

1. Fallow
2. Wheat
3. Beans.

Wheat yields three quarters an acre. The beans are set in rows, at 12 or 14 inches asunder, and kept clean by hand-hoeing: an uncommon instance of good husbandry, with a crop that is succeeded by a fallow: the product five quarters *per* acre.

About *Edgware* and *Stanmore* the ground is chiefly grass, richly manured, it lets from

---

Holderneſſe's is elegantly furnished: the chimney-piece white marble, with fluted *Ionic* pillars of *Siena*; in the frieze, a tablet, representing painting and sculpture, neatly executed. Over it a glass in gilt ornaments, very light, intermixed with porcelain figures. There is an anti-room with books, and a closet out of it, with a case of china, gilt in a very neat and elegant manner. Over these rooms are several bed-chambers and dressing-rooms. Her ladyship's dairy is extremely well contrived for coolness, &c.

from 30 *s.* to 3 *l.* an acre. From hence I entered the great north road at *Barnet*; there joining the country before travelled, and where I shall accordingly take my leave of you for the present.

*   *   *

And now, fir, having finifhed my journey, I muft proceed to give you a general view of the articles of the moft confequence, fcattered up and down in a various manner throughout the preceding minutes: each has in numerous places a very different appearance, owing to variations of foil, culture, &c. but a clear and comprehenfive idea of any one can only be gained by an average of all circumftances: a perfon, who cultivates a plant on a foil peculiarly adapted to it, may probably have a greater fuccefs, than others are to expect: fome likewife might, from contrary reafons, have worfe fuccefs, and yet without proving any thing generally againft the plant: all fuch variations fhould be taken into a general account, and an average drawn, which would then be a fair reprefentation of the culture.

Refpecting

Respecting the products, and other circumstances attending common crops, the rates of labour and provision, and the particulars of farms, which are data for the state of the whole kingdom to be deduced from, with other matters of the same kind, I am happy in finding, from very many persons, whose judgment I have the highest opinion of, as well as from the criticisms of several foreign writers (who must speak unprejudiced) that the deductions I made in the 4th volume of the *Northern Tour*, on this plan, have met with the approbation I could wish, and been pronounced as important a part as any of the work; I shall therefore, in the present case, proceed in the same path, notwithstanding the assertions of some persons, who characterised that volume by mentioning nothing concerning it but *prolixity*; such readers should be referred to *pretty light summer reading for the ladies.*

Without further introduction, I shall proceed to the particulars.

And am, &c.

LETTER XXXII.

CARROTS in the minutes of this Tour make a diftinguifhed figure: I met with fo many experiments on this moft excellent root, that I think there is great reafon to expect it will foon become common hufbandry; which would be one of the moft fortunate circumftances that could poffibly happen to the agriculture of *Britain*. It has been tried in fcarcely any place without being adhered to: Indeed, we may fafely pronounce that whoever does juftice to it in the cultivation, will certainly find it one of the moft profitable crops in the world; but a review of the particulars bringing the moft material points into one view, will beft prove the truth of this affertion.

Mr. *Cope*, at *Arnold, Nottinghamfhire*.
Soil. Rich, deep, dark-coloured fand, at 18 *s.*
Culture. Three earths 12 inches deep. Manures 50 *s.* to 3 *l.* an acre. Hoes at the expence of 30 *s.* to 50 *s.*

Product. 21 Tons.

Use. Feeding and fatting cows, oxen, sheep, horses, hogs. Cows 2 bushels a day. Completely fatted to 12 *l.* 12 *s.* each, and oxen to 20 *l.* Fats hogs completely to 12 and 14 stone (14 *lb.*)

Expences. - - £. 8 9 0

Mr. *Mellish*, Blyth.

Soil. Rich deep sand, at 20 *s.*
Culture. Ploughs for them. Hoes, at 2 *l.* 2 *s.* No manure.
Product. 20 Tons, at 20 *s.* a ton.
Use. Feeding horses and cows, and fattening hogs.

Expences. - - £. 6 2 0
Profit. - - 13 18 9

Mr. *Wharton*, of *Carr-house*.

Soil. Rich sand, at 50 *s.*
Produce. 20 Tons.

Mr. *Stovin*, Doncaster.

Soil. Rich sand, at 40 *s.*
Culture. Trench ploughing from a lay, but turf carried off. Hoed at expence 8 *l.* 8 *s.* 3 *d.*

Product. 6 ¼ Ton, at 4 *l.*
Use. Pigs bought and fatted on them boiled, and then sold; paid 4 *l.* a ton, and feeding cart-horses.

Mr. *Cook, Wheatly.*

Soil. Light loam on lime-stone, 10 inches deep.
Use. Feeding horses, excellent for the wind.

Mr. *Moody, Retford.*

Soil. Rich sand, at 40 *s.*
Culture. Ploughed 12 inches deep; hand-hoed clean, 9 inches asunder.
Product. 20 Tons, at 20 *s.*; also 25 tons, at 20 *s.*
Use. Fatting of oxen of from 80 to 110 stone; four beasts to an acre 14 weeks. No food fattens better; as well as oil cake.

Expences.	-	-	£.7	9	3
Profit.	-	-	15	0	9
And by dung,	-		5	0	0

About *Norwich.*

Soil. A sandy loam, 16 *s.*
Culture. Trench ploughing; manure with 10 loads of long dung. Three hoeings, at 1 *l.* 1 *s.*

Mr. *Fellowes, Shottesham.*

Soil. Light loam.
Culture. Trench ploughed 10 inches; manures with 12 loads of yard dung. Hoes, at 1 *l.* 1 *s.*
Product.
    600 bushels.
    778 ditto.
    350 ditto, being 8 tons 17 C. *wt.*
    ―――
    1728
    ―――
    576 average.

Use. Feeding horses.
Expences. - - £. 5 14 0

About *Saxmundham.*

Soil. Rich sand, at 14 *s.*
Product. 800 Bushels.
Use. Fatting hogs, and feeding horses.

About *Woodbridge.*

Soil. Rich deep sand, at 20 *s.*
Culture. Trench ploughed 12 inches deep; no manuring. Three hand-hoeings, at from 16 *s.* to 21 *s. per* acre.
Product. 698 Bushels, at 6 *d.* £. 17 9 0
Use. Feeding horses; allow a bushel *per* horse *per* day, and give no corn. And fatten hogs completely.

Mr. *Acton*, *Bramford*.
Soil. A sandy loam, at 12 s. 6 d.
Culture. Trench ploughing. No manuring. Three hand-hoeings, 30 s. an acre.
Product.　　　960 Bushels.
　　　　　　　765 Ditto.
　　　　　　　―――
　　　　　　　1725

　　　　　　　862 average.
Which, at 8 d. are,　-　£.25 10 0
Use. Feeding horses.

　　　　Mr. *Hilton*, *Feversham*.
Soil. Rich black loam, at 4 l.
Product. 1000 Bushels.
Expences.　-　-　-　£.9 0 0

　　　　Mr. *Taylor*, *Bifrons*.
Soil. Good loam, at 20 s.
Culture. Ploughed 12 inches. Hand-hoed twice.
Product.　　　8 Tons, at 20 s.
　　　　　　　16 ditto.
　　　　　　　10 ditto.
　　　　　　　―――
　　　　　　　34

　　　　　　　11 average.
Which, at 20 s.　　-　£11 0 0
Use. Feeding horses.

Mr. *Legrand*, *Ash*.

Soil. A sandy loam, at 20 s.

Culture. Ploughing 8 or 9 inches deep; manuring, 80 loads compost, kept clean by hoeing.

Produce.   30 tons.
             20 ditto.
             ―――
             50
             ―――
             25 average.

Use. Horses; a ton *per* week to the team; swine, cows, and fatting wethers.

Expences, - -	£. 9	15 3
Profit, - - -	7	4 9
Value per ton, - -	0	17 0
And *per* bushel, - -	0	0 4¾

Sir *John Hoby Mill*, Bart. at *Bisham*.

Soil. Rich black loam, at 3 *l.*

Culture. Three ploughings very deep, and kept clean by hand-hoeing.

Product. 17 Tons, 12 C. wt. 96 *lb.* or 700 bushels, at 8*d. per* bushel, 25 *l.*

Use. Fattening hogs.

Expences, - -	£. 8	14 0
Profit, - -	16	6 0

Mr. *Burke*, at *Beconsfield*.

Soil. Rich deep loam.

Culture. Well manured and ploughed 16 inches deep, and kept clean by hoeing.

Use. Feeding various cattle, but hogs (even porkers) would not fatten on them.

There is upon the whole a greater variation in thefe minutes than I have met with in moſt articles; but we muſt throw thofe that will admit it into complete views.

The firſt enquiry I ſhall make is into the value of the carrots: all the minutes do not contain this material information; many of them do; but fome valuations being by the ton, and others by the buſhel, I ſhall give both rates, by calculating the buſhel to weigh 56 *lb.* which is the average of many buſhels I have weighed myfelf: in the preceding tour other weights are mentioned : but it was in compliance with the ideas of the various perfons concerned. The rates marked with an afterifm are thofe minuted, the others are calculated.

CROPS.	Value per ton.			Value per bush.	
	l.	s.	d.	s.	d.
Mr. *Cope*, the selling price,	1	0	0	0	6*
Mr. *Mellish*, ditto,	1	0	0	0	6
Mr. *Stovin*, fatting hogs,	4	0	0*	2	0
Mr. *Moody*, fatting oxen,	1	0	0*	0	6
At *Woodbridge*, selling price,	1	0	0	0	6*
Mr. *Acton*, ditto,	1	6	8	0	8*
Mr. *Taylor*, value,	1	0	0*	0	6
Mr. *Legrand*, fatting sheep,	0	14	0*	0	4¼
Sir *J. Mill*, ditto hogs,	1	6	8	0	8*
Average,	1	7	5¼	0	8¼

Upon this table I must remark, that the high price of Mr. *Stovin*'s carrots is by no means to be rejected, because the expenditure was uncommonly accurate: 26 hogs were bought lean and sold from carrots fat, which is of all others the fairest method of trying the value; it is also *weight* not *measure* that was depended on; the latter is not always accurate; and I may further remark, that the value is not at all impeached by the other prices, because none of the other applications were similar: Sir *John Mill*'s crop was given to hogs, but raw, whereas Mr. *Stovin*'s were boiled: there is no absolute authority extant, that boiling will make so great a difference,

difference, but we do not know the contrary. Hence therefore, the price of 4*l.* *per* ton, or 2 *s.* a bushel, must undoubtedly be relied on as accurate, and the superiority of it to the other prices attributed to the circumstances of giving them *boiled* to *hogs.* We may divide the table thus.

	Boiled for hogs.					
	l.	*s.*	*d.*	*l.*	*s.*	*d.*
Mr. *Stovin,*	4	0	0	0	2	0
	Raw to hogs.					
Sir *J. Mill,*	1	6	8	0	0	8
	Fattening oxen.					
Mr. *Moody,*	1	0	0	0	0	6
	Fattening sheep.					
Mr. *Legrand,*	0	14	0	0	0	4
	Selling prices.					
Mr. *Cope,*	1	0	0	0	0	6
Mr. *Mellish,*	1	0	0	0	0	6
Woodbridge,	1	0	0	0	0	6
Mr. *Acton,*	1	6	8	0	0	8
Average,	1	1	8	0	0	6¼
	Feeding horses.					
Mr. *Taylor,*	1	0	0	0	0	6

In the next place, I shall give the products in both tons and bushels. Those marked are the quantities minuted, and the others calculated at 56*lb*. a bushel.

	Tons.	Bushels.
Mr. *Cope*,	*21	840
Mr. *Mellish*,	*20	800
Mr. *Wharton*,	*20	800
Mr. *Stovin*,	*6½	260
Mr. *Moody*,	*22½	900
Mr. *Fellowes*,	14½	576*
Saxmundham,	20	800*
Woodbridge,	17	698*
Mr. *Acton*,	21¼	862*
Mr. *Hilton*,	25	1000*
Mr. *Taylor*,	*11	440
Mr. *Legrand*,	*25	1000
Sir *John Mill*,	*17½	700
	T. C.	
Average,	18 12	744

These products are great, and shew plainly, that carrots will in general yield a very considerable quantity of food. Eighteen tons of so rich and solid food must go very far in fattening or keeping any kind of cattle. But on this head, we have in two articles the exact truth.

Mr.

Mr. *Moody* found that 20 tons fattened four beasts, weighing on an average 95 stone (14 *lb.*) during 14 weeks, each beast having 7 *lb.* of hay *per diem.*

But the fatting season for such large beasts lasting from the first of *November* to the end of *March*, or near it, may be called 20 weeks, consequently an acre of 18 ton 12 *C. wt.* will completely fatten about three beasts during that time; it is not an exact proportion, but near it. Hence we find, that if the carrots are applied to fattening such large oxen, three must be procured to every average acre. The very purchase of the beasts will therefore be near 40 *l. per* acre, besides hay. This shews clearly, that the culture of carrots, for fattening oxen, can be undertaken by nobody that has not a great plenty of money always ready.

In fattening sheep, Mr. *Legrand*'s trials inform us, that 20 wethers, of 30 *lb.* a quarter, will eat a ton a week, and 4 *C. wt.* of hay; and that they are 20 weeks in fatting; the average acre will therefore fat 18 $\frac{1}{2}$. This at 25 *s.* come to 23 *l. per* acre, besides hay. We also find by the same

same gentleman, that four horses should have a ton a week. But at *Woodbridge* they give but 14 *C. wt. per* week. The average of these two accounts is 17 *C. wt.*; the average acre of 18½ tons will therefore feed a team of four horses 21 weeks; that is, from the first of *November* to the end of *March*. Seven weeks, or a third longer, would last till lucerne, &c. was ready, so one acre and one third is sufficient for wintering four horses without oats: this is a very important article.

In feeding milch cows, Mr. *Cope* of *Arnold*, gives each two bushels a day; this is a ton and a half *per* month. In a winter of six months a cow would therefore eat nine tons, consequently an acre would winter feed two cows: but this would by no means answer; for one cow would eat in value 12 *l.* in winter: hence it is clearly proved, that no one but a fool will give a cow meat enough to keep her in good order, of a sort that will fat an ox; for in this instance the cow's butter would cost you perhaps 5 *s.* or 6 *s.* a pound, at the same time that the ox in fat would pay you considerable profit. I never see cows well

well kept in winter (that is on any thing but straw) without being extremely clear, that money is daily loft by them. If they calve early, they muft have hay or green food; for the former they can never pay, and I much queftion whether they near pay even for turnips.

From thefe data we may fee, that a fmall quantity of land, cultivated under carrots, will enable a man to keep great ftocks of cattle. Suppofe, for inftance, that he has ten acres of this root annually, and that he keeps eight horfes, his ftock on carrots may be,

On 2 ⅔ acres, the horfes, - 8
On 3 , acres, fheep, - 60
On 4 acres, oxen, - - 12

In what other hufbandry will ten acres of land be made to winter keep eight horfes, and fatten twelve oxen, of 95 ftone, and 60 wethers, worth 45 s. a-piece? In no other application of the land can any thing like this be done.

In the next place we fhould review the expences, the value of the crops, and the profit.

Crops.	Rent.			Expences.			Value.			Profit.		
Mr. Cope,	0	18	0	8	9	0	21	0	0	12	11	0
Mr. Mellish,	1	0	0	6	2	0	20	0	0	13	18	0
Mr. Wharton,	2	10	0	—	—	—	27	9	6*	—	—	—
Mr. Stovin,	2	0	0	—	—	—	26	0	0	—	—	—
Mr. Moody,	2	0	0	7	9	3	22	10	0	15	0	9
Mr. Fellowes,	0	16	0	5	14	0	19	18	6*	14	4	6
Saxmundham,	0	14	0	—	—	—	27	14	2*	—	—	—
Woodbridge,	1	0	0	—	—	—	17	0	0	—	—	—
Mr. Acton,	0	12	6	—	—	—	28	13	4	—	—	—
Mr. Hilton,	4	0	0	9	0	0	34	6	10*	25	6	10
Mr. Taylor,	1	0	0	—	—	—	11	0	0	—	—	—
Mr. Le Grand,	1	0	0	9	15	3	17	10	0	7	14	9
Sir J. Mill,	3	0	0	8	14	0	23	6	8	14	12	8
Averages,	1	11	7	7	17	7	22	16	0	14	15	6

The first object that calls for our attention in this table, is, the richness of the soil; the average of the rents being a guinea and half an acre; this is an uncommon degree of fertility; besides which natural richness, some of the crops are amply manured; this evidently shews that great success, such for instance, as here appears, much depends on the soil either being naturally extremely fertile, or rendered so by the force of manures. The true carrot soil appears plainly to be the rich black mould, the *putre solum*, at three or four pounds an acre rent. This is the land

---

* These articles valued by the average rate.

land which yields the greatest crops. But carrots, at the same time, thrive nobly in inferior soils. The average rent of the *Saxmundham* ones, Mr. *Fellowes* and Mr. *Acton*, is but 14 *s*. 2 *d*. and yet the average product of those three, is so high as 25 *l*. 8 *s*. 8 *d*.; which shews how well it will answer on land of no extraordinary fertility.

The average expence rising to 7 *l*. 17 *s*. 7 *d*. indicates that the husbandry is correct and spirited; indeed, such noble crops must not be expected without great expences. From that sum we find, that any person who would cultivate ten acres of carrots to advantage, must appropriate 78 *l*. 15 *s*. 10 *d*. to the work, besides the sum requisite for buying cattle, which is about 35 *l*. an acre; or for ten 350 *l*. It is from hence plain, that they will never be much cultivated by common farmers, whose husbandry, in general, is so bad, from a want of money to carry on better.

The product of 22 *l*. 16 *s*. and the clear profit of fourteen guineas an acre, are the material proofs of the excellency of the husbandry. On ten acres you reap a clear advantage (all expences paid) of 147 *l*. 15 *s*.

What

What other culture will equal this? Common husbandry must be extended over a large tract of land to yield such a profit, and what a vast difference between this sum arising from 10 acres, admirably cleaned, and richly manured, and the general run of crops, which foul and exhaust the soil, and are attended by numerous expences arising from the quantity of land. Nor is this the only point, for the dung arising in the expenditure of the crop is of vast consequence in the improvement of other fields. This circumstance leads me to a further examination.

An acre of 20 tons produced, in fattening oxen, as much dung as was worth 5 *l.* expence of straw, for litter, deducted. This new value is therefore exactly 5 *s. per* ton on the crop.

Mr. *Legrand,* of *Ash*, from attending for some years, very minutely, to the improvement of his grass, by fattening sheep on carrots; determines the benefit from each acre of 20 tons, to be 3 *l.*; which is 3 *s. per* ton on the crop.

Mr. *Moody,*	-	-	£.0	5	0
Mr. *Legrand,*	-	-	0	3	0
Average,	-	-	-	0	4	0

Confequently the dung arifing from the crop of 18 ½ tons, comes to 3 *l*. 14 *s*. This taken into the account, and calculated to all the crops, will enable us to have a complete view of their moft important circumftances.

Crops.	Tons.	At per ton.	Product. Value.	Profit.
Mr. Cope,	21	1 4 0	25 4 0	16 15 0
Mr. Mellifh,	20	1 4 0	24 0 0	17 18 0
Mr. Wharton,	20	1 11 5	†31 14 2	— — —
Mr. Stovin,	6 ¾	4 4 0	27 6 0	— — —
Mr. Moody,	22 ½	1 4 0	27 0 0	19 10 9
Mr. Fellowes,	14 ½	1 11 5	22 16 6	17 2 6
Saxmundham,	20	1 11 5	†31 14 2	— — —
Woodbridge,	17	1 4 0	20 8 0	— — —
Mr. A?en,	21 ½	1 10 8	32 19 4	— — —
Mr. Hilton,	25	1 11 5	39 6 10	30 6 10
Mr. Taylor,	11	1 4 0	13 4 0	— — —
Mr. Legrand,	25	0 18 0	22 10 0	12 14 9
Sir . Mill,	17 ½	1 10 8	26 16 8	18 2 8
	T. Cwt. 18 12	*1 11 5	26 10 8	18 18 7

This table includes the moft material circumftances of the experiments on carrots. Had the article, Expences, been complete, the column of profit would have been the fame; but the profit may be calculated in another manner.

---

† There is a fmall difference in thefe products, owing to fractions, one being calculated, originally, from the bufhel, and the other from the ton.

* The old average price with addition of 4 *s*.

Product,	-	-	£.26	10	8
Expences,	-	-	7	17	7
Profit,	-	-	-	18	13	1

Which remainder coming so near to the other average, gives us no slight reason to suppose, that the average of the seven crops, whereof the profit is minuted, is very near the average of the whole thirteen, had they all been expressed.

Thus including the value of the dung in the account, I must be allowed to think totally necessary: It is as much a part of the product as the cash, and a good husbandman will always have it as strongly in view. The best farmers in the kingdom make a very considerable difference between the price of a crop of turnips, to be drawn and carted from the land, and to be fed on it with sheep; in one case they will sell at 30 *s.* but in the other not under 3 *l.* This clearly shews that the manure arising from the crop, they esteem a principal part of it: it is on this account they will have turnips that cost them 40 *s.* or 50 *s.* an acre, and sell them for 30 *s.* Nor is it possible, too often, to inculcate the real importance

portance of hoeing crops, which, in confuming, yield great quantities of manure. It is thefe crops which keep the fields of a farm in fine order, and increafing in fertility: they are the foundation of great products of corn; in a word, the effence of good hufbandry; and I fhould here remark on the preceding trials of carrots, that we do not yet fee the *whole* product refulting from them, for, befides the vaft benefit the land receives from the carrot tillage, and inceffant hoeings, there is the remaining value of the manure, the whole expence of which is, in feveral of the trials, carried to the account of carrots, though all the fucceeding crops of the courfe are greatly benefited by it.

The clear profit of EIGHTEEN GUINEAS *per* acre, on a crop which cleans and ameliorates the ground in a very high degree, is fo confiderable, that all good hufbandmen who are fituated on fands or rich loams, fhould eagerly embrace the culture. I will venture to affert that they, in no other article, will equal it. And as it appears from the experiments, both of Mr. *Moody* and Mr. *Legrand*, that carrots may fucceffively successively be cultivated on the same land with increasing profit; a man who has but one or two fields of the right soil, may every year have those in carrots; which would prove peculiarly advantageous: To extend the idea a little, let us think of an hundred acres of land yielding a profit of near TWO THOUSAND POUNDS A YEAR. Such a space of ground, indeed, so cultivated, would require a capital, appropriated to that alone, of above four thousand pounds; but then the profit would be 50*l. per cent.*

LETTER XXXIII.

THE culture of potatoes is another article of hufbandry highly deferving the attention of all perfons, who are defirous of advancing their hufbandry to perfection. The following minutes will fhew, that few crops can in profit be ranked with them.

Mr. *Kendal,* at *Alfreton.*

Soil. Dry crumbling loam on quarries, at 20 *s.*

Culture. Kept clean by hoeing, &c.

Product. Six hundred bufhels, at 1 *s.*; 30 *l.*

Use. Applies all to fatting brawns, boils them, and mixes two bufhels of rye or barley meal to 20 of potatoes; more fattening than corn alone.

About *Caftleton.*

Soil. Light loam on lime-ftone.

Culture. In rows, and alfo the lazy-bed method; keep them tolerably clean.

Product. Four hundred bushels, at 2 *s.*; 40 *l.*

About *Chesterfield.*

Soil. Hasel loam, at 17 *s.*

Culture. Plough four or five times, and manure 20 loads an acre.

Product. Thirty pounds an acre; this, at the *Castleton* price of 2 *s.* a bushel, is 300 bushels.

Mr. *Wharton, Doncaster.*

Soil. Rich sand, at 50 *s.*

Culture. Plants in equally-distant rows, three quarters of a yard asunder; manures with twelve loads an acre rotten dung; only the knots or eyes used for sets; earthed up with hand-hoes several times.

Produce.   1767, — 242 Bushels.
           1768, — 242
           1769, — 300
           1770, — 719

    Total,   1503

    Average,   375

At 1 *s.* 4 *d.*   £. 24 16 6

Use. Applied chiefly to fattening swine; fats porkers with them; generally boils them, and mixes half a peck barley-meal to six bushels of potatoes; also in half fattening bacon hogs.

Expences,	-	-	£. 9	8	10
Profit,	-	-	15	7	2

Mr. *Cook, Wheatley.*

Soil. Light loam on a lime-stone.

Culture. Planted in rows three feet asunder; manured for with seven loads dung.

Product. 12 *l.* besides the expence of taking up; suppose 13 *l.*; at 1 *s.* 4 *d.* a bushel, it is 195 bushels.

Use. Feeding cows and hogs; the former eat them very heartily, and the milk and butter proved exceedingly good.

Mr. *Moody, Retford.*

Soil. Rich sand, at 40 *s.*

Product. 20 *l.*

About *Bootham,* near *Lincoln.*

Soil. Sandy, at 10 *s.*

Culture. Plant in rows, one foot asunder.

Product. 15 *l.*

Mr. *Arbuthnot, Ravensbury.*

Soil. Rich loam on clay, at 16s.

Culture. In rows, three and a half feet asunder; manured with 15 loads an acre of yard dung; horse and hand-hoed several times, earthing them up often; but they were not planted till *May.*

Product. One hundred and thirty-six bushels, each 80 *lb.* at 2s. 6d. which is 230 bushels, at 48 *lb.* value 17 *l.*

Use. Given to cows instead of hay; porkers were fattened on them, boiled and mashed with a little barley meal.

Expences,	— —	£. 8	13	6
Profit,	— —	8	6	6

Mr. *Taylor,* at *Bifrons.*

Soil. Rich loam, at 20s.

Culture. Planted in rows equally distant, two feet; kept clean by horse and hand-hoeing.

Product. Four hundred bushels, at 9 d.; 15 *l.*

Mr. *Pool,* at *Hook.*

Soil. Stiffish loam.

Culture. Planted eighteen inches square; dunged and hand-weeded.
Product. Six hundred thirty-three bushels.
Use. Fatting hogs; boiled and mixed one third barley meal with two thirds potatoes, beat peafe, and barley alone.

Mr. *Rodney*, at *Alresford*.
Use. Fattened porkers on them boiled, and given alone; nothing could fatten better.

Mr. *Sturt*, *Brownsea*.
Soil. Black moory peat earth, at 4½ d. an acre.
Product. Six hundred bushels, at 2 s.; 60 l.

Mr. *Mawde*, at *Clift*.
Soil. Rich sandy loam, at 20 s.
Culture. Planted in squares of three feet; 20 bushels of sets used.
Produce. Value 21 l.

At *Glastonbury*.
Soil. Good sand, at 40 s.
Culture. Dug into beds, and earthed from the furrows; kept clean by weeding; ten bushel sets to an acre; plant two or three years successively.

Product. Five hundred and forty-four bushels.

In gaining the average of the most material circumstances, I shall begin with the price at which the crop is valued or sold.

	Price per bushel.
Mr. *Kendal*, fatting hogs,	£. 0 1 0
Castleton selling price, -	0 2 0
Mr. *Wharton*, ditto, -	0 1 4
Mr. *Taylor*, ditto, - -	0 0 9
Mr. *Sturt*, ditto, -	0 2 0
Total, - -	0 7 1
Average, - -	0 1 5

This table would have been more satisfactory, had all the prices been the value consumed at home; but the selling rates are not to be despised, since in numerous situations it would be much more beneficial to sell the crop, than to eat them with cattle.

The products are as follow.

	Bushels.	Value.
Mr. *Kendal*,	600	£.30 0 0
Castleton,	400	40 0 0
Chesterfield,	300	30 0 0
Mr. *Wharton*,	375	24 16 6
Mr. *Cook*,	195	13 0 0
Mr. *Moody*,	—	20 0 0
Bootham,	—	15 0 0
Mr. *Arbuthnot*,	230	17 0 0
Mr. *Taylor*,	400	15 0 0
Mr. *Poole*,	633	— — —
Mr. *Sturt*,	600	60 0 0
Mr. *Mawde*,	—	21 0 0
Glastonbury,	544	— — —
Average,	427	25 19 8

These products are very considerable; 26 *l.* an acre on a crop, which like carrots are kept quite clean, and generally manured for very richly, which consequently cleans the land, and as every one knows, greatly improves it, forms upon the whole an object of uncommon importance; and shews that the culture of potatoes cannot be too much promoted. But that the clearer view of the whole may be had, I shall give the other particulars of soil, expences and profit.

THE FARMER's TOUR

Crops.	Soil.	Rent.			Expences			Product.			Profit.		
		l.	s.	d.	l.	s.	d.	l.	s.	d.	l.	s.	d.
Mr. Kendal	Loam	1	0	0				30	0	0			
Castleton	Limest							40	0	0			
Chesterfield	Loam	0	17	0				30	0	0			
Mr. Wharton	Sand	2	10	0	9	8	10	24	16	6	15	7	2
Mr. Cook	Limest.							13	0	0			
Mr. Moody	Sand	2	0	0				20	0	0			
Beotham	Sand	0	10	0				15	0	0			
Mr. Arbuthnot	Loam	0	16	0	8	13	6	17	0	0	8	6	6
Mr. Taylor	Loam	1	0	0				15	0	0			
Mr. Sturt	Moory	0	0	4½				60	0	0			
Mr. Meade	Loam	1	0	0				21	0	0			
Average		1	1	3¼	9	1	2	25	19	8	11	16	10

The foils in general, and in the average, are good; but I shall not divide the table according to the rent, because it is evident, that no useful conclusions could be drawn from it. Mr. *Sturt*'s poor (as commonly reputed) moory foil, yields a vast produce. The *Castleton* lime-stone is not rich, but the product great. A proper foil is plainly as necessary as high rented ones; moors, for instance, that are to be had for a trifle; but ample manuring, and good culture in the cleaning, are of high consequence. It appears from these tables that land at an average of 1 *l.* 1 *s.* an acre will yield 427 bushels *per* acre, worth 26 *l.*

Relative to the methods of culture, the variations in the product seem little to depend on them.

Application of the crop.

This is a point of very great importance; and the preceding minutes offer some valuable intelligence in it.

It appears by Mr. *Kendal*'s experiments, that boiled potatoes, mixed with rye or barley meal, in the proportion of one or two bushels in 20, fatten brawns better than corn alone, and reckoned at the price of 1 *s.* a bushel.

Mr. *Wharton* also boils them for his hogs, and mixes in the same manner; but his proportion is half a peck of meal to six bushels of potatoes; he fattens porkers thus, and half fattens bacon hogs.

Mr. *Kendal*'s proportion is *one tenth* of meal.

Mr. *Wharton*'s *one forty eighth*.

This difference may perhaps account for one fattening brawns, and the other only porkers.

Mr. *Arbuthnot* fattened porkers on them, boiled and mashed with a little barley meal.

One

One third barley meal and two thirds potatoes boiled, with Mr. *Poole*, exceeded peafe and barley alone in fattening hogs; this is very important.

The great object is to know what proportion of meal should be mixed with the mashed potatoes: Now it appears that Mr. *Kendal*'s *tenth* equals Mr. *Poole*'s *third*. Something indeed may be allowed for part of the former being rye meal, which in that cafe may be better than that of barley. The just quantity in all probability lies between a third and a tenth.

Mr. *Rodney*'s intelligence is yet more material; for it appears, that they will fatten porkers as well as poffible, boiled and *given alone*.

Feeding cows has likewife been tried. Mr. *Cook*'s crop was given to milch ones, and the milk and butter proved exceedingly good. Mr. *Arbuthnot*'s were alfo applied in the fame manner to fave hay: but I may here remark, what I did before on carrots, that it is impoffible it should anfwer to give cows in winter a food that will fatten any animal.

Upon

Upon the whole, the grand object of the culture seems to be for fattening hogs; that they will answer in great perfection for this use cannot be more clearly proved, not only for porkers, but even large hogs.

It seems equally clear from these trials, that it is *adviseable* to boil them; and if the hogs are not small, *necessary* to mix a small proportion of barley meal with the mash of the potatoes.

The application of all roots to the food of cattle is the material object; because the difference in good husbandry between selling a crop and using it at home is immense; upon the most moderate computation, one acre of carrots or potatoes (if the cattle are kept well littered) will in the consumption raise dung enough to manure two acres well; the increasing fertility of a farm, a part of which is so applied, wants no illustration: it is an object alone sufficient to change the face of land.

The cultivators of this root should attend more than they have done to the value of a bushel or ton used at home; this is a material point, but much neglected.

LETTER XXXIV.

IN the enquiries I made concerning the culture of madder, I was, upon the whole, very fortunate, for besides the capital experiments of Mr. *Arbuthnot*, whose attention to this plant has been more minute, and his trials on a larger scale than those, I apprehend, of any man in Europe, there are some other articles of it which are very valuable, and the more so, as they were executed on a soil, different from the above-mentioned gentleman's. I shall proceed with the minutes of this culture, as I have done with the preceding ones, and draw them into one view, that the most material circumstances may be comprehended at once.

    Mr. *Arbuthnot*, at *Ravensbury*.
Soil. Sandy loam, more inclinable to clay than mere sand; too wet for turnips, at 16 s.

THROUGH ENGLAND. 125

		Manure.			Total.		
		l.	s.	d.	l.	s.	d.
Expences.	No. 8.	3	10	0	30	8	6
	9.	3	10	0	26	11	0
	10.	3	12	6	23	15	10
	Ditto.	3	12	6	23	17	2
	Ditto.	3	12	6	23	1	6
	12.	2	4	0	23	10	2
	14.	6	0	0	24	17	6
	Ditto.	3	12	0	11	0	6
	15.	6	0	0	24	17	6
		35	13	6	211	19	8
Average,		3	19	3	23	11	11

		Weight.			Value.		
		T.	C.	Q.	l.	s.	d.
Product.	No. 8.	0	12	0	54	0	0
	9.	0	12	0	54	0	0
	10.	0	12	0	54	0	0
	Ditto.	0	8	0	36	0	0
	Ditto.	0	10	0	45	0	0
	12.	0	12	0	48	0	0
	14.	0	15	0	60	0	0
	Ditto.	0	10	0	40	0	0
	15.	0	15	0	60	0	0
Tons,		5	6	0	451	0	0
Average,		0	11	3	50	2	2

	Per acre.			Per acre per ann.		
	l.	s.	d.	l.	s.	d.
Profit.* No. 8.	22	11	6	7	10	6
9.	26	9	0	8	16	8
10.	29	4	2	7	6	0
Ditto.	11	2	10	2	15	8
Ditto.	20	18	6	5	4	7
12.	23	9	10	5	17	5
14.	34	2	6	8	10	7
Ditto.	27	19	6	6	19	10
15.	34	2	6	8	10	7
	210	0	4	61	11	10
Average,	23	6	8	6	17	7

Mr. *Crowe*, at *Feversham*.

Soil. A rich, deep, black mould, at 4 *l.*

Expences. The average of five
crops — — £.39 6 10

	T.	C.	Q.	lb.
Product. Ditto weight,	1	5	0	2

Value, — — £.112 11 1
Ditto *per ann.* 3 years £.41 6 4
Ditto 2 ditto — £.33 9 4
Profit. Ditto, — £.73 1 9
Per acre *per ann.* — £.25 13 11

Mr. *Hilton*, at *Feversham*.

Soil. Ditto.
Product. 18 C. wt. — £.73 10 0

---

* 1 *l. Per* acre deducted for the plants. See Page 232. Vol. II.

Mr. *Reynolds*, at *Addisham*.

Soil. Rich loam, at 20 *s.*
Expences. - - £. 45 0 0
Product. Plants to the amount of 1 *l.* 6 *s.*
Loss. 43 *l.* 14 *s.* 1 *d. per* acre *per*
  ann. - - £. 14 11 4

Mr. *Harrison*, at *Preston*.

Soil. Rich loam, at 20 *s.*
Expences.   22 *l.* 3 *s.* 2 *d.*
Product. 16 C. *wt.* £. 64
     7   28
     ―   ―
     23   92

Average, 11½ 46
Profit. On 16 C. *wt.* 41 *l.* 16 *s.* 10 *d.*; and *per* acre *per ann.* 13 *l.* 18 *s.* 11 *d.* On 7 C. *wt.* 6 *l.*; or *per* acre *per ann.* 2 *l.*
  Average *per* acre, £. 23 18 5
  Ditto *per ann.* - 7 19 5

Mr. *Simmons*, *Osprenge*.
Product. 1 Ton, at 4 *l.*—80 *l.*

Recapitulation.

Expences.

Mr. *Arbuthnot*, *per* acre, - £. 23 11 11
Mr. *Crowe*, - - 39 6 10
Mr. *Reynolds*, - *45 0 0

---

* 35 *l.* For plants.

Mr. *Harrison*,	-	-			22	3	2
Average,	-	-			32	10	5
Average, of No. 1, 2, and 4,					28	7	3

Produce.

	Weight.				Value.		
	T.	C.	Q.	lb.	l.	s.	d.
Mr. *Arbuthnot*,	0	11	3	0	50	2	2
Mr. *Crowe*,	1	5	0	2	112	11	1
Mr. *Hilton*,	0	18	0	0	73	10	0
Mr. *Harrison*,	0	11	2	0	46	0	0
Mr. *Simmons*,	1	0	0	0	80	0	0
Average,	0	17	1	0	72	8	7

Profit.

	Per acre.			Per a. per ann.		
	l.	s.	d.	l.	s.	d.
Mr. *Arbuthnot*,	23	6	8	6	16	7
Mr. *Crowe*, -	73	1	9	25	13	11
Mr. *Harrison*,	23	18	5	7	19	5
	120	6	10	40	9	11
Mr. *Reynolds* loss,	43	14	1	14	11	4
Profit, -	76	12	9	25	18	7
Average of four,	19	3	2	6	9	7
Average profit of the first three,	40	2	3	13	9	11

I think Mr. *Reynolds*'s ill fuccefs fhould come into the account, that too fanguine expectations may not be formed of madder: that it is a moft profitable branch cannot be doubted; but every article of culture is fubject to mifcarriages, and that writer who admits none into his works, is but a deceiver of mankind. In the article carrots, there is one gentleman that gained but 6 ½ tons *per* acre, on a rich fand of 40 s. rent; now fuch a crop muft be confidered as a failure, yet it is regiftered, and I think that Mr. *Reynolds*'s madder ought, in the fame manner, to come into the account, more particularly, as there does not, from his minutes, appear to be any error or mifconduct in the cafe.

Thirteen pounds *per* acre, clear profit, on the other crops, and 6 *l.* 9 *s.* 7 *d.* including his, are either of them articles much fuperior to common hufbandry. The firft fhews, that if total ill fuccefs does not attend the cultivation, the profit to be expected is very great, and highly deferving the attention of all fpirited hufbandmen.

The average expence of the profitable crops is 28 *l*. 7 *s*. 3 *d*. and the profit 40 *l*. 2 *s*. 3 *d*.; this is 142 *l. per cent.* profit in 3 years, or 47 *l. per cent. per ann.* Mr. *Reynolds* including the expence, is 32 *l*. 10 *s*. 5 *d*. and the profit 19 *l*. 3 *s*. 2 *d*.; this is 60 *l. per cent.* in three years, and 20 *l. per cent. per ann.*

Confiderable as this is, carrots exceed it; the average expence of all the crops is 7 *l*. 17 *s*. 7 *d*.; and that of the profit 18 *l*. 18 *s*. 7 *d*.; which is 240 *l. per cent. per ann.* whereas, the profitable madder is but 47 *l*. The fuperiority is therefore immenfe.

LETTER XXXV.

IN fumming up the intelligence I received concerning BURNET, in my tour in 1768, I found the accounts very contradictory; fome ftrongly in favour of this grafs, and others that arraigned it feverely, and treated it as an impofition on the public. The uncertainty about it ftill continues; for I have again found opinions ftrangely various. However, by giving them in one view, the teftimonies will be clearly feen on all fides.

Col. *St. Leger*, at *Parkhill.*

Soil. Deep loam on lime-ftone, at 21 *s.*

Culture. Broad-caft alone; limed and dunged at 5 *l.* expence; weeded at 10 *l.* an acre.

Produce. Seed, hay and ftraw, 8 *l.* 7 *s.* 6 *d.* in three years.

Expences. Twelve pounds thirteen fhillings and fix-pence the firft year.

Ufe. The ftraw cattle in the farm yard eat, but not without wafte; value 3 *s.* a load.

load. Cattle of all forts pined and fell off in their looks in the after-grafs; in *February*, fatting fheep would not touch it; hay eat freely by horfes and cattle; worth 25 s. a load.

Mr. *Stanniforth*, near *Bawtry*.

Soil. Loam on lime-ftone.

Ufe. Kept eight acres three years, but no cattle would touch it; they all broke out of the field when hungry.

Mr. *Hall*, at *Swaith*.

Soil. A good loamy fand.

Culture. Sown with barley; afterwards hand-hoed.

Ufe. Horfes, beafts and fheep, turned into it, but none would touch it.

Sir *Cecil Wray*, *Summer-Caftle*.

Soil. Light loam on lime-ftone.

Culture. Sown with white clover, trefoile, and fine hay feeds; in another piece, fowed it on dead land, with other feeds, and that alone fucceeded.

Ufe. Fed with fheep and other cattle, and always kept as low as the reft; fheep fond of the hay.

Mr. *Reynolds*, at *Addisham*.

Soil. Light loam.

Use. Not liked by cows or beasts, unless mixed with other feeds; but with grass much esteemed, especially by sheep and lambs; and it makes rich butter and milk.

Mr. *Harrison*, *Preston*.

Soil. Rich loam.

Use. Every thing eat it freely; and several sheep were fattened on it.

Mr. *Pool*, at *Hook*.

Use. Tried in small quantities; no cattle would eat it.

Mr. *Anderdon*, at *Henlade*.

Soil. Old rich orchard ground, also clay on lime-stone, and poor land.

Use. Horses, cows, oxen, sheep and pigs, eat it freely. "All cattle, (says Mr. *Anderdon*) eat it green, but are not remarkably fond of it; and when seeded do not care to eat it at all." Fed with oxen, sheep and horses, none eat it greedily, but without waste. In *January*, that which was cut in *December*, good pasture for sheep. Vegetates in winter; no frost hurts it.

Mr. *Clayton, Harleyford.*

Use. Twenty-eight acres laid down, part with burnet, part sainfoine; part white clover, and part bird-grass; the field fed at various seasons with sheep, cows, horses, &c. and they all eat the burnet quite as close as any of the other grasses.

Respecting the quantity of product, and some other circumstances, these experimenters are silent, except Col. *St. Leger*, whose loss arose from sowing it without corn. The only point that these minutes, will allow an inquiry into, is the question, *Will cattle eat it?* And, *Is it a wholesome good food for cattle?*

The contradictions which we here meet with are amazing; it seems to be the fatality of this plant, that its merit or worthlessness are never to be known. As to the variations being precise, and that it is a good pasture in some places, and a bad one in others, this I must be allowed to

suppose

suppose an impossibility, or at least a great improbability: in such a matter, on what are we to reason, unless by similar cases of other plants; now lucerne, sainfoine, clover, trefoile, and those numerous plants, which form what we call natural grass, are eaten every where; they fat beasts, they feed cows, they keep horses and sheep: every man knows what they will do, without enquiring the soil, or other circumstances; and that the same certainty attends burnet, cannot be doubted.

The diversity of accounts must arise from circumstances being unrelated, and in some instances perhaps from prejudice.

Let us for a moment consider the history of the plant. A seedsman produced it, and made considerable sums by selling the seed. This at once accounts for the whole. He and his friends magnified it beyond all bounds: those who were thus deceived, and tricked out of a scandalous price for the seed, were immediately loud in their condemnation of it; and through prejudice would not allow the real merit of the plant, small as it might be. Then came others, who had tried it, and at first reported favourably,

vourably, who piqued at being reprefented in the grofs as fo many fools by their antagonifts, defended themfelves by defending the plant, and of courfe ran their panegyrick too far. Thus it came that the culture has been attended with fuch contradictory accounts: and partly will juftify one in yet attributing fome fmall part of them to prejudice.

But the nature of the plant itfelf will account for fome variations. Cattle may be turned to it after it is got a head and near feeding; then all agree they will not touch it; but who from thence will affert in general, that no cattle will eat it? It is precifely the fame with ray grafs; the feed bents of which are ftubble. What is ray grafs good for as feed after *Midfummer?* The feed of burnet being valuable, much has been feeded, and the *ftraw* has too often been confounded with the *hay*. The original intention of ufing it was for a *winter pafture*, in which feafon cattle will eat and thrive on food, which at other times they will not touch; this has not been fufficiently attended to. On the other hand, fuch great profit has been made by the feed,

feed, that it may have proved something active in recommendations of the plant in general. Cattle may have been turned into a burnet field so hungry, that they might feed on it for a time, without proving it to be good food in general; conclusions of this sort may appear greatly in favour of a plant, and yet prove very little in fact.

From the preceding minutes there are several facts to be deduced, which will lead us to a clearer knowledge of the case.

HORSES.

Col. *St. Leger.* Eat the hay freely.
Mr. *Hall.* Turned into it green, but would not eat it.
Mr. *Harrison.* Eat it freely.
Mr. *Anderdon.* Eat it freely.
Mr. *Clayton.* Eat it as much as other grasses.

The balance of this account is greatly in favour of horses eating it in the common manner of all other food.

SHEEP.

Col. *St. Leger.* Fatting sheep in *February* will not touch it.

Mr.

Mr. *Stanniforth*. Fatting sheep in *February* will not touch it.

Mr. *Hall*. Turned into burnet, but would not touch it.

Sir *Cecil Wray*. Fed readily by sheep; fond of the hay.

Mr. *Reynolds*. Mixed with other grasses much esteemed by sheep.

Mr. *Harrison*. Several sheep fattened on it.

Mr. *Anderdon*. Eat it freely.

Mr. *Clayton*. Fed it as close as other grasses.

From these minutes, we cannot deny burnet to be a good food for sheep; but here are two articles of particular importance. Mr. *Harrison* sold several fat sheep from burnet, and Mr. *Clayton* turned them into 28 acres, sown with various feeds in divisions: the burnet was eaten as close as the rest. These particulars are absolutely decisive. Col. *St. Leger*'s sheep were fat in *February*, when they refused it: from whence we may conjecture, that they were from turnips; so different a food might be refused at first. However, the balance of the intelligence lies much in favour of the grass.

COWS and OXEN.

Col. *St. Leger.* Eat the hay freely.

Mr. *Stanniforth.* Turned in, but would not touch it.

Mr. *Hall.* Ditto.

Sir *Cecil Wray.* Eat it freely.

Mr. *Reynolds.* Makes rich butter and milk.

Mr. *Harrison.* Eat it freely.

Mr. *Anderdon.* Ditto.

Mr. *Clayton.* Ditto.

The same observation is applicable here in a few instances, cows and oxen dislike it; in many they eat it freely.

And upon the whole I shall beg leave to remark, that in general the reports are favourable to this grass: whoever throws the slightest eye over the preceding articles, will see this very clearly; but we may venture to conjecture, that the proper application of burnet is to leave it a good head in autumn ready for sheep in the spring, for them to keep it down as close as possible about two months, upon the plan of ray grass, after that to let it stand for a crop of hay

But the most advantageous method of all

all is, to fow it with other graffes in laying land down to pafture; this appears in the cleareft manner poffible, and is very ftrongly confirmed by the known fact of burnet being fo common a plant in many old meadows highly valued. Sir *Cecil Wray* and Mr. *Reynolds* prove this very ftrongly; and the fine meadow on the *Thames*, of Mr. *Ducket*'s, has a great quantity of burnet in it.

LETTER XXXVI.

SAINFOINE is cultivated in vaftly greater quantities than lucerne, being in many parts of *England* common hufbandry. The reafon of its having obtained this preference is eafy to be conceived; it will thrive to very confiderable profit in the broad-caft mode, fown with corn; which, and not drilling or tranfplanting, is probably the very beft way of cultivating it; but advantageous as for many years great tracts of country have found it, ftill has it not been able nearly to fpread throughout the kingdom, even to this day; which is remarkable. For this reafon, among others, I fhall prefent the reader with the particulars I gained concerning it, in one view, that farmers in countries where it is not yet cultivated, may eafily gain a complete knowledge of the principal circumftances attending it. The foils it yields moft on will appear; the rent of them, and the products that may under given advantages be expected from it.

Place.	Soil.	Rent.	Produce. Loads.	Duration. Years.	Particulars in the cul[...]
1. Hempstead,	loams on chalk and clay	0 10 0	2 ½	20	Manure every [...] year; 50 bushels ashes.
2. Tring,	chalk	0 10 0	2 ½	14	
3. Mr. Kendal,	loam on quarries	1 0 0	2		In drills mixed [...] clover.
4. Col. St. Leger,	loam on limestone	0 5 0	2 load with after-grass 3l. 10s.	16	Mixes some trefo[...] harrows it. Man[...] in 3 or 4 years, [...] bushels of ash[...] 70 foot.
5. Mr. Staniforth,	ditto	0 5 0	1 ½	16	
6. Canwick,	thin loam on limestone	0 7 6	2	20	6 Bushels feed an a[...]
7. Sir Cecil Wray,	ditto	0 5 0	1 ½		Coal ashes did no [...]
8. Sir John Turner,	light loam on chalk	0 10 0	1 ½ 4l. total 4l. 15s.		Clear profit 3l. 15[...]
9. Cheam,	chalk	0 10 0	2	12	20 Bushels foot, at 6[...]
10. Carshalton,	ditto	0 10 0	1 ½	15	
11. Dartford,	ditto	1 0 0	2	16	
12. Feversham,	ditto	0 5 0	1 ½	8	
13. Beaksburn,	light loam on chalk	0 6 0	2	10	30 Bushels foot, a[...]
14. Minster,	ditto	0 10 0	2	8	
15. Alresford,	chalk	0 6 0	1 ½		
16. Critchill,	ditto	0 2 6	2		6 Bushels feed.
17. Mr. Sturt,	ditto	0 2 6	3 5l. in all		
18. Mr. Anderdon,	stoney	0 5 0	1 ½		Best in drills, 8 and [...] inches asunder.

THROUGH ENGLAND.

Places.	Soil.	Rent.	Produce. Loads.	Duration. Years.	Particulars in the culture.
Lining-ton	poor soils		3 tons, at 30 s. and after-grass, at 20 s. 5 l. 10 s.	15	
Cow-			5 tons		
—ley—	chalk	0 11 0	1 ½		Manure with ashes once in two years.
Clay-	various		2, at 30 s. after-grass 8 s. 6 d.		Loams on clay better than on chalk rock.
—tons-	chalk	0 9 0	2	20	Cut twice often without damage. Manure with soot and ashes, 40 bushels per acre.
—rages,		0 8 5	2 ton.	15	

This general table shews, in the clearest manner, that sainfoine is an article of vast consequence to *British* agriculture. Upon and whose average rent is so low as 8 s. 5 d. the product is 2 tons of hay, besides after-grass; which is an amount far exceeding what such sorts can be supposed worth in any other application; and the duration of of fifteen years, gives it a fresh value of no slight consequence.

The value of the aftergrass, and the total crop, are minuted at some places, and deserve attention.

	After-grass.			Total.		
	l.	s.	d.	l.	s.	d.
Colonel *St. Leger*,				3	10	0
Sir *John Turner*,	0	15	0	4	15	0
Mr. *Sturt*, —				5	0	0
Donnington, —	1	0	0	5	10	0
Mr. *Clayton*, —	0	8	6	3	8	6
Average, —	0	14	6	4	8	8

All these soils are very poor, except Sir *John Turner*'s, and that but 10 s. an acre: an annual product of 4 l. 8 s. 8 d. from such land, is carrying the husbandry of it to the highest perfection, and far more than to equal the profit of the best soils in *England* in common management; a slight calculation will explain this.

The total of 4 l. 8 s. 8 d. appears to be a fair general average, for that of all crops is 2 tons, which, at 40 s. is 4 l.; and 8 s. 8 d. for the aftergrass is *low*.

Expences.

		£	s	d
Rent of one acre,	-	0	8	5
Tythe and town charges,	-	0	4	0
Mowing, making, carting, stacking, and thatching,	-	0	10	0
		1	2	5

Produce.

		£	s	d
Total,	- - -	4	8	8
Expences,	- - -	1	2	5
Profit,	- - -	3	6	3

This, I will venture to assert, is infinitely beyond the best common husbandry of the finest clays in *England*. A clear profit of above three guineas an acre, from a crop that is the food of cattle—that lasts 15 years—that may be soon renewed, and whose culture is so cheap and simple. If 10 *s. per* acre *per ann.* be allowed for soot or ashes, (though Col. *St. Leger's* is the only one of these dressed) still no common husbandry will equal it.

It is much to be wished that a culture so greatly advantageous, may spread itself over those numerous tracts of the kingdom, which at present yield but a paltry rent, though

though proper for this noble grafs—If it required being fown in drills and kept clean by horfe-hoeing, or other coftly methods not ufual with the farmer, there would not be reafon for furprize; but a broad-caft crop fown among corn in the fame way as clover, having no ungracious peculiarities in the management, ought to fpread faft. Strange! that landlords fhould be fo infatuated as to poffefs eftates proper for the culture, and yet take no fteps to introduce it.

The world has long been under the influence of an idea, which feems, from thefe minutes, to be perfectly erroneous. It has been thought that no foil is fit for fainfoine, that has not a rock or a ftratum of chalk, &c. very near the furface to ftop its roots. But at *Hempftead* they fow it often upon loams on a clay bottom—and Mr. *Clayton*'s trials prove clearly, that the deeper the foil, the better the crop; loams on clay yielding as much as thofe on chalk. That this grafs thrives admirably on extreme poor and fhallow foils, is undeniable, many of the preceding inftances being ftrong proofs; but I am apt to believe, that a depth of 2 or 3 feet of fine light mould, will

will agree wonderfully well with it, as with every thing elfe. The great point in the foil, is to have it free from fprings and ftagnant water; thefe excepted, I apprehend any foil will do for it; but certainly none like a fine deep light loam on chalk—I fay on chalk, becaufe that is a proof of the drynefs of the land.

Colonel *St. Leger*'s practice of harrowing the fainfoine till it has the appearance of a fallow, an operation he repeats as often as it grows weedy, deferves much attention: fuch a work muft certainly be ufeful to all graffes that will bear it: There is no enemy the fainfoine fears fo much as weeds and natural graffes, it being generally agreed that thefe decide its duration, the plant never dying through mere age; harrowing, therefore, muft, by killing its enemies, add much to its duration.

The manures for it, chiefly recommended, are foot and afhes; but Sir *Cecil Wray*, who is very accurate, tried the latter without finding any benefit from them; this fhould inftigate experimenters to decide the degree of advantage they reap from them.

LETTER XXXVII.

THE moſt important perhaps of the artificial graſſes is LUCERNE, and at the ſame time the leaſt underſtood. Opinions are at this day much divided concerning it, many perſons aſſerting, *on experience*, that it is an incomparable article of culture; and others denying, alſo *on experience*, that it is of any value. This is remarkable among people of fortune particularly, as they may be ſuppoſed to give a plant fair play, by not regretting a little expence. But concerning lucerne, the diverſity of opinions is as great in the higher as the lower ranks. Fortunately, however, I have in this journey met with a variety of intelligence concerning it, that will, when brought into one view, ſet its merit in the cleareſt light; for it has been cultivated on various ſoils in different methods, and applied to ſeveral uſes: the union

union of these particulars will, I flatter myself, give a more distinct knowledge of the subject than is any where else to be found.

Mr. *Stanniforth*, near *Bawtry*.

Soil. Rich light loam on lime-stone.

Culture. Drilled, equally-distant rows, 18 inches asunder, and some transplanted at three feet four inches.

Produce. The drilled maintains five horses *per* acre six months; the transplanted not so good by half; five horses, at 2 *s.* are 13 *l.* an acre.

Mr. *Hall*, at *Swaith*.

Soil. Good loamy land, at 20 *s.*

Culture. Broad-cast with barley, and transplanted in rows, two feet asunder; the first kept clean by harrowing, and the latter by hand-hoeing.

Produce. The broad-cast kept four or five horses 26 weeks; total 11 *l.* 6 *s.*; the transplanted 3 horses, total 6 *l.* 19 *s.* 3 *d.*

Sir *Cecil Wray*, *Summer-Castle*.

Soil. A sandy loam, 12 inches deep on a quarry, at 5 *s.*

Culture. Drilled in rows three feet asunder; kept clean by horse and hand-hoeing.

Produce. Cut five times a year, kept three horses *per* acre six months, or 9*l.*

Sir *John Turner*, *Warham*.

Soil. A light sandy loam, at 7*s.* 6*d.*
Culture. Broad-cast, harrowed every spring, and manured with six loads of rotten dung.
Product. Regularly cut every five weeks; kept five horses 26 weeks, at 2*s.*; 13*l.*
Expences, - - £. 1 14 6
Profit, - - 11 5 6

Mr. *Thompson*, *Norwich*.

Soil. A loamy sand, at 16*s.*
Culture. Drilled in rows, at 18 inches; hand-hoed, &c.
Product. Equal to five loads of common hay.

Mr. *Ramey*, at *Yarmouth*.

Soil. Fine rich light land, at 20*s.*
Culture. Broad-cast, and transplanted in three feet rows, one foot from plant to plant; kept clean for two years.
Product. One horse and a half *per* acre at first.

Dr. *Tanner*, at *Hadleigh*.

Soil. Good lightish loam, at 20*s.*

Culture. Broad-cast, harrowed; manured once in four years, 12 loads.
Duration. It has lasted ten years.
Product. 8 *l.*; mown for horses and cows, and hay, makes excellent butter.

Mr. *Arbuthnot, Ravensbury.*

Soil. Rich black loam, at 40 *s.*
Culture. Broad-cast, harrowed.
Duration. Five years.
Product. In hay, &c. average 11 *l.* 5 *s.*
Profit. Average 6 *l.* 4 *s.* 4 *d.*

Mr. *Butcher,* at *Chalk.*

Soil. Light rich black loam on chalk, at 17 *s.*
Culture. Broad-cast.
Duration. Seven years.
Product. Soils six horses 18 weeks, at 5 *s.*; 18 *l.*

Mr. *Bannister,* at *Chalk.*

Soil. The same.
Duration. Sixteen years.
Culture. Broad-cast.
Produce. Mown thrice a year for hay, six loads at 3 *l.* is 18 *l.*

At *Feversham*.

Soil. Old hop grounds, at 50 s.
Culture. Broad-caſt.
Product. Five loads of hay, &c. 15 l. 15 s.

Mr. *Reynolds*, at *Addiſham*.

Soil. Light loam on chalk.
Culture. Broad-caſt, and drilled, at 18 inches.
Product. Prefers the broad-caſt; it keeps four horſes 23 weeks, at 2 s. 6 d.; 11 l. 10 s.

Mr. *Poole*, at *Hook*.

Soil. Good deep loam.
Culture. Drilled at two feet and 20 inches; could not keep it clean, though he dug between the rows; paring and burning did good.
Product. Cut ſeven times a year.

Mr. *Vernon*, at *Newick*.

Soil. Good loam, at 20 s.
Culture. Drilled, rows two feet; dug twice a year.
Product. Keeps five horſes, at 2 s. 6 d. a week; 14 l. 7 s. 6 d.

	£	s	d
Expences,	3	15	0
Profit,	10	12	6

Mr. *Sturt*, at *Critchill.*

Soil. Strong loam, 18 inches, on chalk.
Culture. Drilled in rows 18 inches afunder; horfe and hand-hoed.
Produce. Cut from three to five times a year; three loads of hay, 9*l.*

Dr. *Lloyd*, at *Puddleton.*

Soil. Good loam, at 10*s.* 6*d.*
Culture. Drilled equally diftant, 18 inches afunder; hoed to one foot in the rows; kept clean by horfe and hand-hoeing, at 22*s.* 6*d.*
Product. Keeps four horfes 18 weeks, at 2*s.* 6*d.*; 9*l.*
Expences, - - £.3 3 6
Profit, - - - 5 16 6
Duration. Has lafted five years.

Mr. *Anderdon*, *Henlade.*

Soil. A rich deep fandy loam, at 20*s.*
Culture. Drilled in equally diftant rows, two feet fix inches afunder; kept clean by horfe and hand-hoeing.

	T.	C.	Q.	lb.
Product, 1767, (the first year)	0	8	0	14
1768,	5	2	0	13
1769,	6	19	2	3
1770,	8	18	3	6
Total,	21	0	1	22
Average,	7	0	0	16

	£.			
1767, At 20s. a ton.	0	8	1½	
1768,	5	2	1½	
1769,	6	19	6	
1770,	9	1	3	
Total,	21	2	10½	
Average,	7	0	11½	

Expences.

1767,	7	0	1
1768,	4	3	10
1769,	2	17	11
1770,	3	11	7
Total,	10	13	4
Average,	3	11	1

Profit.

	£	s.	d.
1767, Loſs,	6	12	0
1768, profit,	1	3	2¼
1769, ditto,	4	9	0
1770, ditto,	5	9	7½
Total,	11	1	10¾
Average,	3	13	11¼

Mr. *Clayton, Harleyford.*

Soil. Stoney loam on clay, and under that chalk.

Culture. Broad-caſt without corn, and drilled in equally diſtant rows, 18 inches aſunder; kept clean by horſe-hoeing, &c. the broad-caſt harrowed and ploughed with a round ſhare.

Product. The broad-caſt, five horſes from middle of *May* till *Michaelmas*; the drilled four; at 2*s.*

	£	s.	d.
Broad-caſt,	9	0	0
Drilled,	7	4	0

Lucerne an infallible cure for the botts in horſes.

Mr. *Burke, Beconsfield.*

Soil. Good ſtoney loam.

Culture. Drilled, the rows equally diftant, 18 inches afunder; kept clean by hoeing.

Product. In 1769, the fecond year, kept two horfes 13 weeks and a half, at 2 *s.* 6 *d.*; 3 *l.* 7 *s.* 6 *d.* In 1770, two horfes 18 weeks, or 4 *l.* 10 *s.*; but it is not near perfection yet.

These articles of intelligence concerning lucerne are upon the whole uncommonly fatisfactory, and will give a clear idea of the importance of the culture. In drawing an average of the whole, it will be proper to begin with the product.

Crops.	Culture.	Cattle kept.	At p. week s. d.	Amount. l. s. d.
Mr. *Staniforth*	Rows 18 inch.	5 Horses 6 m.	2 0	13 0 0
Ditto	Transf. 3 f. 4 in.	5 Horses 3 m.	2 0	6 10 0
Mr. *Hall*	Broad-cast	4 ½ H. 26 week	2 6	11 6 0
Ditto	Transf.rows 2 f.	3 Horses ditto	2 6	6 19 3
Sir C. *Wray*	Ditto 3 feet	3 Ditto 6 m.	2 6	9 0 0
Sir J. *Turner*	Broad-cast	5 Ditto 26 w.	2 0	13 0 0
Mr. *Thompson*	Rows 18 inch.			7 10 0 †
Dr. *Tanner* *	Broad-cast			8 0 0
Mr. *Arbuthnot*	Ditto	Hay, &c.		11 5 0
Mr. *Butcher*	Ditto	6 Horses 18 w.	5 0	18 0 0
Mr. *Bannister*	Ditto	6 L. hay, at 3 l.		18 0 0
Feversham	Ditto	5 Loads		15 15 0
Mr. *Reynolds*	Ditto	4 H. 23 w.	2 6	11 10 0
Mr. *Vernon*	Rows 2 feet	5 H. 23 weeks	2 6	4 7 6
Mr. *Sturt*	Ditto 18 inch.	3 Loads hay		9 0 0
Dr. *Lloyd*	Ditto, ditto	4 H. 18 weeks	2 6	9 0 0
Mr. *Anderdon*	Ditto 2 f. 6 in.	Various	20 a ton	7 0 11½
Mr. *Clayton*	Broad-cast	5 H. 18 weeks	2 0	9 0 0
Ditto	Rows 18 inch.	4 H. 18 weeks	2 0	7 4 0
Mr. *Burke*	Ditto, ditto	2 Ditto 18 w.	2 6	4 10 0
Averages		4 Horses 22 ¼	2 6	10 9 10

† Equal to five loads of common hay.
* Mr. *Ramsy*'s not included, as kept clean only two years; but lucerne seldom is profitable the first year, and inferior the second.

The principal article in this table is the average of the number of horses, and the time they are kept, which I have carefully calculated, and find the proportion to be four horses maintained 22 ¼ weeks on each acre. This is a fact of true importance, and independant of the propriety of weekly charges, or general valuations, which

which are never equally satisfactory. Here we find, that on an average of these numerous crops of lucerne, one acre will maintain four horses soiled in the stable, from the middle of *May* till the end of *October*. I need not remark, that this product is prodigiously great, and forms an object in modern husbandry of the first magnitude.

But that this subject may be as thoroughly understood as possible, I beg leave to observe, that here are two circumstances united, which ought to be somewhat distinguished, though difficult; it is the *product of lucerne*, and the *practice of soiling horses in the stable*. Is the vast benefit here apparent all to be attributed to one or the other, or part to one, and part to the other? and in what degree? These queries I cannot exactly answer; but some light is to be thrown on them by minutes in the preceding Tour, not connected with lucerne, but which I must mention here for elucidating the present point.

Mr. *Hall*, of *Swaith*, tried the application of clover to soiling horses, and two acres kept six during 19 weeks, or three *per* acre that

that time, which at 2 s. 6 d. is 7 l. 2 s. 6 d. In the field he remarked, that the six horses would have had nine acres.

Mr. *Ramey*, of *Yarmouth*, made the same experiment. Seven acres of clover keeps 20 horses, seven cows, five calves, &c. 17 weeks; the horses and cows at 2 s. 6 d. a week, the amount 9 l. 2 s. 1 d. *per* acre.

And from a comparison with his tenants feeding clover in the field, Mr. *Ramey* found, that five acres soiled, lasted as long as 30 eaten in the field.

These two experiments are very important, and directly to the point in question. Mr. *Hall*'s clover paid him 7 l. 2 s. 6 d. *per* acre, Mr. *Ramey*'s 9 l. 2 s. 1 d. These are prices never heard of for clover in common management; and advance very nearly to the products of lucerne.

Mr. *Hall*,	-	£.7	2	6
Mr. *Ramey*,	-	9	2	1
Total,	-	16	4	7
Average,	-	8	2	3½

This is to 10 l. 9 s. 10 d. the average of lucerne, nearly as four to five. So if lucerne pays

pays 5*l.* clover in this way may be expected to pay 4*l.* This difference is by no means so great as has been generally supposed between the two plants; and if other attendant circumstances are taken into the account, will totally disappear. For it must be considered, that these accounts of lucerne are taken from the third, fourth, fifth, or after years of it; whereas the first and second are losing or at least much inferior. Further, it is to be considered, that the clover products are without any expences, except the rent and mere mowing and carrying; no preparatory years of loss, no horse or hand-hoeing, none of that attention to cleaning, which with lucerne is almost without bounds. If all these circumstances be duly considered, lucerne *applied in the manner of the preceding crops* will by no means be condemned, but the greatness of the products will be much attributed to the soiling. This idea is rather confirmed than contradicted by the products of hay. Mr. *Arbuthnot*'s was in the season four loads an acre; Mr. *Bannister*'s two loads; at *Feversham* five loads; Mr. *Sturt* three loads; average of these,

these, four and a half; which is not more in quantity than clover, at two mowings on the same soils.

Upon the whole, I am desirous that a merit, which seems principally to depend on a most excellent practice, that of soiling, be not attributed as a peculiarity to lucerne; and I venture this the rather, as I much wish that these ingenious farmers would decide the *real value* of the plant, not by estimations of the weekly feeding horses, but the feeding or fattening sheep and small beasts, so that we may have other value than that vague one of *so much per week*.

I shall conclude these remarks with the expences and profit.

Crops.	Applic.	Expence.			Product.			Profit.		
		l.	s.	d.	l.	s.	d.	l.	s.	d.
Sir J. Turner	Soiling	1	14	6	13	0	0	11	5	6
Mr. Arbuthnot	Hay	5	0	8	11	5	0	6	4	4
Mr. Vernon	Soiling	3	15	0	14	7	6	10	12	6
Dr. Lloyd	Ditto	3	3	0	9	0	0	5	16	0
Mr. Anderdon	Ditto	3	11	1	7	0	$11\frac{1}{2}$	3	13	$11\frac{5}{4}$
Averages		3	8	11	10	18	3	7	10	5

The less is necessary to be observed on this, as I have already hinted how much is to be attributed to the *application*.

But let me not forget to remark, that the point in which lucerne seems moſt important is *duration*. It laſts many years, ſo that a man may keep juſt land enough for his purpoſe of ſoiling, without being plagued with corn crops; this cannot be with clover, and where it ſuits is an invaluable circumſtance.

LETTER

LETTER XXXVIII.

IN this review, CLOVER muſt not be forgotten; the uſe it is of to many parts of the kingdom is ſo great, as to be one of the pillars of good huſbandry; and yet it has not been able to make its way through all the counties: this graſs is ſo truly ſerviceable to the farmer, that a clear knowledge of its product and value are the only means of ſpreading the culture, and of improving it where known.

Place.	Soil.	Rent.			Loads.		Value.			Sundry circumſtances
		l.	*s.*	*d.*	1ſt cut	2d cut	*l.*	*s.*	*d.*	
1. *Hempſted*	Loams	0	10	0		3¼				50 Buſhels of aſhes.
2. *Tring*	Ditto on chalk	0	10	0		4				
3. *Bliſworth*	Clay	0	16	0						Oats better after feeding than mowing.
4. *Quenby*	Clay	0	18	0			One acre white, fat 4 to 7 large ſheep			
5. *Alfreton*	Clayey	1	0	0	2					Feed the firſt.
6. *Formark*	Sandy loa.	0	15	0			4	0	0	
7. *Lawton*	Loam on lime-ſton.	0	8	0	2					
8. *Gateford*	Sand	0	10	0		4½				
9. *Blythe*	Ditto	0	10	0		2				
10. Mr. *Wharton*	Ditto	2	10	0		4	6	0	0	
11. Mr. *Hall*	Sandy loa.	0	10	0			10	10	0	White clover for feed and ſeed.

Place.	Soil.	Rent.			Loads.			Value.			Sundry circumstances
		l.	s.	d.	1st cut	2d cut	av	l.	s.	d.	
12. Wombwell	Sandy loa.	0	16	0			4				The best wheat after mowing.
13. Retford	Sand, &c.	0	12	6	2						
14. Dunham	Sandy, &c.	0	17	0			4				
15. Bootham	Various	0	10	0			3				
16. Canwick	Lime-sto.	0	7	6			3				
17. Summer-castle	Loam on lime-st.	0	10	0			2½				
18. Walpole	Clay	0	17	0			2				White clover.
19. Muffingham	Sandy	0	8	0	1½						Better wheat than if fed the whole year.
20. Sherringham	Sandy loa.	0	15	0	1						
21. Aylsham	Ditto	0	14	0	2						
22. Earlham	Ditto	0	16	0							Mow all twice, that the wheat may be the better.
23. Bracon Ash	Clayey	0	15	0	2	1	3				
24. Mr. Bevor	Ditto	0	16	0			3	6	0	0	
25. Shottesham	Sandy loa.	0	14	0			3	3	0		
26. Fleg Hundred	Ditto	0	15	0							The best wheat after mowing.
27. South of Beccles	Ditto	0	12	0			2				
28. Saxm. to Woodbridge	Sand	0	14	0			3				
29. Mr. Acton	Sandy loa.	0	12	6			4½				
30. Hadleigh	Clayey lo.	0	15	0	2						Feed much with hogs, which they find very profitab. Also for seed, 4 to 8 bush. best wheat after feeding, but not so clean.
31. Hastead	Clayey	0	14	6	1¼						
32. Colchester	Sandy gravel	0	16	0	2			4	4	0	
33. Youngsberry	Heavy	0	12	0	1½	1	2½				Reckon wheat best after feeding.
34. Petersham	Sandy	1	0	0			3½				
35. Morden	Clay	0	12	0			3				
36. Cheam	Chalk	0	10	0	1½						
37. Cuddington	On ditto	0	17	0			3				
38. Carshalton	Ditto	0	10	0			3				Best wheat after feeding.
39. St. Mary Cray	Loam	0	14	0			3				
40. Minster	Rich dit.	0	17	0							Mixt with trefoile, keeps four large sheep *per* acre; better wheat after trefoile than clover.
41. Burwash		0	10	0	1½						
42. Findon	Light loa.	0	13	6	2						

Place.	Soil.	Rent. l. s. d.	Loads. 1st cut	2d cut	av.	Value. l. s. d.	Sundry circumstances
43. Mr. *Turner*	Clay		1½				Feeds much with hogs; 9 acres paid 50l. even fows and pigs.
44. *Isle of Wight*	Loam	1 0 0	1½				
45. Ditto	Dit. ftoney	0 10 0	1¼				
46. *Gilbury*	Ditto	0 10 6	1½				
47. *Critchill*	Loam	0 10 0	2¼				
48. *Moreton*	Ditto	0 12 0	1¼				Moft ray; feed it the fecond year.
49. *Leigh*	Clay	0 12 6	1¼				
50. *Taunton-vale*	Clay	1 0 0	1¼			2 10 0	
51. *Bridgwater*	Clay		2				
52. *Donnington*	Loam	0 15 0	2½			At 30s. a load	No difference in the wheat, whether mown or fed.
53. *Harleyford*	Various	0 11 0	1½	1½	3		Wheat is better after mowing than feeding.
54. *Beconsfield*	Ditto	0 9 0			4		
Averages		0 14 0	C. 35½	C. 22	C. 64	5 4 0	

Upon thefe averages it is to be remarked, that the profit of clover appears to uncommon advantage in them. On the average of fo many foils, many of them poor ones, for the firft mowing to yield 1 ton 13 C. wt. 2 quarters, is a circumftance moft valuable to a farmer; and that even this product is below the truth, had the totals of the two cuttings been feparated, appears from the average total being more than the firft and fecond together.

The importance of a grafs that is of fo hardy a nature, as to bear fowing with corn,

corn, and subject to scarcely any failures,—that will the very first year yield 3 ton 4 *C. wt.* of hay at two mowings — that will last one or perhaps two years longer, if it suits the farmer — that is for wheat a better preparation than the finest fallow, requiring at the same time but one ploughing — all these circumstances unite to render clover an object of the highest consequence to these kingdoms; and cannot but amaze one to reflect, that there are various parts of them, wherein it is yet unknown. And it is miserable to think of so many common fields yet remaining, where the farmers are tied down to most unprofitable courses to the exclusion of this noble grass.

Suppose the clover hay on an average to be worth but 40*s.* a ton, the product of hay amounts to 6*l.* 8*s. per* acre, which considering the low expences is great. Whatever price is named to suit any neighbourhood, still the profit will be uncommonly high.

Nor let it be forgotten, that these advantages are gained by a crop, which may be all, and usually is, consumed by cattle at home; hence opens new views of its profit: the farmer is enabled to keep great ſtocks of cattle on ſoils, where he could not otherwiſe have any; raiſing much dung, and keeping his land in great heart.

The comparative advantage of the two applications of the clover, *mowing* and *feeding,* relative to the wheat that ſucceeds, is in favour of the former. I am not ſurprized at this, for mowing will always make the land cleaner from weeds, an effect particularly obſerved at *Haſtead*; but the ſhade of a thick crop is the great object in ſummer; be it what it may, it will breed ſo putrid a fermentation in the ſoil, as to work a far greater and infinitely more regular improvement, than the random dunging and ſtaleing of cattle*. All experience proves the benefit of thick ſhade in ſummer. That this compariſon may be the better underſtood, I ſhall compare the practice with the ſoil.

---

* I have treated the point of feeding and mowing meadows at large, in my *Courſe of Experimental Agriculture,* Vol. II. p. 372.

Place.	Soil.	Which best.
Blisworth	Clay	Feeding
Wombwell	Sandy loam	Mowing
Massingham	Sand	Mowing
Earlham	Sandy loam	Ditto
Fleg hundred	Ditto	Ditto
Hastead	Clayey	Feeding
Youngsberry	Clayey	Ditto
Carshalton	Chalk loam	Ditto
Beconsfield	Loams	Mowing

If we were to reason on this point, we should naturally say that feeding must be best on light soils, and mowing on heavy ones; because the one wants to be trodden to make them more compact, and the other to be opened and rendered loose, the universal effect of mowing crops. But in this table such an idea is not justified: the advantages of mowing are so superior, that they succeed even on sandy loams much better than feeding. The *Hastead* feeding should be thrown out of the question; because they acknowledge that the crops are cleanest after mowing.

But as several places appear on the side

feeding, and three of them on clays, which it is impoſſible to be ſo, let me 1eſt, that ſome gentleman will accurately the point, by fairly dividing a field, feeding one half through the year, mowing the other twice for hay.

LETTER

LETTER XXXIX.

IN the Tour I made through the North of *England*, in the year 1768, I gained an uncommon variety of intelligence, concerning the culture of the great *Scotch* cabbage, which it was very remarkable had been planted for several years in *Yorkshire* by many spirited gentlemen, and applied by them constantly to husbandry uses, without the publick knowing that such a plant existed. The registers of experiments, which I inserted in that Tour, kindled a curiosity throughout many counties, to try the merit of it, which has produced more experiments, several of which I am favoured with in the present work. Perhaps I may venture to hint, that this circumstance is one proof of the utility, which may possibly attend such an undertaking as this of publishing provincial and local customs, for the information of the nation in general.

Besides

Besides several trials on the *Scotch* cabbage, I have met with another sort, the *North American*, cultivated by some gentlemen in *Northamptonshire*, *Derbyshire*, &c. which seems to bid fair to be a most capital article of *British* husbandry, as appeared in the preceding minutes.

Bringing all my intelligence concerning cabbages into one view, will assist the reader in completing the idea of the culture, which he may have gained from the experiments, registered in the *Six Months Tour*.

Mr. *Booth*, at *Glendon*.

Soil. A red, light, rich loam, at 10 s.

Sort. The *Dutch* cabbage.

Culture. Sows in *August*, and the latter end of *February*; pricks out both; plants the first in *March*, and the latter in *May* or *June*; plants in squares of two feet; keeps clean by hand-hoeing; gives a year's fallow, ploughing 12 inches deep in *October*, and manures with 40 loads an acre.

Product. The *Dutch* cabbage comes to so high as 40 *lb*.

Use. Feeds them on the ground with rams.

Duration. They generally decay in *January.*

Mr. *Kendal,* at *Alfreton.*

Soil. Rich loam on quarries, at 20 s.

Culture. In *March* he plants beans in single rows, four feet asunder, and after that sets a row of cabbages between the rows of beans; keeps them clean by earthing up.

Product. Twenty cart loads *per* acre, worth about 6 *l.* They rise some to 23 *lb.*

Use. Given to cows, which yield vastly more milk on them than on any other food, and the cream and butter have not the least bad taste; gives half a cart-load a day to seven or eight cows.

Sir *Robert Burdett, Formark.*

Soil. Rich sandy loam, at 20 s.

Sort. The *North American.*

Culture. Digs two spits deep, and richly manures and limes; planted in rows three feet every way, the first week in *April*; kept quite clean from weeds by hand-hoeing.

Product. Many of them 50 *lb.* each.

    Average in 1769,   -   35
    In 1770,   -   -   - 30

The latter is - 65 tons *per* acre.
The former,   - 76 ditto.
                 ———
                 141
                 ———
                 70 Average.
                 ———

Value in 1769, by fatting oxen and sheep, 39*l.* 8*s.* which is *per* ton 10*s.*

	£	s	d
	39	8	0
Sixty-five tons, at 10*s.*	32	10	0
Total, -	71	18	0
Average value *per* acre,	36	0	0

Fatting great oxen and sheep: never beasts fatted better or sooner.

ation. In perfection the beginning of *October*; and none lasts longer than *January*.

Col. *St. Leger,* at *Parkhill.*

Thin loam on lime stone, at 2*s.* 6*d.*

Great *Scotch.*

ure. Planted on a summer fallow; ploughed six times, and manured with 12 loads an acre of rotten dung; rows four feet by 20 inches.

Seed

Seed part sown in *September* and part in *February*; the first twice pricked out; the second at once into field hand and horse-hoed.

Use. They were given to dry cows, calves and sheep; they all did exceedingly well on them.

Product. One acre was more than as good as three of turnips; and as the average of the latter is 35 s. the cabbages amount to 5 l. 5 s.

Mr. *Mellish*, at *Blyth*.

Soil. Rich sand, at 20 s.

Sort. Great *Scotch*.

Culture. Manured for 12 loads an acre farm yard compost; sown in *February*, and planted the end of *May* in squares of two feet; kept clean by hand-hoeing.

Product. Average value 7 l. *per* acre.

Use. Sheep bought lean at 14 s. and sold from them fat at 21 s.

Mr. *Wharton*, *Carr-House*.

Soil. Rich sand, at 20 s.

Sort. Great *Scotch*.

Culture. Sown in *August*, pricked out

in *October*, again in *March*, and into field the middle of *June*; land prepared by five ploughings and 10 loads an acre of farm-yard dung; kept clean by horse and hand-hoeing.

Product. Average cabbage 21 *lb*. 12 *oz*. or 47 tons *per* acre.

Use. Given to fatting beasts, milch cows, young cattle, and swine; for beasts they answered but indifferently; cows give a vast quantity of milk, but strong, though ventilated; but kept pigs and in excellent order till put up to fatting; answered best in this manner. Mr. *Wharton* on the whole prefers a crop of turnips worth 3 *l.* suppose the acre of 47 tons worth about 50 *s*. it may be called 1 *s*. a ton.

Candidates for Doncaster *Premium.*

Mr. *Crowle*,	-	54½ Tons
Mr. *Wright*,	-	51¼
Mr. *Wharton*,	-	46¼
Mr. *Hervey*,	-	29
Mr. *Turner*,	-	28¼
Mr. *Hewet*,	- -	14

Mr. *Hall*, at *Swaith*.

Soil. Rich loam, at 20 *s*.

Sort. Great *Scotch.*

Culture. Well fallowed and manured as for turnips; sown in *February,* and planted in *June* in rows four feet asunder, and two feet from plant to plant; kept quite clean by horse and hand-hoeing.

Product. Came to the average weight of 12 *lb.* which is 29 tons 13 *C. wt.* the value 3 *l.* or 2 *s.* a ton.

Use. Fattening sheep, which throve well on them.

Mr. *Howman, Bracon-Ash.*

Soil. A strong clay.

Sort. Turnip cabbages and *Reynold's* cabbage turnip.

Culture. Sown in *April,* and planted in *July*; those that were left in the seed-bed the best; frost destroyed the turnip cabbage.

Use. Horses, cows and sheep, eat them very freely.

Mr. *Fellowes,* at *Shotteſham.*

Soil. Sandy loam.

Sort. Great *Scotch.*

Culture. Sown in *March,* and planted in *May,*

May, in squares of two feet six inches; manured with 20 loads dung an acre.

Product. Fifteen tons 16 *C. wt.* 88 *lb. per* acre.

Mr. *Acton*, at *Bramford*.

Soil. Good turnip loam.

Sort. Great *Scotch*, sown for but proved a bad sort; and *Reynolds*'s cabbage turnip; sown first week in *April*; planted in *June*; the *Scotch* three feet by two; *Reynolds*'s two by 18 inches; kept as clean as a garden.

Product. The common cabbage 2*l.* 16*s.* 10¼*d.* by feeding cows, at 2*s.* a week.

Use. Milch cows; and the butter excellent, without any taste.

Mr. *Arbuthnot*, at *Mitcham*.

Soil. Brick earth loam.

Sort. Various kinds.

Culture. Ploughed 14 inches deep, and planted in *September*, rows equally distant, 18 inches and two feet, and the plants one foot in the rows; kept perfectly clean.

Product. 2*l.* 18*s.* 6*d.*

Use. Feeding ewes and lambs in *April* and May.

Sir *Thomas Hales, Beakſbourn.*

Sort. The *Lombardy* cabbage.
Product. They riſe to 60 *lb.* a cabbage.

Mr. *Reynolds,* at *Addiſham.*

Soil. Light hazel loam.
Sort. Great white cabbage, and alſo the cabbage turnips.
Culture. Ploughs deep, and plants in rows of two feet by 20 inches; ſows in *April,* and plants in *June.*
Product. Of the cabbage turnip, on an average, 33 tons, at 4*s.* 6*d.* a ton, or 7*l.* 8*s.* 6*d. per* acre. 1 *C. wt.* better than 2 *C. wt.* of common turnips.
Use. Of great utility in feeding all ſorts of cattle; and late in the ſpring, cows give fine and ſweet butter.

Mr. *Taylor, Bifrons.*

Soil. Good loam, at 20*s.*
Culture. Plants them between the rows of beans.
Product. 3*l.*

Mr. *Jeffart, Minster.*

Soil. Rich loam, at 17*s.*
Sort. *Reynolds*'s cabbage turnip.
Culture. Rows two feet by 20 inches, horse and hand-hoed.
Product. Thirty-five tons, and five of sprouts.
Duration. Fed off with sheep late in *April.*

Mr. *Edward Pett, Minster.*

The same soil, sort and culture; crop exceedingly fine.

Mr. *Anderdon, Henlade.*

Soil. Good loam, at 20*s.*
Sort. Turnip cabbage, cabbage turnip, great *Scotch*, and boorcole.
Duration. The turnip cabbage kept sound, and without any mealiness, till *May*, and sheep fonder of them than of turnips; both this and *Reynolds*'s increases vastly in weight by green shoots, *without the root being the worse*; *Reynolds*'s is heavier five times over by being left.

	T.	*C.*	*Q.*	*lb.*
Product. Brown boorcole,	6	7	0	16
Scotch, - -	6	17	3	0
Common turnips, -	11	14	0	0

Sir *John Mill*, *Bisham*.

Soil. Rich deep black loam, at 3 *l.*
Sort. Unknown.
Culture. In rows three feet by two, kept clean.
Product. Nineteen tons; common turnips 24 tons.

Earl of *Holdernesse*, *Sion*.

Soil. Good loam.
Sort. Large winter cabbage from *Newbury*.
Culture. Planted in squares of four feet; horse-hoed both ways.
Product. Many from 25 to 30; at the average of 15 *lb.* 18 tons 4 *C. wt. per* acre.
Use. Fattening oxen.

THROUGH ENGLAND. 181

Crops	Rent (l. s. d.)	Rows	Tons	Value (l. s. d.)	Duration	Application	Sort
Mr. *Bactb*	0 10 0	2 Feet square				Sheep	*Dutch*
Mr. *Kendal*	1 0 0	4 F. equal dist.		6 0 0	*Jan.*	Cows	*American*
Sir R. *Burdet*	1 0 0	3 Feet square	70	36 0 0		Oxen	*Scotch*
Col. St. *Leger*	0 2 6	4 F. by 20 inc.		5 5 0		Various	Ditto
Mr. *Mellifh*		2 Feet square		7 10 0	*Jan.*	Fat sheep	Ditto
Mr. *Warton*	1 0 0			2 10 0		Various	Dit:o
Mr. *Creole*			47				Ditto
Mr. *Wright*			54½				Ditto
Mr. *Hervey*			51½				Ditto
Mr. *Hall*	1 0 0	4 Feet by 2	29	3 0 0		Fat sheep	Ditto
Mr. *Fellowes*	0 16 0	2 F. 6 in. sq.	15½				Ditto
Mr. *Afton*	12 6	3 F. by 2	33	2 16 10		Cows	Unknown
Mr. *Arbuthnot*	0 16 0	2 F. equal dist.		2 18 8	6 *May*	Sheep	Cabbage turnip
Mr. *Reynolds*	0 15 0	2 F. by 20 in.		7 8 0	6 *May*	Various	*Aberdeen*
Mr. *Taylor*	1 0 0			3 0 0			Cabbage turnip
Mr. *Jeffart*	0 17 0	2 Feet by 20 in.	40		*April*	Sheep	Boorcole
Mr. *Anderson*	1 0 0		6¼				*Scotch*
Ditto			6¼				Unknown
Mr. *J. Mill*	1 0 0	3 by 2	19				Ditto
E. of *Holdernesse*	3	4 Feet square	18			Oxen	
Averages	0 19 4		T. C. 32 6	7 11 10			

The average weight, exclusive of Sir *Robert Burdet*'s, 29 tons 4 *C. wt.* value 4*l.* 8*s.* 9*d.* The amazing product of this *American* cabbage opens a new world in husbandry, and being so peculiar, must be thrown out of the question. The other crops do not, upon the whole, raise so great an idea of this husbandry, as upon other occasions have appeared: but upon this

variation

variation I must observe, that here are so many sorts of cabbages, that they may, and certainly do, differ as much as cabbages and turnips: on this account, the table must be divided into sorts, that we may thereby know what conclusions are to be drawn from each.

North American.

	Tons.	Value.		
		l.	*s.*	*d.*
Sir *R. Burdet*,	70	36	0	0

True Scotch.

	Tons.	*l.*	*s.*	*d.*
Col. *St. Leger*,	–	5	5	0
Mr. *Mellish*,	–	7	0	0
Mr. *Crowle*,	54¼	–	–	–
Mr. *Wharton*,	47	2	10	0
Mr. *Wright*,	51½	–	–	–
Mr. *Harvey*,	29	–	–	–
Mr. *Hall*,	29½	3	0	0
Average,	42	4	8	9

Cabbage turnip.

	Tons.	*l.*	*s.*	*d.*
Mr. *Reynolds*,	33	7	8	6
Mr. *Jessart*,	40	–	–	–
Average	36	–	–	–

Various sorts.

	Tons.	Value.		
		l.	*s.*	*d.*
Mr. *Kendal*,	-	6	0	0
Mr. *Fellowes*,	15¼	-	-	-
Mr. *Acton*,	-	2	16	10
Mr. *Arbuthnot*,	-	2	18	6
Mr. *Taylor*,	-	3	0	0
Sir *John Mill*,	19	-	-	-
Earl of *Holderness*,	18	-	-	-
	17	3	18	5

The laſt of theſe tables muſt be conſidered only as a general proof, that any kind of cabbage will, in good management, turn out a profitable culture.

The true *Scotch*, in point of weight, makes a great figure; the average product of 42 tons, ſhew what an immenſe quantity *per* acre may be expected of this cabbage under a good culture. But in the value, the caſe is very different.

But here we muſt remark, that the average 4 *l.* 8 *s.* 9 *d.* takes in a crop on a thin limeſtone, of only 2 *s.* 6 *d.* an acre; it is aſtoniſhing it ſhould come to 5 *l.* 5 *s.*; two other articles that decide it, are Mr. *Wharton* 47 tons for 2 *l.* 10 *s.* and Mr. *Hall* 29½ for 3 *l.*; the firſt, 1 *s.* a ton, the ſecond, 2 *s.*; by the way, a difference of *half* is very great, and ſhews that no juſt rule of valuation has been followed. Here I ſhall draw into one view the value, *per* ton, of all that contain the information.

	£	s	d
Sir *Robert Burdet*,	0	10	0
Mr. *Wharton*,	0	1	0
Mr. *Hall*,	0	2	0
Mr. *Reynolds*,	0	4	6
Average,	0	4	4

But how extravagant the difference of cabbages, paying with one perſon 1 *s.* and with another 10 *s.*! Such variations prove how little we know the real honeſt truth. But as to the 1 *s.* I leave it to any perſon of half an hour's winter experience in huſbandry, to judge if a ton of green food can be worth ſo little; whether a ton of hay at 40 *s.* can go as far as 40 ton of cabbages!

I ſhall, however, include it, and take the average of 4 *s.* 4 *d.* as a valuation of thoſe crops whoſe weight is minuted, but not the value, and give thereby as full a view of theſe experiments as poſſible.

	Tons.	Value.			
		l.	*s.*	*d.*	
Mr. *Kendal*,	-	6	0	0	
Sir *R. Burdet*,	70	36	0	0	
Col. *St. Leger*,	-	5	5	0	
Mr. *Mellish*,	-	7	0	0	
Mr. *Wharton*,	47	2	10	0	
Mr. *Crowle*,	54½	11	16	0	at 4*s*. 4*d*.
Mr. *Wright*,	51½	11	3	0	at 4*s*. 4*d*.
Mr. *Hervey*,	29	6	5	0	at 4*s*. 4*d*.
Mr. *Hall*,	29½	3	0	0	
Mr. *Fellowes*,	15¼	3	8	0	at 4*s*. 4*d*.
Mr. *Acton*,	-	2	16	10	
Mr. *Arbuthnot*,	-	2	18	6	
Mr. *Reynold*,	33	7	8	6	
Mr. *Taylor*,	-	3	0	0	
Mr. *Jeffart*,	40	8	13	0	at 4*s*. 4*d*.
Sir *J. Mill*,	19	4	2	0	at 4*s*. 4*d*.
Earl of *Holderneſſe*,	18	3	18	0	at 4*s*. 4*d*.
Average,	37	7	7	3	

In the application of the crop, there is some very material intelligence that we can fully depend on.

COWS.

Mr. *Kendal*. They give more milk than any other food. Cream and butter have not the least taste.

Mr. *Wharton*. Give vast quantities of milk, but strong.

Mr. *Acton*. The butter excellent, without the least taste.

Mr. *Arbuthnot*.* The butter, while the cows were fed on the cabbages from *Northamtonshire*, was exceedingly good, but tasted strong the moment they were put to the *Scotch*.

Mr. *Reynolds*. They give sweet butter and milk.

The point of sweet butter is still undecided, from Mr. *Arbuthnot*'s discovering a difference between sorts.

OXEN.

Sir *Rob. Burdet*. Fats them as quick and well as possible.

Earl of *Holdernesse*. Fats them well.

SHEEP.

Sir *Rob. Burdet*. Fatted them well.

Col. *St. Leger*. Did extremely well on them.

Mr. *Mellish*. Sheep bought lean, at 14 *s*. and sold fat from them, at 21 *s*.

Mr. *Hall*. Fat sheep throve well on them.

---

* Not in the minutes, but I have received the information since.

HOGS.

Mr. *Wharton*. Found them of very great utility (beyond turnips) in keeping a large ſtock of ſtore ſwine.

From all which it clearly appears, that cabbages are uncommonly beneficial in feeding and fattening oxen and ſheep, and keeping ſwine.

GENERAL OBSERVATIONS.

It may be thought very ſurprizing, that a vegetable cultivated by ſuch numbers of perſons, ſhould not yet be thoroughly known; but if the caſe is well conſidered, it will not be difficult to account for ſuch ſeeming contradictions; and this enquiry may perhaps lead the way to more accurate ideas in future.

The culture of cabbages, as food for cattle, has been proſecuted under a general idea of ſupplying the place of turnips late in the ſpring; and this notion has run through the cultivators of all the various ſorts, and at both the ſeaſons of ſowing; hence has ariſen one grand error in the culture, and from which ſeveral of the enemies of cabbages have been led into their miſtakes.

The

The culture of this plant for late spring food—and the most profitable culture of it in general, are perhaps very different things. From attentively considering the various intelligence I have received, I am clearly of opinion, that cabbages ought to be used before they decline in the leaf, that is, while all their loose leaves are fresh and green; this will universally be before *Christmas*; and if planted in the spring, at *Michaelmas*, then should fat oxen or sheep be put to them without the least view to late spring food; and that this will prove the most profitable conduct, I have not a doubt.

The vast importance of 40 or 50 tons of food well adapted to the autumn fatting of cattle is unaccountably lost sight of, for rambling after late spring food, which is quite another enquiry, and perhaps of much inferior importance. And this strange infatuation leads people to value crops by their use in the spring, which ought to have been consumed before *Christmas*. A gentleman weighs part of a crop in *November*; it turns out 40 or 50 ton; he leaves it to the spring, when it pays him only 40 *s*. or 50 *s*.; then, says he, cabbages are worth only

only 1 *s.* or 2 *s.* a ton; forgetting, that inftead of 40 tons, he has not, at the time of confuming, perhaps 20.

I am led into thefe reflections from Mr. *Crowle*'s getting above 50 tons; and, as I am informed, reporting very unfavourably of the culture. How ftrange is this! Is it poffible for a man to be poffeffed of 50 tons of what will undeniably fatten both oxen and fheep, and yet not know what to do with it? Here comes in another confideration.

Gentlemen keep cows for their families; fome milked, fome dry—young cattle—hogs, &c. &c. their cabbages are fometimes confumed in a mifcellaneous manner, and turn out unprofitable: no wonder; it would be fo with any other food: thefe applications, if accurately accounted for, are all unprofitable; four or five acres go one knows not how, that (referved for the purpofe) would have fattened, perhaps, 20 oxen or 100 wethers.

For thefe reafons I am induced to declare, that cabbages have not fair play till they are applied to fattening cattle or fheep—and at the time when the crop is in perfection. Is not this opinion ftrongly corroborated

rated by the great profit made by those gentlemen who thus apply their crops?

That the true *Scotch* cabbage will stand till *May* without bursting or sprouting, I know to be an undeniable fact; but if weighed in *December*, and again in *May*, there will be a wonderful difference.

In my Northern Tour, I spoke of feeding cows, but I am inclined to change my opinion, partly from a winter's experience, and partly from reflection: an animal that yields little or nothing for half the year, can never pay for a winter food that will fat an ox which pays a daily profit from the hour of putting up.

Upon the whole, I beg leave to recommend a better consideration of *the application* of cabbages, than seems hitherto to have been practised by many cultivators: gaining great crops seems very well understood; but what we now want, is to discover the value of them, in which enquiry, let me particularly mention the *completing the fatting of oxen, or wethers that have had the summer's grass.* Putting lean cattle or sheep to cabbages, will tell you nothing, and it is the same with turnips.

LETTER XL.

THE culture of Turnips being among the clearest proofs of good husbandry, when managed on the principles found most advantageous in the well cultivated counties, deserves particular attention. It cannot fail of being useful to see the average products of this root under various circumstances.

Places.	Soil.	Rent. l. s. d.	Value hoed. l. s. d.	Ditto unhoed. l. s. d.	Sundry circumstances.
1. Hempstead,	stoney loam	0 10 0	2 2 0		Feed all with sheep.
2. Tring,	loam on chalk	0 10 0	2 10 0		Ditto.
3. Blisworth,	clayey, &c.	0 14 0	2 0 0		Ditto.
4. Glendon,	red loam	0 10 0	2 2 0		
5. Quenby,	clay	0 18 0	2 5 0		
6. Dishley,	loam	0 16 0	3 0 0		Ditto.
7. Formark,	sandy ditto	0 15 0	2 10 0		
8. Chatsworth to Tiddswell,	loam	1 0 0	4 0 0		Many unhoed not so high.
9. About Tiddswell,	limestone loam	0 15 0		3 5 0	Various uses.
10. Chesterfield,	hazel loam	0 17 0	1 17 6		Ditto.
11. Lawton,	limestone	0 8 0		1 15 0	One acre will finish the fatting four beasts of 40 stone in stalling.

Places.	Soil.	Rent.			Value hoed.			Ditto unhoed.			Sundry circumstances.
		l.	s.	d.	l.	s.	d.	l.	s.	d.	
12. Gateford,	sand	0	10	0	3	5	0	1	15	0	One acre will, in stalling, fatten 5 or 6 beasts.
13. Blythe,	ditto	0	10	6				2	0	0	
14. Doncaster,	ditto	2	10	0				2	0	0	
15. Broadsworth,	limestone	0	6	0				1	5	0	
16. Woombwell,	sand loam	0	16	0	2	7	6				Both feed and carry off
17. Retford,	sand	0	12	0				2	4	0	
18. Bootham,	gravel	0	10	0				1	15	0	
19. Canwick,	limestone	0	7	6				2	0	0	
20. Sir Cecil Wray,	ditto	0	7	0	2	5	0				Twice successively, the first 40s. the second 50s.
21. Runcton,	sandy	0	14	0	1	10	0				
22. Massingham,	ditto	0	8	0	1	7	0				400 fat sheep will eat an acre every day; one acre drawn and carried to bullocks will go as far as three on the land.
23. Snettisham,	ditto	0	12	0	1	15	0				
24. Burnham to Wells,	ditto	0	14	0	2	10	0				
25. Warham,	ditto	0	10	0	1	10	0				Fat beasts of 50 stone in the field; barley better than after sheep alone.
26. Earlham,	ditto	0	16	0	2	0	0				
27. Bacon Ash,	clayey	0	15	0	2	0	0				
28. Mr. Bevor,	ditto	0	16	0	3	3	0				Feeds his horses on them to great advantage; ½ an acre will winter a cow.
29. Shottesham,	loam	0	14	0	2	2	0				
30. Flegg,	sandy loam	0	15	0							Buy lean beasts at 5l. about Michaelmas and put them to turnips; sell fat in April, at 8l. 8s. or 9l. Three rood will fatten a beast of 40 stone, (14 lb.) or Norfolk wethers.

Places.	Soil.	Rent. l. s. d.	Value hoed. l. s. d.	Ditto unhoed. l. s. d.	Sundry circumstances.
31. Mr. Ramey,	sandyloam	0 15 0	3 0 0		
32. Beccles,	sandy	0 12 0	1 10 0		
33. Saxmundham,	ditto	0 16 0	1 10 0		
34. Mr. Acton,	ditto loam	0 12 6	1 15 0		
35. Hadleigh,	loam	0 15 0	1 11 6		
36. Hastead,	clayey	0 14 6	2 0 0		
37. Colchester,	loam	0 16 0	3 0 0		One acre will, in the field, fatten a beast of 40 or 50 score.
38. Youngsberry,	clayey &c.	0 12 0	1 15 0		
39. Petersham,	sandy	1 0 0	2 10 0		
40. Morden,	clay	0 12 0	1 10 0		
41. Cheam,	chalk	0 10 0	1 15 0		
42. Carshalton,	ditto	0 10 0	2 0 0		
43. St. M. Cray,	ditto loam	0 14 0	2 5 0		
44. Feversham,	rich loam	1 0 0	2 0 0		
45. Beaksburn,	chalk	0 10 0	3 0 0		
46. Isle Thanet,	rich loam	0 17 0	3 0 0		
47. Mr. Poole,	clayey	0 10 0			Has kept 30 beasts 3 months on 5½ acres drilled.
48. Findon,	light	0 13 6	1 7 6		
49. Isle Wight,	loam	1 0 0	3 0 0		
50. Ditto,	stoney	0 10 0	2 0 0		
51. Critchill,	limestone	0 10 0		1 10 0	
52. Moreton,	loam	0 12 0		2 0 0	
53. Came,	dit. on ch.	0 5 0		1 10 0	
54. Bridport,	loam	2 0 0		1 10 0	
55. Leigh,	clay	0 12 6		1 10 0	
56. Taunton,	ditto	1 0 0		1 0 0	
57. Kingsdown,	loam		2 10 0		
58. Rundway,		0 16 0	2 5 0		
59. Donnington,	ditto	0 15 0	1 11 6		
60. Beconsfield,	loam	0 9 0	1 15 0		
Averages,		0 14 1	2 3 10	1 16 9	

It is much to be regretted that so many places should continue in the unprofitable practice of not hoeing: In this comparison, the hoed ones are the most valuable, notwithstanding the general circumstance of being scarcer in countries that do not hoe.

General average of hoed and unhoed, 2 *l.* 2 *s.* 5 *d.*

LETTER XLI.

THE intelligence on the culture of Hops, inserted in the preceding minutes, well deserves to be drawn into one point of view, being much more important, upon the whole, than any account of them I remember to have read; particularly in respect of the expences and produce. The general opinions concerning hops are extremely various; some have an idea of their being prodigiously profitable, while others assert it to be a culture that answers poorly; and this diversity is found even in the midst of the hop grounds of *Kent*. A want of knowledge in these points is generally owing to the cultivators not keeping regular accounts.

Place.	Soil.	Rent.	Expences.	Produce	Value.	PerCw.	Profit.
		l. s. d.	*l. s. d.*	*T. C. Q.*	*l. s. d.*	*l. s. d.*	*l. s. d.*
Mr. *Brown*, *Ordsal*,	black bog, 3 feet deep	3 0 0	10 0 0	0 8 0	72 0 0	9 0 0	62 0 0
Mr. *Jacob*, *Feversham*,	rich black mould	3 10 0	23 15 0	0 10 0	30 0 0	3 0 0	6 5 0
Sir *T. Hales*,	rich loam	3 0 0	23 9 6	0 8 2	44 4 8	5 4 1	20 15 2
Preston,	ditto	1 0 0		0 7 0	36 8 7	*5 4 1	
Canterbury,	ditto black	3 0 0		0 11 0	57 4 11	*5 4 1	
Hawkhurst,	loam	1 0 0		0 7 0	21 0 0	3 0 0	
Averages,		1 18 10	19 1 6	0 8 2	43 9 8	5 2 0	29 8 0

* Supplied from the preceding price.

The great point in this table, is the profit made by planting hops in a bog, which is amazing; and although 9 *l.* seems an extravagant rate, yet if we take 5, the product will be 40 *l. per* acre, and the profit 30 *l.*; an improvement which should make the possessors of such wastes reflect on what they have in their power to execute.

In less favourable circumstances, hops appear to be a most profitable article, and much to exceed common husbandry. If the column of profit was complete, the great advantage of them would be more striking, as may easily be conceived from that of product.

LETTER XLII.

IN several parts of the minutes of this Tour are inserted the register of various experiments in the new husbandry, on drilling wheat, barley, oats, pease, beans, turnips, &c. and the journey passed thro' a part of *Kent*, in which drilling most crops is common husbandry; it will therefore be proper to draw into one point of view all the intelligence received of this kind. Some material circumstances may appear from such a review, which would not otherwise be gained; for the average of many persons trials on various soils, and performed with various instruments, must give a better idea of the drill culture, than the trials of a single person confined to one soil, and using perhaps but one or two implements. It is grown of more consequence than ever, to have just ideas of the real merit of drilling, as the partizans of the culture become every day more numerous — as experiments very successful are frequently published,

lished, and as the *London* and *Dublin* Societies *seem* pretty much to patronise it. The latter, to my great surprize, thinks no other object worthy recommending to the very ingenious Mr. *Baker*, than the comparison of the broad-cast and drill husbandry; although I will venture to assert, that the providing winter and spring green food for cattle; the comparative merit of manures, and the culture of the artificial grasses, are any of them of ten times the importance. The new husbandry receiving such particular attention at present, without the real merit of it being generally known, should make one anxious to lay before the publick, in as clear a light as possible, the result of the information received concerning it.

Tring. The better sort of farmers drill pease in rows two feet, and hand-hoe twice; product 35 bushels; and clean so well, that wheat always follows; in the common way the product but 20 bushels.

Mr. *Booth.* Drills pease, and hand-hoes; product one quarter and a half *per* acre.

Col. *St. Leger.* Dibbled beans in double rows,

rows, eight inches, with 18 inch intervals; hand-hoed well.; product greater than ever known in the common way; wheat followed, which yielded 27 bushels an acre.

Mr. *Hall.* Rouncival peafe, rows 18 inches afunder; clean as a garden, and finer than any broad-caft.

Leverington. Many farmers drill their beans, 10 pecks *per* acre, inftead of four bushels fown; clean by horfe-hoeing; crops four quarters inftead of three, and wheat follows; as clean as a garden.

Walpole. Drill beans in every fourth furrow; kept clean by horfe and hand-hoeing; much finer crops than common.

Mr. *Canham.* Ditto, product five and a half quarters *per* acre, and then five quarters of wheat over 60 acres.

Mr. *Fellowes.* Wheat in equally diftant rows, 18 inches afunder; kept quite clean; product *per* acre two quarters five bushels.

Saxmundham. Beans in drills, hoed twice; product four and a half quarters.

Woodbridge. Peafe drilled, and kept quite clean by hand-hoeing; product three and a half quarters; beans dibbled in rows, equally diſtant, 16 or 18 inches; hand-hoe at 8 *s*.; product of the horſe bean from five to ſeven and a half quarters, and of *Windſor* ticks four or five quarters, at 40 *s*. to 3 *l*. a quarter.

Colcheſter. Peaſe drilled; hand-hoe them as clean as a garden; get to ſix quarters an acre, average four; dibble beans in rows, nine inches aſunder; keep them clean as peaſe; crops from five to 10 quarters; average ſix and a half.

Mr. *Ducket.* Drills his turnips from 12 inches to two feet aſunder; wheat and oats from nine to 12 inches; keeps them clean by hand-hoeing; the crops much better than in the broad-caſt mode; ſows clover before the laſt hoeing, and hoes it in.

Mr. *Arbuthnot.* Drills wheat, barley, peaſe, beans, and turnips; four rows of wheat in general, at ſix inches, on ridges three and a half feet wide; ſome double rows; peaſe and beans various diſtances; turnips at two and

and three feet; average product of
drilled wheat, 23 bushels; of beans
27 and a half; of barley one quarter
seven bushels; peafe have not fucceeded; turnips middling.

Mr. *William Neal.* Drilled hotspur peafe,
the rows equally distant, 10 inches;
broad-cast at same time.

		£	s.	d.
Product, drilled,		3	0	0
Broad-cast,	-	2	5	0
Superiority,	-	0	3	0

The price 8 s. a bushel.

St. Mary Cray. Peafe they drill in equally
distant rows, two feet.

Dartford. Peafe and beans drilled and
hand-hoed; product from four to six
quarters an acre.

Northfleet. Peafe and beans drilled, and
hand and horse-hoed; wheat after
them; product, peafe four to seven
quarters; beans four to eight.

Sittingburn. Peafe and beans drilled, hand
and horse-hoed: product, peafe three
and a half quarters; beans, five to
eight quarters.

Feversham. Peafe and beans drilled in rows,
18 inches

18 inches afunder; hand-hoe the peafe, and horfe and hand-hoe the beans; crops from five to feven quarters; average five and a half.

Beakfburn. Drill peafe and beans equally diftant, at 20 inches; both horfe and hand-hoe them; product three and a half quarters peafe, and five of beans.

Mr. *Taylor.* Wheat equally diftant, 10 inches afunder; hand-weed and horfe-hoe with a narrow fhim; product four quarters *per* acre; beans in double rows, at 16 inches, on four feet ridges; horfe-hoed; crop four quarters: in this method he plants cabbages in *June*, in the middle of the intervals, and horfe-hoes them after the beans are off; crop four quarters, and cabbages 3*l.* Oats in equally diftant rows, 11 inches afunder; hand and horfe-hoed, and clover harrowed in; the crop four and a half quarters; and the cleaneft clover in the country.

Mr. *Reynolds.* Turnips in equally diftant rows, 18 to 24 inches afunder; horfe and hand-hoed, the crops better than broad-caft ones, up to 38 tons *per* acre. Wheat in equally distant rows, one foot, horse and hand-hoed; product 20 bushels, broad-cast adjoining 14; the former exceeded the latter by 1*l.* 11*s.* 9*d. per* acre.

Preston. Beans in rows, 18 to 24 inches; kept quite clean by horse and hand-hoeing; crops five quarters; wheat always after them.

Isle of Thanet. Beans drilled and horse-hoed; crop four to five quarters, on an average.

Margate ditto. Wheat, barley and oats, equally distant, nine inches; hand and horse-hoed with a shim; beans and pease 16 to 24 inches: crops; beans four and a half quarters, pease four quarters, wheat four quarters, barley to eight quarters; five and a half average.

Minster ditto. Wheat, barley, and oats, ditto: crops, wheat three and a half, barley five and a half, oats seven, pease four quarters, beans four; wheat after pulse.

Dover. Beans, at 18 inches, hand and horse-hoed; crop four quarters; wheat after.

Sandgate. Beans drilled, hand and horse-hoed; crop four quarters; wheat after them.

Mr. *Poole.* Tried *Tull*'s wide intervals for many years; but found repeatedly, that they would not anfwer; he then contracted them to equally diftant, which have proved regularly profitable.

Wheat, barley, and oats, at nine inches.

Peafe, double rows, at nine inches, with intervals of two feet; turnips at 20 inches; crops of barley, five to feven quarters.

Mr. *Turner.* Beans drilled, hand-hoes once; crops, four to feven quarters; average five.

Mr. *Anderdon.* Wheat double rows, on five feet ridges; produced *per* acre,

No. 15. Clear crop,	B. 10	2	0
No. 16. Another crop,	8	3	1
No. 17. Another, —	19	0	0
No. 18. Another,	13	2	0
No. 19. Another,	8	0	1
Average, —	12	0	0

Profit and loss on these crops.

No. 15. Profit,	£. 1	3	1
No. 16. Ditto,	1	4	2
No. 17. Ditto,	1	1	5
No. 18. Ditto,	1	15	5
No. 19. Ditto,	0	4	0
Total,	5	8	1
Average,	1	1	7

Broad-cast compared with it.

	Produce. B.P.G.	Profit. l. s. d.
No. 15, Broad-cast,	13 2 0	2 10 2
Drilled,	10 2 0	1 3 1
Superiority,	3 0 0	1 7 1
No. 16, Drilled,	8 3 1	1 4 2
		Loss.
Broad-cast,	4 0 1	1 0 10
Superiority,	4 3 0	2 5 0

No. 15, Rent,	£. 1	0	0 *per* acre.
No. 16,	0	5	0
No. 17,	0	12	0
No. 18,	0	12	0
No. 19,	0	10	0

BARLEY.

No. 21. Four and 8 rows on a ridge produced *per* acre clear crop, — B. 20 0 0
Profit, — £. 2 2 0
No. 22. Equally diftant rows, at one foot, produced 3 quarters 2 bufhels.
No. 21. Compared with broad-caft.
It produced, clear crop, B. 22 0 0
Drilled, 20 0 0

Superiority, — 2 0 0

Profit, broad-caft, £. 2 4 8½
Ditto, drilled, — 2 2 0

Superiority, — 0 2 8½

OATS.

Drill and broad-caft compared.

Four and 8 rows on a ridge, produced clear, B. 27 2 1 5
Broad-caft, — 21 3 4 4

Superiority, 5 3 0 1

Drilled, profit, — £. 0 19 3
Broad-caft, — 0 2 0

Superiority, — 0 17 3

BEANS.
Broad-cast and drilled compared.

		B.		P.
Broad-cast, gross crop,		35		2
Drilled,	-	15		1
Superiority,	-	20		1

		£.		
Broad-cast, profit,		3	17	4¼
Ditto drilled,	-	0	17	9¼
Superiority,	-	2	19	7

Another drilled crop produced eight bushels *per* acre.

PEASE.
Broad-cast and drilled compared.

No. 27. Broad-cast, clear
crop,   -   B. 15 3 0 0
Drilled,   -   8 2 7 0

Superiority,   -   7 0 1 0

No. 28. Drilled, Increase
per acre,   -   B. 0 2 7 0
Loss, broad-cast,   3 0 5 0

Superiority,   -   3 2 6 0

M. *Coombs.* Drills peafe in rows equally diftant, 20 inches; cleans them by horfe and hand-hoeings; product 30 bufhels *per* acre.

Donnington. Drill their peafe, rows equally diftant, 15 inches; hand and horfe-hoe; product four quarters.

Beans at 18 inches, hand-hoe; crop four and a half quarters.

Mr. *Cowflade.* Wheat in equally diftant rows, 18 inches, hand-hoed; the crop three and a half quarters.

Another crop at one foot, hand-hoed, three and a half quarters; broad-caft adjoining five quarters.

Drills all his peafe and beans; product four and a half quarters.

Reading. Drill their peafe at 18 inches, and hand-hoe; the crop three and a half quarters.

Harleyford. Peafe drilled, equally diftant rows, and horfe-hoed; crop three and a half quarters.

Mr. *Clayton.* Wheat equally diftant, five inches, hand-hoed; not equal to broad-caft.

Having

Having thus given a general review of all the trials in drilling, we must, in the next place, draw each crop into one view, that the clearer idea may be had. I shall begin with

BEANS.

Crops.	Distance.	Seed	Produc. Q. B.	What follows.
Leverington		2½	4 0	Wheat
Mr. *Canham*	Every 4th fur.		5 4	Ditto 5 qrs
Saxmundham			4 4	
Woodbridge	16 or 18 inch.		6 2	Wheat
Colchester	9 Inches		6 4	Ditto
Mr. *Arbuthnot*	Various	2	3 3½	Ditto
Dartford			5 0	Ditto
Northfleet			6 0	Ditto
Sittingburn			6 4	Ditto
Feversham	18 Inches		5 4	Ditto
Beaksburn	20 Inches		5 0	Ditto
Mr. *Taylor*	Double rows, 16 inc. on 4 feet ridges		4 0	Barley
Preston	18 to 24 inch.		5 0	Wheat
Thanet			4 4	Ditto
Ditto	16 to 24 inch.		4 4	Ditto
Ditto			4 0	Ditto
Dover	18 Inches		4 0	Ditto
Sandgate			4 0	Ditto
Mr. *Turner*			5 0	
Mr. *Anderdon*			1 3	
Donnington	18 Inches		4 4	
Mr. *Cowslade*			4 4	
Average			4 4	

From this account the importance of the drill culture of beans is sufficiently clear: four and a half quarters an acre are a product far beyond the average of broad-cast crops. But the bean is peculiarly adapted to this husbandry; the stalks are strong, keep erect, and no weather has power to beat them down, or even to entangle them like wheat; so that the horse-hoe is admitted with the greatest ease, and without any damage, which is seldom the case with any other corn crop; and that horse-hoeing is of infinite consequence in improving the crop, and keeping the land quite clean, has never been doubted; indeed the constant practice of all the *Kentish common farmers* shews clearly enough that they find it highly profitable.

But the advantage, perhaps, the greatest of this careful bean culture is that crop being made a fallow for wheat; all *Kent* concurs in this course; it is the same with the best farmers in the marsh-land clays of *Norfolk:* let any person judge of the merit of that husbandry, which makes the fallow year yield four and a half quarters of beans *per* acre, which are certainly a product of above 5*l.* The same regular practice

practice finds the advantage of sowing wheat after them, which would not be the case, if they were not to all purposes a real fallow.

What an amazing difference is there between this most advantageous practice, and the course of, 1. Fallow, 2. Wheat, 3. Beans; which is yet the practice throughout the *Vale* of *Aylesbury*, and many other clay countries! And in which the beans are sown broad-cast, and weeded by sheep. What shameful, execrable husbandry!

PEASE.

Crops.	Distance.	Produce Q. B.	What follows.
Tring	2 Feet	4 3	Wheat
Mr. *Booth*		1 4	
Woodbridge		3 4	
Colchester		4 0	Wheat
Mr. *Neal*	10 Inches	3 0	
Dartford		5 0	Wheat
Northfleet		5 4	Ditto
Sittingburn		3 4	Ditto
Beaksburn	20 Inches	3 4	Ditto
Thanet	16 to 24 in.	4 0	Ditto
Ditto		4 0	Ditto
Mr. *Anderdon*		1 1	
Mr. *Coombs*	20 Inches	3 6	
Donnington	15 Inches	4 0	
Mr. *Cowslade*		4 4	
Reading	18 Inches	3 4	
Harleyford		3 4	
Average		3 5	

Drilling in this table alſo appears a moſt beneficial culture for peaſe; three quarters five buſhels are a great crop; and many products riſing from four to more than five ſhew how advantageous the practice is. Every one muſt be ſenſible, that the broad-caſt mode will not on an average nearly equal it.

WHEAT.

Crops.	Diſtance.	Produce Q. B.	
Mr. *Fellowes*	18 Inches	2 5	
Mr. *Arbuthnot*	4 Rows at 8 in. on 3½ feet ridges	2 7	Horſe-hoes
Mr. *Taylor*	10 Inches	4 0	Ditto
Mr. *Reynolds*	12 Ditto	2 4	
Thanet	9 Ditto	4 0	Ditto
Ditto	Equally diſt.	3 4	Ditto
Mr. *Anderdon*	2 Rows on 5 f.	1 4	Ditto
Mr. *Cowſlade*	18 Inches	3 4	Hand-hoe
Ditto	1 Foot	3 4	
Average		3 1	

The product of wheat thus cultivated, on compariſon with the old method in general, is not here ſo much the object, as the general importance of admitting the hand and horſe-hoe; which keeps the land clean and in much finer order than it can be in the broad-caſt way.

BARLEY and OATS.

Crops.	Sort.	Distance.	Prod.	
Mr. *Arbuthnot*	Barley	Double rows, 3, 4, and 5 feet ridges	1 7	Horse
Mr. *Taylor*	Oats	11 Inches	4 4	Ditto
Thanet	Barley	9 Ditto	5 4	Ditto
Ditto	Ditto	Ditto	5 4	Ditto
Ditto	Oats	Ditto	7 0	Ditto
Mr. *Poole*	Barley	9 Inch	6 0	Hand
Mr. *Anderdon*	Barley	1 Foot	3 0	
Ditto	Oats	Ditto	3 3	
Average			4 4	

It is very clear from this table, that close drilling is on dry soils very beneficial, since the *Kentish* farmers have invented horse-hoes (shims) that will work in nine inches; and one practice of great importance (so great indeed that without it any product would be comparatively useless) is the sowing clover over the crop, and covering it by the last hoeing, hand or horse; which is much superior to the common mode of rolling it in.

Comparisons of the old and new methods.

Several of the preceding gentlemen have formed comparative trials between the two modes, which must by no means be passed over.

214 THE FARMER's TOUR

	Crops.	New husbandry, what	Superiority in Product	In cash. l. s. d.	Product old. Q. B. P.	Product new. Q. B. P.
Mr. *Arbuthnot*	Wheat	2 Rows on 4 f. ridges	Old ½ bushel	0 15 1½	1 2 0	2 1 2
Ditto	Wheat	4 Rows on 3½ feet	Old 2½ pecks	0 3 1½ the new	1 4 0	3 7 1½
Ditto	Barley	2 Rows on 3 feet	Old 2 bushels	0 18 10	2 4 0	2 1 0
Mr. *Neal*	Pease	10 Inches	New 3 bushels	—	2 5 0	3 0 0
Mr. *Reynolds*	Wheat	1 Foot	New 6 bushels	1 11 9	1 6 0	2 4 2
Mr. *Anderson*	Wheat	2 Rows on 5 feet	Old 3 bushels	1 7 1	1 5 2	2 2 2
Ditto	Ditto		New 4¾ bush.	2 5 0	4 1 3	3 3 1
Ditto	Barley		Old 2 bushels	0 2 8	6 0 2	4 2 0
Ditto	Oats	Equally	New 5¼ bush.	0 17 3	5 3 3	5 3 1
Ditto	Beans		Old 20¼ bush.	2 19 7	3 2 1	2 7 1
Ditto	Pease		Old 7 bushels	1 7 3	7 3 1	3 2 1
Ditto	Ditto		New 3½ bush.			
Mr. *Cowflade*	Wheat	1 Foot	Old 1½ qrs.	5 0 0	0 3 4	0 1 0
				2 4 3½	2 0 3	7 1

New product,   £. 2 7 1
Old ditto,   —   2 4 3

   Superiority,   0 2 2

	£	s	d
In cash, new superior,	0	3	1
Ditto,	1	11	9
Ditto,	2	5	0
Ditto,	0	17	3
Total,	4	17	1

Average, — £. 1 4 3

	£	s	d
Ditto old ditto,	0	15	1
Ditto,	0	18	10
Ditto,	1	7	1
Ditto,	0	2	8
Ditto,	2	19	7
Total,	6	3	3

Average, — £. 1 4 7

I do not offer these tables as satisfactory evidence, but only as hints to shew that the comparison should be further enquired into. The real truth is, that drilling and horse-hoeing on the *Kentish* system of close rows, are most advantageous; but the broad-cast much exceeds the *Tullian* system of wide intervals.

Upon the drill husbandry in general,

as it appears in the minutes of this Tour, I have to remark, that the methods pursued in *Kent*, with relation to beans and pease, seem to deserve universal imitation; because I know not any soils or circumstances that can make an exception. The same observation is undoubtedly to be made with respect to wheat, barley, and oats, on such soils as drilling is practised on in *East Kent* and the *Isle of Thanet*, viz. light loams, dry enough, always to be ploughed and kept on the flat; as they do with their turnwrest ploughs, leaving not one furrow in a whole field: the success there met with in this husbandry is so great, that no unfavourable conclusions can possibly be allowed: and I may further remark, that success also depends much on the implements used being strong, simple, and *in commom use:* this is the case in *Kent*, where drill ploughs, and variety of horse-hoes, are found in every farm yard.

But on soils, that are so heavy or wet as to require ridge work, I am clear from these minutes, that (beans excepted) the broad-cast mode will be found much the

most

moſt profitable; and I may alſo affirm, that in reſpect of good implements for the drill culture, no part of the kingdom, *Kent* excepted, though not the Society's room, is near perfection.

LETTER

LETTER XLIII.

GAINING certain information concerning the rental of the kindom is one of the moſt important objects of this Tour; ſuppoſed amounts, varying in different periods, have for this century paſt been calculated by ingenious political arithmeticians, and numerous important reflections founded on the reſult: I apprehend the neceſſity of calculating on *real* authority, inſtead of ſuppoſition, whenever it can be gained, muſt be manifeſt to every one, and in proportion as the reflections of thoſe politicians are of conſequence, ſo much will be the advantage of calculating the average, from the various minutes of this and ſimilar journeys.

Fom *North Mims*, through *St. Alban's*, and *Hempſtead* to *Tring*, within four miles of *Ayleſbury* the ſoil is of moderate fertility; rents from 5 *s*. to 20 *s*. but principally at 10 *s*; the average I reckon 11 *s*. This is a tract of 28 miles through the country, which *Ellis* calls the *Chiltern*. From thence, through the vale, 14*s*. About *Hockston* 16*s*. *Winslow* from 28*s*. to 3*l*. average 35*s*.; thence to *Buckingham* 15*s*.; from *Buckingham*, through *Towcester* to *Northampton*, is also rich clay about *Towcester*, and five miles towards *Northampton*, from 20*s*. to 3*l*. average 28*s*. Here we must stop: this is a line of 37 miles, all a very rich soil; the average of the averages is 21*s*. and is I believe near the truth.

From *Blisworth*, about which rents are 8*s*. to 20*s*. average 12*s*. through *Northampton*, the country improves; it is a fine red loam; for some miles from *Northampton*, from 20*s*. to 40*s*.; average 25*s*. About *Hazelbeach*, inclosed, 15*s*. to 25*s*.; but some large open fields from 2*s*. 6*d*. to 8*s*. will reduce the other to 16*s*. From *Hazelbeech* to *Kettering* the same. About *Glendon*, the average 15*s*. From *Hazelbeech* to *Quenby Hall* mostly grazing country; inclosures 18*s*. open fields 10*s*. average of both 15*s*. About *Tilton* on the hill 16*s*. From *Tilton* to *Leicester* and *Loughborough* chiefly grazing, 16*s*. About *Dishly* various soils, 16*s*.

16 s. From thence to *Nottingham* the same.

Here ends the rich country; it is a line of 129 miles; average of the whole, as nearly as I can calculate, 17 s.

From *Nottingham* to *Arnold* about the town some rich at 30 s.; about *Arnold*, at 18 s. but much forest at 5 s. general average 14 s. To *Mansfield* by *Newstead* waste forest land; we must not call the rent more than 2 s. 6 d. This is a tract of 26 miles, the average of which is not above 7 s. 6 d.

From *Mansfield* to *Alfreton* is inclosed and rich, 18 s.; about *Alfreton* 20 s.; to *Derby*, on an average, 16 s; about *Derby*, 18 s; from *Radburn*, about *Formark*, 17 s.; to *Ilam*, *Longford*, &c. 10 s.; from *Derby* towards *Matlock*, 16 s.; about *Matlock* 8 s. to 40 s.; average 12 s. from thence to *Chatsworth* 15 s.; about the latter place 20 s. from *Chatsworth* to *Tiddswell*, most of it inclosed, and cultivated, from 5 s. to 30 s. average 14 s; about *Tiddswell*, 15 s.; thence to *Chesterfield* much at 12 s. to 15 s. but as there are some waste tracts, we must not reckon this line at more than 10 s. About *Chesterfield*

Chesterfield at 17*s.*; from *Chesterfield*, to *Lawton* and *Parkhill*, by *Worksop*; as part of this tract was included in my last Tour, I must allow for it, that no part of the kingdom may be reckoned twice; the average I shall call 10*s.* About *Gateford*, forest, 3*s.*; old inclosures 12*s.* 6*d.*; average 10*s.*; for some miles around *Blyth* 10*s.*; to *Doncaster* ditto; about that town 50*s.*; from *Doncaster* to *Broadsworth*, around the latter; a limestone at 6*s.*; about *Wombwell*, through a large tract, 16*s.*; about *Barnsley* and *Warth* 18*s.* Returning southward we come to *Retford*, about which place the rents are from 5*s.* to 40*s*; average 14*s.*; from *Retford*, great tracts, towards *Clumber* and *Thoresby*, waste, call it 2*s.* 6*d.* From *Durham* to *Lincoln* 17*s.* and part 10*s.*; average 12*s.*

Here ends a tract of various country, the extent 344 miles; I have calculated the proportions, and find the average 13*s.* 6*d.*

About *Lincoln* 4*l.*; *Bootham* 10*s.*; *Canwick* 6*s.*; to *Summer* castle, and about it 6*s.* 6*d.*; *Lincoln* to *Sleaford* 12*s.* This is is a tract of poor land of 50 miles, the average of which is 12 s.

At *Sleaford* begins the richer country; about *Swinehead*, at 22 s.; to *Long Sutton* 20 s.; from *Barton*, on the *Humber*, to *Long Sutton*, 100 miles, at 20 s.; *Long Sutton* to *Leverington* 20 s.; thence to *Lynn* 16 s. This is a tract of 149 miles, at 20 s.

From and about *Lynn* to *Runcton* 17 s.; to *Massingham* 7 s. 6 d.; from *Lynn* to *Snettisham* 2 s. 6 d.; about *Snettisham* 10 s.; thence to *Warham* 10 s.; from *Warham* to *Holt* 14 s.; about *Blakeney* and *Sherringham* 15 s.; to *Melton*, some 14 s. but commons will reduce it to 12 s.; to *Aylsham* 14 s.; to *Norwich* 12 s.; about *Norwich* 16 s.; thence to *Bracon Ash* 15 s.; *Norwich* to *Yarmouth* 14 s.

This line of country extends through the county of *Norfolk*; the distance is 150 miles, and the average is 11 s. 6 d.

To *Beccles* 12 s.; from thence to *Yoxford* 12 s.; about *Saxmundham* 14 s. A large tract near *Woodbridge*, sheep-walks, 4 s. 6 d. other lands 16 s.; the average I reckon about 10 s.; *Woodbridge* to *Ipswich* 13 s.; about

about *Bramford* 12 s. 6 d.; to *Hadleigh* 13 s. around that place 15 s.; to *Lavenham* 12 s. to *Stow Market* 10 s. 6 d.; from *Lavenham* to *Haſtead* 9 s. to 20 s.; average 14 s.; from *Hadleigh* to *Colcheſter* 14 s.; from thence to *Witham* 13 s.; to *Chelmsford* 11 s.; thence to *Dunmow* 12 s.; *Dunmow* to *Hockerill* 15 s.; *Dunmow* to *Braintree* 15 s.; ditto to *Thaxtead* and *Clare* 15 s.; *Hockerill* to *Ware* 15 s.; about *Youngsberry* 12 s.; thence to *North Mims* 10 s.

This is an extent of 224 miles, and the average rent is 13 s.

From *London* to *Peterſham*, 40 s.; thence to and about *Mitcham*, 15 s.; about *Cheam*, 10 s. *Cuddington*, 15 s. to *Carſhalton*, 10 s. about *St. Mary's Cray*, 14 s. *Dartford*, &c. 20 s. Here we enter the fine *Kentiſh* loams on chalk. To *Northfleet*, 20 s. to *Chalk*, 17 s. to *Sittingburn*, 15 s.; about *Feverſham* many hop-grounds at 3 l. 10 s.; but a ſmall diſtance, ſome at 12 s. average 20 s.; to *Maidſtone*, 10 s. to *Canterbury*, 10 s. the *Iſle of Sheepy*, 11 s.; *Canterbury* to *Beakſburn* much good land at 20 s. and ſome hop grounds; but much chalky hill at 6 s.; call it 15 s. About *Addiſham*, 6 s.; to to the *Isle of Thanet*, by *Preston*, 18 s.; at *St. Nicholas* in the island, 20 s.: northward towards *Margate*, 12 s.; to *Minster* 17 s.; the marsh land in the southern part, 20 s.; from *Sandwich* to *Deal*, 17 s.; from thence to *Dover* the soil declines much; we may reckon it at 10 s.: towards *Hythe*, 15 s.; about *Sandgate* the crops are good; we may suppose it 10 s.; about *Hythe*, the hills 8 s. 6 d. the lower grounds 20 s. average, 15 s.; half way to *Romney*, 15 s.; *Romney* marsh, 70,000 acres, at 20 s.

Here ends *Kent*, and a line of country, all good, of 219 miles, in which, for the sake of including them, I call the *Isle of Sheeppy* 15 miles, and *Romney* marsh as much: the average rent is 15 s. 9 d.

About *Rye*, 17 s. 6 d. to *Hawkhurst*, 12 s.; from thence to *Battle*, 16 s. to *Burwash*, 10 s.; from thence to *Lewis*, various; some pretty rich, but much waste about *Heffel*; I do not reckon the average more than 8 s. *Lewes* to *Hook* and *Sheffield-Place*, about the latter, 10 s. suppose the whole, 7 s. 6 d. *Lewes* to *Brighthelmstone*, all downs, 4 s.; thence to *Steyning*, the same; from *Steyning* to *Arundel*, 13 s. 6 d. the inclosed, but the downs into the bargain, I calculate the average at 6*s.* From *Shoreham* by *Walberton* to *Chichester,* 25 miles, at 20*s.* At *Bignor Park,* 10*s.*; thence to *Chichester* lower, as much down: I calculate it at 7*s.* 6*d.* About *Chichester,* 40*s.* to *Havant,* 18*s.* to *Portsmouth,* much poor chalk: we will call it on an average with the rich lands, 12*s.*

The *Isle of Wight,* 12*s.* 6*d.* From *Southampton* to *Alresford,* 8*s.* from *Alresford* to *Crux Easton,* 5*s.* ditto to *Portsmouth,* 10*s.* ditto to *Basingstoke,* 7*s.* ditto to *Andover,* 6*s.* From *Redbridge* to *Gilbury,* and then to *Lymington,* several minutes; but *New Forest* takes up so considerable a part of the country, that it reduces the rent of the rest infinitely; I shall not calculate this line at more than 2*s.* 6*d.* From *Lymington* to *Christchurch,* 17*s. Christchurch* to *Winborn,* 20*s. Christchurch* to *Ringwood,* 12*s.*

Here ends *Hampshire,* and a line of extremely various country, extending 329 miles, including 30 in the *Isle of Wight:* the average is 10*s.* 9*d.*

From *Ringwood* to *Critchill,* the good 10*s.* but much common reduces it to 8*s.*

To *Poole*, much good land, but the last four miles waste; from *Poole* to *Charbro'*, for six or seven miles, waste; inclosures there 20*s.*; this whole tract I shall reckon at 7*s.* 6*d.* Many wastes to *Wareham*, and also to *Moreton*; 2*s.* 6*d.* I think, is high enough to rate it. About *Moreton*, 12*s.* to *Dorchester*, two minutes, 20*s.* and 10*s.* 6*d.* all inclosed; the average I shall call 12*s.* 6*d.* About *Came*, 11*s.* to *Ridgway-hill*, 7*s.* thence to *Weymouth*, 15*s.* About *Milbourn*, 10*s.* to *Blandford*, 8*s.* Around *Milton-Abbey*, 8*s.* 6*d.* From *Dorchester* to *Bridport*, across Mr. *Hardy*'s farm of 11,000 acres, at about 5*s.* the last four miles at 40*s.* To *Mapperton*, 20*s.* About *Brammerton*, 20*s.* To *Sherbourn* and *Yeovil*, 20*s.* To *Dorchester*, 10*s.* *Bridport* to *Axminster*, 12*s.*

Here I leave *Dorsetshire*; this is a line of 154 miles, and the average rent is 10*s.* 9*d.*

From *Axminster* to *Leigh*, 18*s.* thence to *Ilminster*, 13*s.* from *Leigh* to *Taunton*, 16*s.* *Taunton-Dean* vale, 20*s.* thence to *Milverton*, 17*s.* 6*d.* to *Bridgwater*, 20*s.* *Bridgwater* to *Axbridge*, 27*s.* 6*d.* *King's Sedgmoor*,

Sedgmoor, 2 s. 6 d. *Quantoc* hills, suppose 6 d. at *Glastonbury*, 20 s. to 40 s. to *Wells*, 25 s. from *Bridgwater* thither I shall call 17 s. At *Compton*, 25 s. To *Bath*, none under 20 s. say 22 s. 6 d. From *Wells* thither, 20 s.; about that city for some miles, 30 s.

This line extends through *Somersetshire* 160 miles, and the mean rent is 18 s. 6 d.

From *Bath* to *Melksham*, but one minute, 10 s. to 40 s. but there being much down, I shall not call it more than 12 s. Thence to *Devizes*, 25 s. thence to *Marlbro'* at *Bundway*, 16 s. 6 d. *Bishops Cannons*, 15 s. *Overton*, 16 s. average, 15 s. 10 d. but I shall call it no more than 13 s. From *Marlbro'* to *Hungerford*, 15 s. 6 d. This line across *Wiltshire* is 44 miles, and the medium rent, 16 s.

From *Hungerford* to *Newbury*, 13 s. the *Vale of White Horse*, 20 s. *Newbury* to *Reading*, 17 s. about *Reading*, 20 s. to *Harleyford*, 15 s. This tract of *Berkshire* is 62 miles, and the average 16 s. 9 d.

Harleford to *Beconsfield*, 7 s. 6 d. around that place, the arable 7 s. the grass 17 s. 6 d. suppose the medium 14 s. From *Uxbridge* to *Barnet*, two minutes, the grass 25 s.

25s. to 40s. and 30s. to 3l.; and arable 12s. 6d. The medium, as there is much grafs, I calculate at 25s. It is a line of 27 miles at 17s.

Recapitulation.

	Miles.	Rent.		
		l.	s.	d.
From *North Mims* to the vale of *Aylesbury*, thro' the *Chiltern*, -	28	0	11	0
Thro' the vale to *Blisworth*,	37	1	1	0
From *Blisworth* to *Nottingham*, -	129	0	17	0
From *Nottingham* to *Mansfield*, -	26	0	7	6
From thence to *Lincoln*,	344	0	13	6
Through the poor parts of *Lincolnshire*, -	50	0	12	0
To *Lynn*, through the rich clays of *Lincolnshire* and and *Norfolk*, -	149	1	0	0
Through *Norfolk*, -	150	0	11	6
Through *Suffolk, Essex*, and *Herts*, - -	224	0	13	0
From *London*, through part of *Surry* and *Kent*,	219	0	15	9
Through *Sussex* and *Hampshire*, -	329	0	10	9
Through *Dorsetshire*,	154	0	10	9
Through *Somersetshire*,	160	0	18	6
Through *Wiltshire*, -	44	0	16	0
Through *Berkshire*, -	62	0	16	9
Ditto *Buckinghamshire* and *Middlesex*, -	27	0	17	0

I have calculated thefe proportions, and find the average rent to be juſt 14*s*. an acre.

It gives me pleaſure to find, that this very extenſive tract of country is, upon an average, let at ſo good a rent. That of the counties travelled in my laſt Tour was but 11*s*. 9*d*. Hence we find, how much richer, and better cultivated, this part of the kingdom is.

	Miles.	Rent.
		l. s. d.
That part of the country travelled in the *Six Weeks Tour*, of which minutes of *rent* were taken, was	459	0 12 7
Ditto in *Tour through the North of England*,	1451	0 11 9
The part of the preſent journey that contains *rent*, -	2067	0 14 0
	3977	

In this line through *England*, of near four thouſand miles, the general average is 13*s*.

LETTER XLIV.

THE Products of Corn require very little introduction; it is not only a matter of much curiosity to know the average, but also of great public utility to be informed of the variations and the circumstances on which they depend. In the following sheets I throw those of white corn into progressive tables, according to the rent of the land.

Rents to 10s. an acre.

Place.	Rent.	Wheat.	Barley.	Oats.	Rye.	Aver.	Sundry circumstances
	l. s. d.						
Hempstead,	0 10 0	25	40	48		37	Much good husbandry in general.
Tring,	0 10 0	25	24	48		32	
Haselbeech,	0 6 0	12	24	22	16	18	Open fields.
Glendon,	0 10 0	15	32	16		21	
Quenby,	0 10 0	24	34	64		40	Open fields, rich clay.
Lawton,	0 8 0	18	24	32		24	Much open field and bad husbandry.
Gateford,	0 10 0	22	36	40	24	30	
Blythe,	0 10 0	24	32	40	24	30	

THROUGH ENGLAND.

Places.	Rent. l. s. d.	Bushels. Wheat.	Barley.	Oats.	Rye.	Aver.	Sundry circumstances
Mr. Wharton at Wheatly,	0 10 0	15	24	32	24	23	
Broadsworth,	0 6 0	15	20	24	15	18	
Bootham,	0 10 0	16	24	36	24	25	Execrable husbandry.
Canwick,	0 7 6	23	28	26	20	24	
Sir Cecil Wray,	0 7 0	20	40			30	
About Summer castle,	0 7 0	20	34	24		26	
Massingham,	0 8 0	24	34			29	Good husbandry, light sand.
Warham,	0 8 6	24	36			30	Ditto.
Cheam,	0 10 0	24	32	40		32	
Carshalton,	0 10 0	24	32	32		29	
Burwash,	0 10 0	24		32		28	
Framfield,		16		36		26	
Sheffield Place,	0 10 0	24	32	28		28	
Isle of Wight,	0 10 0	20	32	32		28	
Alresford,	0 8 0	16	30	32		26	Thin loam on chalk hills.
Critchill,	0 10 0	22	24	32		26	
Came,	0 5 0	17	20	24		20	
Milbourn,	0 10 0	16	24	24		21	
Milton Abbey,	0 8 6	16	24	27		22	
Beconsfield,	0 9 0	16	24	24		21	
Average,	0 8 10	20	29	32	21	26	

Rents from 10 s. to 15 s. an acre.

Places.	Rent.	Bushels. Wheat.	Barley.	Oats.	Rye.	Aver.	Sundry circumstances.
Aylesbury,	0 14 0	15	16			15	Very bad husbandry on rich clay, open fields.
Buckinghamsh.	0 15 0	16	16			16	
Blisworth,	0 12 0	20	28	40	24	28	

		Bushels.				
Places.	Rent.	Wheat. Barley. Oats. Rye. Aver.				Sundry circumstances.
Raaburn,	0 14 0	23 44		48	38	
Formark,	0 15 0	24 40			32	
Retford,	0 12 6	26 40			33	
Runcton,	0 14 0	20 28	40	22	27	
Snettisham,	0 12 0	24 24	32	28	27	
Burnham to Wells,	0 14 0	36 36			36	
Sherringham,	0 15 0	26 28			27	
Melton,	0 14 0	28 32			30	
Aylsham,	0 14 0	26 32	46		34	Very good husbandry.
Bracon Ash,	0 15 0	28 32	40		33	
Mr. Bevor,	0 15 0	36 44			40	
Shottesham,	0 14 0	20 28			24	
Mr. Fellowes,	0 14 0	28 32			30	
Flegg Hundred,	0 15 0	28 32	40		33	
South of Beccles,	0 12 0	16 20	32		21	
Saxmundham,	0 14 0	22 32	32		28	Good land well cultivated.
Bramford,	0 12 6	26 32	36		31	Good husbandry.
Mr. Acton,	0 12 6	32 40			36	
Hadleigh,	0 15 0	32 34	34		33	
Hasted,	0 14 6	20 24	28		24	
Boreham,	0 11 0	24 40	48		37	
Dunmow to Hockerill,	0 15 0	28 40	48		38	
Hockerill to Ware,	0 15 0	34 48			41	
Youngsbury,	0 12 0	20 30	32		27	
Morden,	0 12 0	24 32	40		32	
St. Mary Cray,	0 14 0	24 40	44		36	Fine loam on chalk, and good husbandry.
Sittingbourn,	0 15 0	28 40			34	
Beaksbourn,	0 14 0	28 28	32		29	
Isle of Thanet,	0 14 0	32 40			36	Rich loam, chiefly drilled and hand-hoed.
Near Dover,	0 15 0	24 32			28	
Rye,	0 15 0	24 40	44		36	
Thence to Hawkhurst,	0 12 0	24	36		30	

Places.	Rent. l. s. d.	Bushels. Wheat.	Barley.	Oats.	Rye.	Aver.	Sundry circumstances.
Hawkhurst,	0 12 0	20	30	32		27	
Findon,	0 13 6	24	36			30	
Tilbury,	0 10 6	20	28	32		26	
Moreton,	0 12 0	18	24	24	12	19	Very bad management.
Leigh,	0 12 6	20	25	24		23	
B. Canons,	0 15 0	32	32	32		32	
Donnington,	0 15 0	24	32	40		32	
Harleyford,	0 11 0	24	36	38		32	
Stanmore,	0 12 6	24				24	
Averages,	0 13 6	25	32	36	21	30	

Rents from 15s. to 20s.

Places.	Rent. l. s. d.	Bushels. Wheat.	Barley.	Oats.	Rye.	Aver.	Sundry circumstances.
Hockson,	0 16 0	24	16			20	
Mr. Booth,	1 0 0	17	56	72		48	Excellent husbandry and much cattle.
Dishley,	0 16 0	28	36	48		37	
Alfreton,	1 0 0	30	35			32	
Chatsworth to Tiddswell,	1 0 0	33	24			28	
Tiddswell,	0 16 0	25	44	56		41	
Chesterfield,	0 17 0	26	36	52		38	
Wombwell,	0 16 0	24	48	40		37	Very fine rich loam.
Leverington,	0 18 0	28	44*			36	* Barley big.
Walpole,	0 17 0	24	60			42	
Earlham,	0 16 0	20	28	32		26	
Woodbridge,	0 16 0	32	44	40		38	Admirable management.
Mr. Aspin,	1 0 0	40	40			40	
Colchester,	0 16 0	28	48	64		46	Ditto.
Petersham,	1 0 0	24	32	40	24	30	
Cuddington,	0 17 0	24	32	40		32	

Places.	Rent.			Bushels.				Sundry circumstances.
	l.	s.	d.	Wheat.	Barley.	Oats.	Rye.	Aver.
Near *Dartford*,	1	0	0	32	64	52		49	Fine loam on halk, and excellent husbandry.
Northfleet,	1	0	0	32	48	60		47	Ditto.
Feversham,	1	0	0	32	40	48		40	
Preston,	0	18	0	32	32			32	Fine rich loam, and much drilling and horse-hoeing.
Isle of Thanet,	1	0	0	32	40			36	Ditto chiefly drilled.
Ditto,	0	17	0	28	40	56		41	Ditto.
Sandwich to *Deal*,	0	17	0	28	32			30	Some drilled, but in general inferior to the island.
Hythe,	1	0	0	24	32			28	
Walberton,	1	0	0	32	32			32	
Mr. *Turner*,				28	40	48		38	Rich stiff clay.
Havant,	1	0	0	24	36			30	
Isle of Wight,	1	0	0	32	44	48		41	
Ditto,	1	0	0	32	44	64		47	Very fine sandy loam.
Ditto,	1	0	0	32	40	66		46	Ditto.
Charborough,	0	16	0	26	30	36		30	
Mapperton,	0	16	0	16	24	32		24	
Axminster,	0	18	0	20	30	30		27	
Taunton,	1	0	0	20	25			22	Rich clay.
Halswell,	0	18	0	15	18	25		19	Very bad husbandry.
Bridgwater,	1	0	0	20	30			25	
Rundway,	0	16	6	28	28	28		28	
Overton,	0	16	0	28	32			30	
Marl. to *Hung.*	0	15	6	16	24	32		24	
Vale W. Horse,	1	0	0	40		48		44	
Reading,	1	0	0	26	40	48		38	
Averages,	0	17	10	26	36	46	24	34	

Rents above 20 s. an acre.

Place.	Rent.			Bushels.				Sundry circumstances.
				Wheat.	Barley.	Oats.	Rye.	Aver.
	l.	s.	d.					
Doucaster,	2	10	0	30	48	80	34	48	Rich sand.
Swinehead,	1	2	0	28	24	32		28	
Chichester,	1	10	0	32	36	64		44	
Bridport,	2	0	0	30	32	40		34	
Compton,	1	5	0	30	30	40		33	
Averages,	1	13	4	30	34	51	34	37	

Recapitulation.

	Rent.			Bushels.				
				Wheat.	Barley.	Oats.	Rye.	Aver.
	l.	s.	d.					
Rents to 10 s.	0	8	10	20	29	32	21	26
Ditto 10 s. to 15 s.	0	13	6	25	32	36	21	30
Ditto 15 s. to 20 s.	0	17	10	26	36	46	24	34
Ditto above 20 s.	1	13	4	30	34	51	34	37
General average,	0	14	9	24	32	38	22	30

Upon this table, which is the average of such numerous articles, I must, in the first place, observe, that the rent coming within 9 d. of the article rent, alone, unmixed with other circumstances, is a confirmation that our calculations are probably accurate. The general average products are of,

Wheat, 3 quarters,

Barley, 4 ditto,
Oats, 4 quarters 6 bushels,
Rye, 2 quarters 6 bushels,
And the medium of all these, 3 quarters 6 bushels,

They shew that throughout the countries now travelled, both soil and culture are GOOD. The former alone could not have so general an effect; the latter is of great consequence, as appears by the regular gradation of products in proportion to rent, which is remarkably unbroken; in wheat totally; in barley, except one slight variation; oats unbroken; rye the same; and the average of them also.

But I should here remark, that a circumstance is to be remembered which is very important, and raises these products much; it is, that the table includes very numerous minutes from some whole counties, particularly *Norfolk*, *Suffolk*, *Essex*, and *Kent*, where summer fallows are extremely rare; hence these products are the more considerable, from being gained in so many places, without the attendant loss of fallows; this circumstance raises them to be superior to those in the Northern Tour, though,

what

what is very remarkable, wheat and barley, in the average product, is the same in both.

Respecting the proportion between the *rent* and average products of all white corn, the following table will shew it.

Rent.			Prod.	Rent per bushel.		
l.	s.	d.		l.	s.	d.
0	8	10	26	0	0	4
0	13	6	30	0	0	$5\frac{1}{4}$
0	17	10	34	0	0	$6\frac{1}{4}$
1	13	4	37	0	0	$10\frac{1}{4}$
Average,			30	0	0	$5\frac{1}{4}$

Product, though it rises with rent, is not at all proportioned to it: 17 s. 10 d. is about the double of 8 s. 10 d.; the latter producing 26 bushels; the former should yield 52, whereas it is only 34, and the same with all the rest. But the consideration which explains this difficulty is the expence of cultivation; the land that yields the 26 bushels, costs as much in every thing but rent, as that which produces the 37; consequently a small increase of product will make it answer much to the farmer, to give a great apparent increase of rent, because *that* is the *only increase*.

LETTER XLV.

I Shall, in the next place, beg leave to lay before you the average products of peafe and beans, diftinguifhing the hoed and the unhoed; from the comparifon between them, we fhall probably be able to draw fome conclufions of importance.

Rents to 10*s. an acre.*

Place.	Rent. l. s. d.			Peafe unho.	Peafe hoed.	Bean unho.	Bean hoed.	Sundry circumftances.
Hempfteed	0	10	0	25				Drill and hoe fome.
Tring	0	10	0	20	35	30		
Hazelbeach	0	6	0	12				
Glendon	0	10	0	32		32		
Quenby	0	10	0			24		
Lawton	0	8	0	22		21		
Gateford	0	10	0	22				
Broadfworth	0	6	0	14				
Bootham	0	10	0	24				
Canwick	0	7	6	14				
Sir C. Wray	0	7	0	16				
Summer-Caftle	0	7	0	16		24		
Warham	0	8	6	20				
Cheam	0	10	0	24				
Carfhalton	0	10	0	20		28		
Sheffield Place	0	10	0	24				
Ifle of Wight	0	10	0	28				
Alresford	0	8	0	16				
Beconsfield	0	9	0	20		20		
Averages	0	8	9	20	35	25		

THROUGH ENGLAND.

Rents from 10s. to 15s. per acre.

Place.	Rent. l.	s.	d.	Pease unho.	Pease hoed.	Bean unho.	Bean hoed.	Sundry circumstances.
Aylesbury	0	14	0			28		
Buckingham	0	15	0			24		
Blisworth	0	12	0			28		
Radburn	0	14	0	28				
Runcton	0	14	0	20				
Snettisham	0	12	0	16				
Aylsham	0	14	0	28				
Fleg Hundred	0	15	0	20				
Sou. of Beccles	0	12	0			32		
Bracon Ash	0	15	0	24				
Saxmundham	0	14	0		24		36	Many in drills, but all well hand-hoed. Fine sandy soil.
Hadleigh	0	15	0	20		20		
Hastead	0	14	6	20				
Boreham	0	10	6		24		40	
Dunmow to Hockeril	0	15	0	24		32		
Ditto to Ware	0	15	0			28		
Youngsberry	0	12	6	16		20		Very bad managem.
Morden	0	12	0	16				
Sittingburn	0	15	0		28		52	All drilled, and hor. and hand-hoed.
Beaksburn	0	14	0		28		40	All ditto, the beans rich manured.
Isle of Thanet	0	14	0		32		36	Ditto.
Dover	0	15	0				32	Drilled and hor. hoe.
Sandgate							32	
Rye	0	15	0	28			40	The beans bro. cast, but twice hand-ho.
To Hawkhurst	0	12	0				36	
Gilbury	0	10	6	20				
Moreton	0	12	0	16				
Donnington	0	15	0		32		36	Drilled and hor. ho.
Harleyford	0	11	0			28		Ditto.
Stanmore	0	12	6				40	In rows.
Averages	0	13	10	21	28	26	38	

Rents from 15s. to 20s. an acre.

Place.	Rent. l. s. d.	Pease unho.	Pease hoed.	Beans unho.	Beans hoed.	Sundry circumstances.
Hockston	0 16 0			24		
Mr. Booth	1 0 0		12	40		Drills and hoes the pease.
Disbley	0 16 0			28		
Chesterfield	0 17 0	20				
Wombwell	0 16 0	24		32		Fine loam.
Leverington	0 18 0			24	32	
Walpole	0 17 0				40	Drilled and hoed.
Earlham	0 16 0	24				
Woodbridge	0 16 0		28		50	Many drilled, & al kept as clean as a garden.
Colchester	0 16 0			32	52	Generally in drills all kept garden clean.
Petersham	1 0 0			32		
Mr. Arbuthnot	0 16 0				28	Drilled and ho. hoed
Cuddington	0 17 0	16		20		
Dartford	1 0 0		40		40	All drilled and hand and horse-hoed.
Northfleet	1 0 0		44		48	Ditto, ditto
Feversham	1 0 0		28		44	Ditto
Preston	0 18 0				40	Ditto
Isle of Thanet	1 0 0				36	Ditto
Ditto	0 17 0		32		36	Ditto
Hythe	1 0 0				40	
Mr. Turner					40	Drilled & hand hoed
Isle of Wight	1 0 0			40		Broad-cast dunged
Ditto	1 0 0	24				
Mapperton	0 16 0	12		24		
Taunton	1 0 0	20		20		Set beans promisc.
Mr. Anderdon	1 0 0		10		11	Drilled & hand h.
Mr. Coombs	1 0 0		30			Ditto.
Halswell			14		20	
Bridgewater	1 0 0		25		30	
Vale W. Horse	1 0 0			40	40	
Reading	1 0 0		28			Drilled & horse h.
Averages	0 18 4	19	29	27	38	

Rents above 20 *s. an acre.*

Place.	Rent. l. s. d.	Peafe unho.	Peafe hoed.	Bean unho.	Bean hoed.	Sundry circumstances.
Swinehead	1 2 0			24		
Chichester	1 10 0	28				
Compton	1 5 0	16				

Recapitulation.

	l. s. d.	Peafe unho.	Peafe hoed.	Bean unho.	Beans hoed.
Rents to 10 s. an acre	0 8 9	20	35	25	
Ditto from 10 s. to 15 s.	0 13 10	21	28	26	38
Ditto from 15 s. to 20 s.	0 18 4	19	29	27	38
General average,	0 14 3	20	29	26	38

		Bufhels.
Peafe, hoed,	- --	29
Ditto unhoed,	- -	20
Superiority,	-	9
Beans, hoed,	- -	38
Ditto unhoed,	-- -	26
Superiority,	- -	12

It is impoffible too repeatedly to inforce the neceffity of hoeing peafe and beans; every review we take of the hufbandry of the kingdom abounds with frefh proof of the real importance of this culture: is it not aftonifhing, that fo many tracts of country should remain in so barbarous a state, as to persist in the contrary mode of slovenliness?

Suppose the price 3s. a bushel, the superiority *per* acre, is 1l. 7s.; and in beans 1l. 16s. though the extra expence of hoeing in most cases is saved in the seed: but suppose it came to 7s. an acre, there is 1l. *per* acre saving on the pease; and 1l. 9s. on the beans: is not this a most striking contrast!

But by means of keeping them clean, they in one case are a fallow, followed by wheat or barley; in the other a *crop* succeeded by a fallow. This difference must be decisive to the least attentive reader: if it was calculated through a course, the importance of it would appear much greater than may at first be conceived. As I enlarged particularly on this point in my *Northern Tour* (from the minutes of which the same observations were deduced) it is the less necessary to be particular here.

LETTER XLVI.

THE quantities of SEED used for the production of both corn and pulse, are an essential article in their culture. This is an object very important in two respects; first, the general application of the whole crop; and secondly, to discover, if we can, the portions that are most advantageous. There is no point in agriculture about which opinions vary more, nor any in which a greater difference is found in practice: when this is the case, it is always useful to discuss the variations—to attempt to discover their reason—and the quantities most beneficial, either absolutely in themselves, or relatively to soil; this I shall attempt in the following tables.

Place.	Rent. *l. s. d.*	Wheat Seed	Wheat Crop	Rye Seed	Rye Crop	Barl. Seed	Barl. Crop	Oats Seed	Oats Crop	Peafe Seed	Peafe Crop	Beans Seed	Beans Crop
1. *Hempstead,*	0 10 0	3	25			4	40	4	48	3	25		
2. *Tring,*	0 10 0	2½	25			4	24	3½	48	4	20	3	30
3. *Blisworth,*	0 12 0	2½	20	2	24	5	28	5½	40			5	28
4. *Hazelbeech,*	0 6 0	2¼	12	3	16	2	24	6	22	6	12		

			Wheat.		Rye.		Barl.		Oats.		Pease.		Beans.	
Place.	Rent.		Seed.	Crop.	Seed.	Crop.	Seed.	Crop.	Seed.	Crop.	Seed.	Crop.	Seed.	Crop.
	l.	s.	d.												
5. Glendon,	0	10	0	2½	15			4	32	5	16	5	32	4½	32
6. Mr. Booth,	1	0	0	2	17			2½	56	3½	72			4	40
7. Quenby,	0	10	0	2	24			4	34	7	64			5	24
8. Diſhley,	0	16	0	2	28			4	36	5	48				
9. Radburn,	0	14	0	2	23			4	44	4½	48				
10. Tiddſwell,	0	16	0	3	25			4	44	7	56				
11. Cheſterfield,	0	17	0	2½	26			4	36	4¼	52	3¾	20		
12. Lawton,	0	8	0	2½	18			3	24	3	32	2½	22	4	21
13. Gateford,	0	10	0	2½	22	2	24	3	36	4	40	2½	22		
14. Blythe,	0	10	0	3	24	3	24	3	32	3	40				
15. Wombwell,	0	16	0	2¼	24			3½	48	5	40	3	24	4	32
16. Bootham,	0	10	0			2	24	3	24	4	36	3	24		
17. Canwick,	0	7	6	2½	23	2	20	4	28	4	26	3	14		
18. Leverington,	0	18	0	2	28			3	44					4	24
19. Runcton,	0	14	0	3	20	1½	22	3	28	4	40	4	20		
20. Snettiſham,	0	12	0	3	24	3	28	2½	24	4	32				
21. Warham,	0	8	6	3¼	24			3	36			3	20		
22. Aylſham,	0	14	0	2½	26			4	32	4½	46	4	28		
23. Earlham,	0	16	0	3	20			3	28	4	32	4	24		
24. Bracon Aſh,	0	15	0	2½	28			3	32	4	40	3	24		
25. Flegg,	0	15	0	3	28			3	32			3	20		
26. Bramford,	0	12	6	2	26			3	32	4	36				
27. Haſtead,	0	14	6	2	20			4	24	4	28	2	20		
28. Colcheſter,	0	16	0	2½	28			4	48	5	64	2*	32	2*	5
29. Youngsberry,	0	12	0	2¼	20			4	30	4	32	4	16		
30. Mr. Arbuth-not,	0	12	0*	3½P	*23									2*	2
31. Beaksburn,	0	14	0	2¾	28			3	28	4	32	3*	28		
31. *Thanet,	0	17	0	*2½	28			2½*	40	2½*	56	4*	32	2¼*	31
32. Hawkhurſt,	0	12	0	3	20			4	36	5	32				
33. Sheffield Place,	0	10	0	3	24			5	32	5½	28	4	24		
34. Walberton,	1	0	0	3	32			5½	32						
35. Mr. Turner,	0	10	0	2	28					4	48			4*	4
36. Iſle Wight,	1	0	0	2¼	32			4	44					1½	4
37. Ditto,	0	10	0	2½	20			4	32	4½	32	3½	28		
38. Alreſford,	0	8	0	3½	16			4¼	30	5½	32	4	16		
39. Gilbury,	0	10	6	2½	20			4	28	4½	32	4	20		
40. Critchill,	0	10	0	3½	22			5	24	6	32				
41. Moreton,	0	12	0	3	18	2	12	4	24	4	24	4	16		
42. Came,	0	5	0	3	17			4½	20	5	24				

'ace.	Rent. l. s. d.	Wheat. Seed.	Wheat. Crop.	Rye. Seed.	Rye. Crop.	Barl. Seed.	Barl. Crop.	Oats. Seed.	Oats. Crop.	Pease. Seed.	Pease. Crop.	Beans. Seed.	Beans. Crop.
3. inton,	1 0 0	2¼	20			3¾	25			3½*	20	4½	20
4. unington,	0 15 0	2¼	24			3	32	4	40	4*	32	3*	36
5. rleyford,	0 11 0	3	24			3½	36	4	38	3*	28		
5. onsfield,	0 9 0	2¼	16			3½	24	3	24	3½	20	4	20
verages,	0 13 0	2½	23	2¼	21	3½	32	4¼	38	3½	23	3½	31

The numbers marked * are drilled.

Having thus drawn the general averages, all in the next place compare the products with the respective quantities of seed, inning with

WHEAT.

Products from two bushels of seed.

ce.	Crop.	Place.	Crop.
6.	17	No. 18.	28
7.	24	26.	26
8.	28	27.	20
9.	23	35.	28

Average product 24 bushels.

From 2¼ and 2½ bushels of seed.

ce.	Crop.	Place.	Crop.
2.	25	No. 28.	28
3.	20	29.	20
5.	15	31.	28
1.	26	36.	32
2.	18	37.	20
3.	22	43.	20
7.	23	44.	24
2.	26	46.	16
4.	28		

Average product 23 bushels.

246 THE FARMER's TOUR

From 2 ¼ and 3 bushels of seed.

Place.	Crop.	Place.	Crop.
No. 1.	25	No. 31.	28
4.	12	32.	20
10.	25	33.	24
14.	24	34.	32
15.	24	39.	20
19.	20	41.	18
20.	24	42.	17
23.	20	45.	24
25.	28		

Average product 22 bushels.

From 3 ¼ and 3 ½ bushels of seed.

Place.	Crop.	Place.	Crop.
No. 21.	24	No. 38.	16
30.	23	40.	22

Average product 21 bushels.

From 2,	24
2 ¼ and 2 ½,	23
2 ¾ and 3,	22
3 ¼ and 3 ½,	21

A more unbroken degradation could not have happened; and though there is not a proof, that the cause is the quantity of seed, yet there is much reason to suppose small portions a part of good husbandry, and attendant on rich soils. When the land is rich, and the husbandry good, it is evidently proved, that two bushels of wheat

wheat seed are preferable to any larger quantity, and of course that there is a great waste when more is used.

BARLEY.
From 2 to 3 bushels of seed.

Place.	Crop.	Place.	Crop.
No. 4.	24	No. 21.	36
6.	56	23.	28
12.	24	24.	32
13.	36	25.	32
14.	32	26.	32
16.	24	31.	28
18.	44	31*.	40
19.	28	44.	32
20.	24		

Average product 32 bushels.

From $3\frac{1}{2}$ to 4, both inclusive.

Place.	Crop.	Place.	Crop.
No. 1.	40	No. 27.	24
2.	24	28.	28
5.	32	29.	30
7.	34	32.	36
8.	36	36.	44
9.	44	37.	32
10.	44	39.	28
11.	36	41.	24
15.	48	43.	25
17.	28	45.	36
22.	32	46.	24

Average product 33 bushels.

From 4½ and 5 bushels.

Place.	Crop.	Place.	Crop.
No. 3.	28	No. 38.	30
33.	32	40.	24
34.	32	42.	20

Average product 27 bushels.

From 2 to 3	-	32
3½ to 4	-	33
4½ and 5	-	27

From hence it appears, that from 3½ to 4 bushels, are attended with the greatest products. This is very consistent with the common ideas of improved husbandry.

OATS.

From 2½ to 3½ bushels of seed.

Place.	Crop.	Place.	Crop.
No. 2.	48	No. 31.*	56
6.	72	46.	24
14.	40		

Average product 48 bushels.

From 4 and 4½ bushels of seed.

Place.	Crop.	Place.	Crop.
No. 1.	48	No. 19.	40
9.	48	20.	32
12.	32	23.	32
13.	40	24.	40
16.	36	26.	36
17.	26	27.	28

Place.	Crop.	Place.	Crop.
No. 29.	32	No. 39.	32
31.	32	41.	24
35.	48	44.	40
37.	32	45.	38

Average product 35 bushels.

From $4\frac{1}{4}$ to 5, both inclusive.

Place.	Crop.	Place.	Crop.
No. 5.	16	No. 22.	46
8.	48	28.	64
11.	52	32.	32
15.	40	42.	24

Average product 40 bushels.

Upwards of 5 bushels.

Place.	Crop.	Place.	Crop.
No. 3.	40	No. 33.	28
4.	22	38.	32
7.	64	40.	32
10.	56		

Average product 39 bushels.

From $2\frac{1}{2}$ to $3\frac{1}{4}$	48
4 and 4	35
$4\frac{1}{4}$ to 5	40
above 5	39

This table is so full of contradictions, that no conclusions to be relied upon, are to be drawn from it.

It may indeed be divided,

From $2\frac{1}{2}$ to $4\frac{1}{2}$	41
above $4\frac{1}{2}$	39

From which something may be slightly conjectured.

Let me here remark on the quantities of wheat, barley, and oat seed, that the smallest portions appearing the most advantageous, is partly owing to several places being included where the corn is drilled and hoed; in which mode, less seed will undoubtedly do, than broadcast.

PEASE.

From 2 ½ to 3 bushels.

Place.	Crop.	Place.	Crop.
No. 1.	25	No. 24.	24
12.	22	25.	20
13.	22	27.	20
15.	24	28.	32
16.	24	31.	28
17.	14	45.	28
21.	20		

Average product 23 bushels.

From 3 to 4 bushels of seed.

Place.	Crop.	Place.	Crop.
No. 2.	20	No. 31.*	32
11.	20	33.	24
19.	20	37.	28
22.	28	38.	16
23.	24	39.	20
29.	16	41.	16

lace.	Crop.	Place.	Crop.
o. 43.	- 20	No. 46.	- 20
44.	- 32		

verage product 22 bushels.

Above 4 bushels of seed.

lace.	Crop.	Place.	Crop.
o. 4.	- 12	No. 5.	- 32

verage, - 22 bushels.

From $2\frac{1}{2}$ to 3	-	23
3 to 4	-	22
above 4	-	22

BEANS.

From 2 to 3 bushels of seed.

lace.	Crop.	Place.	Crop.
o. 2.	- 30	No. 31. *	- 36
28.	- 52	36.	- 40
30.	- 27	44.	- 36

verage product 37 bushels.

From 3 to 4 bushels of seed.

'lace.	Crop.	Place.	Crop.
o. 6.	- 40	No. 18.	- 24
12.	- 21	35.	- 40
15.	- 32	46.	- 20

verage product 29 bushels.

Above 4 bushels of seed.

'lace.	Crop.	Place.	Crop.
lo. 3.	- 28	No. 7.	- 24
5.	- 32	43.	- 20

verage product 26 bushels.

From 2 to 3, - 37
3 to 4, - 29
above 4, - 26

With both peafe and beans, fmall quantities of feed muft, beyond a doubt, be the moft beneficial. Where the crops are fown thin, they generally hand-hoe, which very thick fowing excludes; befides, the bean is fo ftrong and branching a plant, that a few of them well cultivated, will cover much ground: which is not the cafe with white corn.

Recapitulation.

The moft advantageous portions of feed appear to be,

Wheat, 2 bufhels.
Barley, 3 ½ to 4 ditto.
Oats, 2 ½ to 3 ¼ ditto.
Peafe, 2 ½ to 3 ditto.
Beans, 2 to 3 ditto.

LETTER XLVII.

THE article of TILLAGE is worthy of the utmost attention, that it may be known what is the average draught of the kingdom, the expence and other circumstances, also the comparative strength applied to different soils. The result of a similar enquiry in my *Northern Tour* shewed, that this comparison turned out merely a matter of chance; probably it will do the same now; but it is always of consequence, to know the degree, as well as the certainty of the fact: I shall at the same time include the expence of keeping horses, which is an object strangely neglected by the writers of husbandry, though a very material part of rural oeconomics. The soil I shall characterise under the three distinctions of sand, loam, and clay; oxen must be reckoned as horses.

Place.	Soil.	Draug.	Work.	Dep. in.	Price s.	Price d.	Prop. per 100	Expence keeping. l.	s.	d.	Time of breaking Stubbles.
1. Hempstead	Loam	4	1¼	5	7	0	5	15	0	0	After Christmas.
2. Tring	Ditto	4	1¼	6	5	0	5				Christmas.
3. Aylsbury	Clay	4		3							
4. Hockston	Loam	4½	1								
5. Bliswortb	Clay	3½	1¼	3	5	0	7	10	0	0	April.
6. Haselbeech	Clay	4	1	4							After Christmas.
7. Glendon	Loam	4	1	2¼	8	0	9½	10	0	0	Ditto.
8. Quenby	Clay	4	1	3	8	0	7	12	0	0	Ditto.
9. Dishley	Loam	5½	¾	6	7	6	10	10	0	0	March.
10. Mr. Bakewell	Loam	2	1								
11. Alfreton	Loam	3½	1	4	6	0	8	10	0	0	Christmas.
12. Radburn	Clay	5	¾	4	7	0					April.
13. Tiddswell	Loam	2½	1	3½	6	0	10	6	0	0	February.
14. Chesterfield	Loam	3	1	3	6	0		6	10	0	April.
15. Lawton	Loam	3½	1	4	5	0	6	7	0	0	January.
16. Gateford	Sand	2	1	5	5	0	6	10	0	0	December.
17. Blythe	Sand	2	1¼	5	4	0	6	13	0	0	November.
18. Doncaster	Sand	2	1	5	4	6					
19. Broadsworth	Loam	2½	1	3	3	6	10				
20. Wombwell	Loam	2	1¼	8	4	6	8				November.
21. Bectham	Loam	2	1¼	3½	4	6	8				Lady-Day.
22. Canwic	Loam	2	1	4	4	0	12				Ditto.
23. Summer-castle	Loam	2	1	4½	4	0	4				
24. Swinehead	Clay	2	1								
25. Leverington	Clay	2	1	3¾	3	3	6	7	0	0	
26. Runcton	Sand	2	2	½	4	0	8				February.
27. Massingham	Sand	2	2		2	6					
28. Snettisham	Sand	2	2	5	2	6	4	5	0	0	November.
29. Warham	Sand	2	2½	4	2	6	6	6	6	0	February.
30. Aylsham	Sand	2	2	4	2	6	5	5	10	0	After Christmas
31. Earlham	Sand	2	2	5	2	6	6				Autumn.
32. Bracon-Ash	Loam	2	1	3	2	6	8				Ditto.
33. Flegg	Sand	2	1½	4	2	6	6	6	0	0	Christmas.
34. Woodbridge	Sand	2	1½								Michaelmas.
35. Hadleigh	Loam	2	1	6			7				Autumn.
36. Hastead	Clay	2	1	4½	4	0	6	7	0	0	April.
37. Colchester	Loam	2	1½	5½	4	0	4				Autumn.
38. Youngsberry	Clay	4	1	4½	6	6	4	10	10	0	After Christmas.
39. Morden	Clay	4½	1	5	10	0					
40. Cheam	Loam	4½	1	5	8	6	5				
41. Carshalton	Loam	3½	1		7	0	5				
42. Feversham	Loam	4	1¼	5	7	0	6	8	0	0	Autumn.
43. Beaksburn	Loam	4	1	5	7	0	5				
44. Hawkhurst	Clay	4	1	4½	8	0	10				
45. Sheffield-place	Clay	4	1	4	7	0	8				
46. Walberton	Clay	3½	1	4½	6	0	6				Autumn.
47. Isle of Wight	Loam	4	1		6	0	6				Autumn.
48. Ditto	Loam	4	1		5	0	5				
49. Ditto	Loam	5	1½	4	7	0	9	15	0	0*	Autumn.
50. Alresford	Loam	4	1	4	8	0	5				Autumn.
51. Gilbury	Clay	4	1	4	6	0	8				Christmas.
52. Critchill	Loam	4	1	4	6	6	4				Christmas.
53. Morcton	Loam	3½	1	4	5	0	5	15	0	0*	

* Including decline of value.

Place	Soil	Draught	Work	Dep. in.	Price s. d.	Prop. per 100	Expence keeping l. s. d.	Time of breaking Stubbles
4. Came	Loam	4	1	4	5 0	4		
5. Milton Abbey	Ditto	4	1	5	7 6	6		
6. Mapperton	Ditto	4	1			8		
7. Leigh	Clay	4	¼	3½	5 0	6		
8. Taunton	Clay	5		4½	4 6	16	7 10 0	May.
9. Wells to Bath	Loam	6						
0. Rundway	Loam	4						
1. Overton	Ditto	4						
2. Donnington	Clay	4	1	5	6 0	5		November.
3. Reading	Loam	4						
4. Harleyford	Ditto	4	1	6½	9 0	6		November.
5. Beconsfield	Ditto	5	1	5	7 6	6		Christmas.
Averages,		3⅓	1⅙	4½	5 6	6¼	9 4 0	

It is remarkable, that the average draft of this Tour should be exactly the same as in the *Northern* one: three and one third are a much greater strength than necessary, especially as a very considerable part of the journey is through sandy countries.

The depth of four and a half inches on an average appears to be very little, if considered with the least attention to the length of the roots of all crops. We do not possess clear and decisive experiments (and I much question whether the points will ever be precisely known) that will enable us to pronounce, what is in general the proper depth on all soils. Those who urge the propriety of deep tillage, quote instances,

instances, in which it is succefsful. In this Tour the experiments of Mr. *Arbuthnot*, Mr. *Burke*, and Mr. *Ducket*, are as fatisfactory as poffible, in proving that deep ploughing is excellent; but then on the other hand, what is to be faid to places, where very fhallow ploughing is attended with equal, and perhaps much fuperior fuccefs?

These are not matters, in which reafon fhould decide, though it may fometimes interfere: experiments moft carefully made (which by the way would be infinitely difficult) can alone fpeak it authoritatively. But let us for a moment endeavour to reconcile the apparent contradictions, between the trials of particular gentlemen, and the general refult of various tillage.

I conceive, that deep ploughing demands better hufbandry, particularly refpecting manures, than fhallow ploughing; and that depth, which with certain excellent farmers is advantageous, would with inferior managers be pernicious.

Let it in the firft place be confidered, that in manuring a field, you mix the manure with the upper ftratum of the earth ufually moved in tillage; fuppofe you plough four inches deep, and lay on 20 loads of dung, you confequently mix that portion of manure with the loofe earth of four inches. But fuppofe 20 loads are fpread on eight inches of depth, will the crops be the fame? I apprehend not. That there is a certain advantageous proportion between given quantities of manure, and given quantities of earth ftirred by the plough, on which they are fpread, cannot be doubted; for all the earth that is moved ought to be mixed or impregnated with the manure; but this cannot be, if by ploughing deeper you raife more loofe earth, without increafing your dung.

Manures will foon be mixed with the earth, as deep as you plough, and if they are not proportioned to the mould, the plants growing in it will thrive only in proportion to the richnefs of that compoft, which fupports them. This will appear very clear, if we fuppofe a greater depth than common; for inftance, two feet: if inftead of ploughing, as formerly, fix inches, you ftir two feet, but manure the fame as before, 20 loads an acre. Now is it not very plain, that this manure, which was proportioned to the body of earth moved in six inches, must be almost lost in that of two feet? and the effect would be (without recurring to fowerness of foil, &c.) a bad crop.

If the depth of ploughing should depend on that, to which the roots of field vegetables run, two feet may as well be named as one; for it is well known they will, in a fine bed of mould, be two feet long.

This reafoning induces me to think, that the quantities of manures ought to be proportioned to the depth of tillage. If 20 loads were a good dreffing, when the land was ploughed four inches deep, moft affuredly it will not when it is ftirred twelve.

But it may further be confidered, that in proportion as the loofe foil is diftant from the air, or rather from its beneficial influence, in fuch proportion will it require another fuperiority of manuring, and all other efforts of good hufbandry, to correct that fowerness, which it will undoubtedly have. The fyftem of deep ploughing is very incomplete, and indeed means little,

if

If the loose earth is not one uniform mass, the same as it always is in common management; to have it in that state, it must be equally manured, and equally turned to the sun with the shallower soils.

Those who laugh at the mention of the lowerness of the under strata, talk equally against reason and experience. Those who really understand this point rationally, tell you, that an unusual depth should be gained in the beginning of a fallow, and that the first crop ought not to be wheat or barley, but hardier plants. Does not this shew the real state of the case? And if this lowerness is once admitted, the preceding reasoning is surely just, that proportionate means must be used, not only to cure it at first, but to prevent its return.

Hence therefore we find, that both parties are consistent: farmers, who change the depth alone, say ploughing deep is pernicious; and they are certainly right: gentlemen, who are more spirited in their general management, apply manures with a more liberal hand, and give more plentiful and better tillage, say it is excellent, and therein speak equal truth; but keep the points separate; and do not in the lump recommend very deep tillage, as common in conversation, and the pages of most writers, without attendant explanations.

That the average of this Tour, four and a half inches, is too shallow, I am clear in my own mind; though there is no proof of it; the greater depths of five, and upwards, are in those parts, where there is the best husbandry. Besides, 6 or 8 inches are turned over by the lightest ploughs with a pair of horses, with near as much ease as 4 and a half, and consequently would be kept in as good order in every respect of expofition; six or eight inches, according to soil, may be found deep enough for any common crop under *common management*; but when trench-ploughing, or any greater depth, that requires really more than two horses, then great expences are the confequences of that depth, and much larger quantities of manure requisite to gain, I may venture to say, *the same products*.

The proportion of six and a half horse to 100 acres arable is, upon the whole, no objectable: it is much more moderat than nine and a third, the average of the *Northern Tour*.

Nine pounds four shillings, the average expence of horses (but including only two places, where decline of value is reckoned) makes this part of the expence of tillage 59*l.* 16*s. per* 100 acres of arable, or very near 12*s. per* acre: an enormous article, which shews in the strongest manner, how much it behoves every man to keep no more horses than absolutely necessary.

As to the time of breaking the fallows, it is an object of much more importance than commonly imagined among farmers. I will not pretend to assert, which season is best, but undoubtedly one must be superior to the rest on certain soils. The modern writers of husbandry speak in this respect as in all others; generally they raise a hurly burly: oh! you are all mad for not ploughing them at *Michaelmas*. Why? says the farmer. But these gentlemen there beg to be excused; for as to an experiment, that clearly proves this point, I aver there is not a single one. It is true, you have an hundred reasons; but this dependance on reason is the curse of agriculture:

culture: it has pestered the world long enough, and ought at last to give way to experiment. If I am asked, what is the proper season, I can only confess my ignorance, and offer like my brethren some *reasoning*.

From the observations I have made, I am clear, that it is in certain cases *wrong* to break a stubble in autumn. On a wet soil, in proportion as an early spring sowing is important, directly in that proportion is this autumnal ploughing wrong. Suppose I have a corn stubble, which I intend sowing in spring with beans or hardy pease; and suppose further, what no man can contradict, that it is of particular moment to get such seed into the ground in *February*, if the weather will permit; in this case, the stubble must not be touched; for if it is, the *proportion* of time will be the end of *March*, on an average, instead of the middle of *February*; for that land, which will break up from stubble quite in molds, will not allow a horse to tread it, if ploughed the autumn before. Two circumstances unite here to recommend sowing on one earth; first, getting the seed early into

the

the ground; and fecondly, on fine tilth, if I may fo call it; for let him who ploughed in autumn, fow at the fame time with another who did not plough then, and the former fhall fow in garden moulds, the latter in mortar.

The arguments in favour of autumnal ploughing turn much on the benefits of a winter expofition to the atmofphere; that the fine *nitrous* affairs may come in full play. All this founds extreamly well; but plough half a wheat ftubble in *October*, and leave the other half till the fpring to fow on one earth: all other circumftances equal, which will be the beft crop? This is a plain queftion: where is the man that can anfwer it? Here again we have reafon and chemiftry, but not farming experiment. On many foils, your tillage land is in winter a mafs of mud, from the eafy admiffion of rain, owing to the tillage, but if left unploughed, it fhoots off the water, and remains dry: why fhould not this be an advantage?

But to reverfe the medal, a cafe is to be ftated, wherein the autumnal tillage appears to be of particular importance. If the land is not to be sown till *Midsummer*, or summer fallow for wheat at *Michaelmas*; the preceding reasoning will not be just. You then do not want to get on early in the spring, and of course can leave the land till it is perfectly dry, suppose till the middle or end of *April*, then an earth will make it as fine as any garden, at the same time that it destroys all those weeds, which have vegetated since the autumnal sowing; and the fineness you then gain is a great preparation for having a full crop to kill by the end of *May:* thus, when a fallow has for its object the killing seed weeds, the land ought certainly to be ploughed in *October*. But Mr. *Arbuthnot*'s experiments prove very clearly, that this fineness in spring must never be an object, if there is much couch in the land, as the very contrary system of exposing the soil in huge clods to a whole summer's sun is then most effectual.

The great error of the generality of common farmers is not distinguishing between these cases, but using that method, which is prescribed by the custom of the neighbourhood, indiscriminately for all sorts of

of foils; and whether foul with couch or feeds.

I shall, in the next place, compare the three foils of clay, loam, and fand.

CLAY.

Place.	Draft.	Work.	Depth.	Price. s.	d.	Per 100 acres.
No. 3	4		3			
5	3½	1¼	3	5	0	7
6	4	1	4			
8	4	1	3	8	0	7
12	5	¾	4	7	0	
24	2	1				
25	2	1	3¾	3	3	6
36	2	1	4½	4	0	6
38	4	1	4½	6	6	4
39	4½	1	5	10	0	
44	4	1	4½	8	0	10
45	4	1	4	7	0	8
46	3½	1	4½	6	0	6
51	4	1	4	6	0	8
57	4	¾	3½	5	0	6
58	5		4½	4	6	16
62	4	1	5	6	0	5
Average,	3½	1	4	6	2	7

LOAM.

Place.	Draft.	Work.	Depth.	Price s.	Price d.	Per 100 acres.
No. 1	4	1¼	5	7	0	5
2	4	1¼	6	5	0	5
4	4½	1				
7	4	1	2¼	8	0	9¾
9	5½	¾	6	7	6	10
10	2	1				
11	3½	1	4	6	0	8
13	2½	1	3½	6	0	10
14	3	1	3	6	0	
15	3½	1	4	5	0	6
19	2½	1	3	3	6	10
20	2	1¼	8	4	6	8
21	2	1¼	3½	4	6	8
22	2	1	4	4	0	12
23	2	1	4½	4	0	4
32	2	1	3	2	6	8
35	2	1	6			7
37	2	1½	5½	4	0	4
40	4½	1	5	8	6	5
41	3½	1		7	0	5
42	4	1¼	5	7	0	6
43	4	1	5	7	0	5
47	4	1		6	0	6
48	4	1		5	0	5
49	5	1½	4	7	0	9
50	4	1	4	8	0	5
52	4	1	4	6	6	4
53	3½	1	4	5	0	5
54	4	1	4	5	0	4
55	4	1	5	7	6	6
56	4	1				8
59	6					

Place.	Draft.	Work.	Depth.	Price. s. d.	Per 100 acres.
No. 60	4				
61	4				
63	4				
64	4	1	6½	9 0	6
65	5	1	5	7	6
Averages,	3½	1	4½	6 0	6½

SAND.

	Draft.	Work.	Depth.	Price. s. d.	Per 100 acres.
No. 16	2	1	5	5 0	6
17	2	1¼	5	4 0	6
18	2	1	5	4 6	
26	2	2	4½	4 0	8
27	2	2		2 6	
28	2	2	5	2 6	4
29	2	2¼	4	2 6	6
30	2	2	4	2 6	5
31	2	2	5	2 6	6
33	2	1½	4	2	6
34	2	1½			
Averages,	2	1½	4½	3 10	6

Recapitulation.

Clay	3½	1	4	6 2	7
Loam	3½	1	4½	6 0	6½
Sand	2	1½	4½	3 10	6

Upon this little table I muſt congratulate the reader, on the proportions being ſo regular, and in very few inſtances broken; we find that in many particulars, the nature of the ſoil is, as it ought to be, a guide. From loam and clay to ſand, every column is unbroken; and from clay to loam the price and ſtrength *per* 100 acres decline, as the ſoil is light; but the ſame number of horſes in a plough, and the daily work being the ſame in theſe ſoils, is a contradiction.

I ſhould however obſerve, that ſand being in every particular ſo much below the other ſoils, is greatly, I apprehend, owing to ſuch numerous minutes in *Norfolk* and *Suffolk*, where their management is ſo good.

Reſpecting the compariſon between horſes and oxen, ſome minutes were taken, which will tend to throw a light on that part of rural oeconomy.

Mr. *Cook.* Three oxen in harneſs plough as much as four or five horſes.

Lawton. Four oxen in a plough, and will do as much as four horſes.

Wombwell. Four in a plough; but horſes gain ground among them.

Bootham and *Canwick*. Oxen laid afide.

Rye. Many oxen ufed; they increafe every year. On dry land better than horfes, but not on wet foils, not from weight, but going double. An ox put to work at three years old, then worth 6*l.* work him two years, and he is then worth 10*l.* This makes the annual expence of an ox only 2*l.* 8*s.* 4*d.* that of a horfe 10*l.* 15*s.* 6*d.* fuperiority of the ox 8*l.* 7*s.* 2*d.* One horfe cofts as much as four and a half oxen. On ftraw alone they do fix hours work.

Hawkhurft. Oxen moft ufed; they prefer them greatly.

Sheffield-Place. Oxen beft on light foils, becaufe they do not go in a row on heavy ones.

Taunton. Horfes kept as cheap as oxen, for no oats given; but every ox improves 50*s.* a year in his growth.

Sir *Charles Tynte.* Four oxen in harnefs do the work of fix or feven and one horfe.

Donnington. Oxen do not anfwer fo well as horfes.

Mr. *Burke.* Four oxen in harnefs, as much as four to fix horfes of the farmers.

The first object here that requires attention, is the importance of working oxen in harness. Mr. *Cook*'s, Sir *Charles Tynte*'s, and Mr. *Burke*'s intelligence on this head, is as clear, satisfactory, and decisive, as any one can wish. With Mr. *Cooke* three oxen do as much as four or five horses in the farmer's team. With Sir *Charles Tynte* four perform the work of six or seven in yoaks and a horse; and with Mr. *Burke* four equal five or six farmers horses. From all which, and the particulars mentioned at large, it is evident, that the old objection against oxen of being slow, has in this way no foundation; of which indeed I was an eye witness at Mr. *Cooke*'s, seeing his oxen walk as fast in a heavily loaded cart, as any horses could do. This therefore is the proper method of using oxen, and in which the supposed superiority of horses in so many counties would at once vanish: in this method also the objection to them, on account of poaching, is answered; that comes from their being in yoaks necessitated to tread the land in some cases; but in harness they are worked like horses at pleasure, either in pairs, or one before another. Reason tells us that it would be amazing were this superiority not found;

for

for in yoaks, besides the weight on their necks, which is very grievous, they draw unequally, if one ox hangs back, or is in any polition, except exactly even with his fellow, both muſt be wrung, and draw in a twiſted pofition, in which it is impoſſible for them to exert their ſtrength, and he who moſt exerts himſelf, ſuffers more from the tranſverſe poſition of the yoak and bow, than from carrying moſt of the weight. For all which reaſons, united with thoſe general advantages that attend oxen, however worked, it is much to be wiſhed, that the practice may become general.

Even in yoaks, their ſuperiority to horſes in profit is very clearly decided in two places. About *Rye* each ox improves 50 *s. per ann.* while worked: it is exactly the ſame at *Taunton*. At the former the expence of an ox 2 *l.* 8 *s.* 4 *d.* of a horſe 10 *l.* 15 *s.* 6 *d.* ſuperiority of the ox 8 *l.* 7 *s.* 2 *d.* or four and a half to one. Now no two horſes can poſſibly do the work of nine oxen, yoak them how you will; but where will the compariſon be, if you ſuppoſe theſe oxen in harneſs? under the ſame advantages mentioned of the above three gentlemen?

I surely need not observe, that the mere contrary assertions of the other places cannot be thought to counterbalance such minute comparisons.

The prejudice against oxen met with in many places, that have left off using them, have arisen either from the high prices of live stock, as observed in my last Tour, or from the ridiculous practices of using an immoderate number in a plough, even to a dozen, until the beasts made such a string, that two or three drivers were necessary. Such unprofitable customs, in which the ploughmen and labourers heartily concurred, from always liking to work in a posse, brought the custom of them in general into disuse, and horses were naturally preferred; but a preference founded on such absurd comparisons, must not be accepted by the more enlightened parts of the kingdom.

If the use of oxen in no greater drafts than really necessary, once comes to be understood, they will be more generally ploughed than at present; but especially if the working them in harness becomes common. The circumstance of each ox, in a proper system, paying 50 *s. per ann.*

in his growth, and the horse on the contrary growing annually worse; the one subject to numerous disorders, the other to scarcely any; the one requiring oats, and in some counties eating them in enormous quantities, up to 10 or 12 bushels *per* week to a team of four; the other never having any; the one requiring good hay, besides his oats; the other supporting six hours work on good straw alone; the one requiring no slight expence in cleaning and attendance; the other wanting neither. If all these, and some other points, are considered with the attention they deserve, the facts asserted by the *Rye* farmers, that one horse costs as much as four and a half oxen, will be thought no extravagant idea: and let any one reflect on the preceding minutes, and determine if there is any such difference in their service. In harness, an ox appears clearly to be as good as a horse; but if he is only half as able, what a prodigious advantage is it to save two and a half in four!

LETTER XLVIII.

THE first object in the farmers live stock, that demands attention, is SHEEP. An animal of such immense importance to the agriculture, manufactures, and commerce of the kingdom, cannot be too minutely considered;—the points materially to my purpose, are the average products and profit—and the causes of the variations, which an attentive review may possibly discover; all these circumstances ought clearly to be known, in order to carrying the advantage, accruing from sheep, as high as possible. There are some great evils in this part of our domestic œconomy, but they must be fully known, before any one can attempt a cure.

Place.	Rent. l. s. d.	Flocks.	Profit. l. s. d.	Fleece. lb.	Value of Fleece. s. d.	R
1. *Hempstead*,	0 10 0	20 to 300	0 14 0			
2. *Tring*,	0 10 0		0 10 0	4		
3. *Blisworth*,	0 12 0	60—160	0 10 0	6½		
4. *Glendon*,	0 10 0	100—500	0 9 6	5		
5. *Quenby*,	0 10 0	40—120	0 8 9		2 3	
Ditto,		fat stock	0 14 0	8	4 0	
6. *Tilton*,	0 15 0	ditto	0 14 0	8		Floods and
7. *Distley*,	0 16 0	80—120	0 13 0	6½	3 0	Floods.

THROUGH ENGLAND.

ace.	Rent.			Flocks.	Profit.			Fleece.	Value of Fleece.		Re'.
	l.	s.	d.		l.	s.	d.	lb.	s.	d.	
...reton,	1	0	0	60 to 140					4	0	
...burn,	0	14	0		0	4	6	4¼	1	6	Lime, and limestone sand.
...dswell,	0	16	0	100—1000	0	6	0		1	6	
...sterfield,	0	17	0		0	12	0	4			Springs.
...ton,	0	8	0	80—100				4½			
...ford,	0	10	0	200—2000	0	5	0	3			
...he,	0	10	0	100—500	0	9	0	4			
...mbwell,	0	16	0	fatting	0	7	6*	13			Quick growing grass.
...ham,	0	10	0	50—200	0	6	6	2¾	1	6	
...wick,	0	7	6	50—500	0	6	8		1	8	
...ner	0	8	0	100—1000	0	19	0		3	0	
...nehead,	1	0	0	fatting	0	15	6	9½	5	6	
...Sutton,	1	0	0	ditto	1	0	0		6	0	
...rington,	0	18	0	100—600	0	19	0		4	0	
...ton,	0	14	0	100—450	0	9	6		1	6	Water on land in winter.
...ingham,	0	8	0	300—1700	0	8	6		1	0	
...isham,	0	12	0	200—800	0	8	0		1	0	
...ham,	0	8	6	500—700	0	10	3		1	3	
...am,	0	14	0		0	8	0	3½			
...ham,	0	16	0	300—600	0	8	6		1	0	
...ad,	0	14	6	20—80	0	10	0				
...sbury,	0	12	0	100—400	0	11	0	6	3	0	Floods on grass.
...en,	0	12	0		0	8	6		1	6	
...m,	0	10	0	100—300	0	12	6		3	6	
				wethers							
				ewes	1	10	6		2	6	
...alton,	0	10	0	200—2000	0	15	0		2	0	
...sham,	1	0	0						7	0	
...burn,	0	14	0	100—300	0	10	0				
...ld	0	10	0		1	0	0				
...erton,	1	0	0								Herbs that grow in wet places.
...ight,	1	0	0	300—1200	1	0	0		2	0	
...,	0	10	0	1000—1500	0	12	8		2	0	Springs and fogs.
...ford,	0	8	0	300—1500	0	12	0		2	0	
...bill,	0	10	0	100—1000	0	10	6				
...bro'	0	15	0	400—500	0	11	0		2	0	

* Only winter.

276 THE FARMER's TOUR

Place.	Rent.			Flocks.	Profit.			Fleece.	Value of Fleece.		Rot.
	l.	s.	d.		l.	s.	d.	lb.	s.	d.	
42. Moreton,	0	12	0	500 to 1000	0	10	0		2	0	Watered meadver rot in spring, but after-grass sur rots till the tumn wateri after which f The worst l for rotting, cu by watering.
43. Came,	0	11	0	500—13000	0	8	6		2	6	
44. Milbourn,	0	10	0	2000	0	10	0	3½	2	6	
45. Ditto,	0	10	0		0	8	6		1	8	
46. Milton Abbey,	0	8	6	400—1700	0	11	0	4	2	6	
47. Near Dorchester a flock,	0	5	6	13000	0	10	0		2	6	
48. Mapperton,	0	16	0	100—700	0	9	0		2	0	
49. Leigh,	0	12	6	100—700	0	15	3		2	6	Stagnant water low meads, much rain in mer on clays.
50. Taunton,	1	0	0	20—100	0	8	6				
51. Kingsdown,	0	15	0		0	14	6		2	0	
52. Cannons,	0	15	0		0	12	0				
53. Donnington,	0	15	0	to 3 or 400	0	12	6		2	6	All watered n rot, turn in you will. Sp have nothi do with it. ewe ever while it h lamb by the
54. Beconsfield,	0	13	0	to 3 or 400 fat stock	1	0	0		2	0	
Averages,	0	13	0		0	11	8	5½	2	8	

Here we find that the average profit on sheep throughout this Tour, amounts to 11s. 8d. the average fleece to 5 ½ lb. and the value of it to 2s. 8d. The profit is, I think,

think, very low, considering how rich a tract this journey runs through; but few parts of rural management seem less understood than this of sheep; for in *Dorsetshire*, where they boast of nothing else, I before shewed how near they were to be a losing article. To discover what circumstances have the greatest influence, I shall divide the table according to profit.

Profit to 5 s.

Place.	Rent.			Flocks rise to	Profit.			Fleece. lb.	Value.	
	l.	s.	d.		l.	s.	d.		s.	d.
No. 9.	0	14	0		0	4	6	$4\frac{1}{4}$	1	6
13	0	10	0	2000	0	5	0	3		
Average,	0	12	0		0	4	9	$3\frac{1}{2}$	1	6

Profit from 5 s. to 10 s.

Place.	Rent.			Flocks rise to	Profit.			Fleece. lb.	Value.	
	l.	s.	d.		l.	s.	d.		s.	d.
No. 2.	0	10	0		0	10	0	4		
3.	0	12	0	1600	10	0		$6\frac{1}{2}$		
4.	0	10	0	5000	9	6		5		
5.	0	10	0	1200	8	9			2	3
10.	0	16	0	1000	6	0			1	6
14.	0	10	0	600	9	0		4		
15.	0	16	0		0	7	6	13		
16.	0	10	0	200	6	6		$2\frac{1}{2}$	1	6
17.	0	7	6	500	6	8			1	3
22.	0	14	0	450	9	6			1	6
23.	0	8	0	1700	8	6			1	0
24.	0	12	0	800	8	0			1	0

278 THE FARMER's TOUR

Place.	Rent. l. s. d.	Flocks rise to	Profit l. s. d.	Fleece. lb.	Value. s. d.
No. 26.	0 14 0		0 8 0	3½	
27.	0 16 0	600	0 8 6		1 0
28.	0 14 0	80	0 10 0		
30.	0 12 0		0 8 6		1 6
34.	0 14 0	300	0 10 0		
42.	0 12 0	1000	0 10 0		2 0
43.	0 11 0	5000	0 8 6		2 6
44.	0 10 0	2000	0 10 0	3½	2 6
45.	0 10 0	2000	0 8 6		1 8
47.	0 5 6	13000	0 10 0		2 6
48.	0 16 0	700	0 9 0		2 0
50.	1 0 0	100	0 8 6		
Average,	0 12 0	1540	0 8 8	5¼	1 9

Profit from 10s. to 15s.

Place.	Rent. l. s. d.	Flocks rise to	Profit l. s. d.	Fleece. lb.	Value. s. d.
No. 1.	0 10 0	300	0 14 0		
5.	0 10 0	fat	0 14 0	8	4 0
6.	0 15 0	ditto	0 14 0	8	
7.	0 16 0	120	0 13 0	6½	3 0
11.	0 17 0		0 12 0	4	
25.	0 8 6	700	0 10 3		1 3
29.	0 12 0	400	0 11 0	6	3 0
31.	0 10 0	300	0 12 6		3 6
32.	0 10 0	2000	0 15 0		2 0
38.	0 10 0	1500	0 12 8		2 0
39.	0 8 0	1500	0 12 0		2 0
40.	0 10 0	1000	0 10 6		
41.	0 15 0	500	0 11 0		2 0
46.	0 8 6	1700	0 11 0	4	2 6
49.	0 12 6	700	0 13 3		2 6
51.	0 15 0		0 14 6		2 0

Place.	Rent.			Flocks rise to	Profit.			Fleece. lb.	Value.	
	l.	s.	d.		l.	s.	d.		s.	d.
No. 52.	0	15	0		0	12	0			
53.	0	15	0	400	0	12	6		2	6
Average,	0	12	0	878	0	12	8	6	2	5

Profit from 15s. upwards.

Place.	Rent.			Flocks rise to	Profit.			Fleece. lb.	Value.	
	l.	s.	d.		l.	s.	d.		s.	d.
No. 18.	0	8	0	1000	0	19	0		3	0
19.	1	0	0	fat	0	15	6	9½	5	6
20.	1	0	0	ditto	1	0	0		6	0
21.	0	18	0	600	0	19	0		4	0
35.	0	10	0		1	0	0			
37.	1	0	0	1200	1	0	0		2	0
54.	0	13	0	400fat	1	0	0		2	0
Average,	0	15	0	800	0	19	0	9½	3	9

Recapitulation.

Place.	Rent.			Flocks rise to	Profit.			Fleece. lb.	Value.	
	l.	s.	d.		l.	s.	d.		s.	d.
To 5s.	0	12	0	2000	0	4	9	3¼	1	6
5s. to 10s.	0	12	0	1540	0	8	8	5¼	1	9
10s. to 15s. exclusive.	0	12	0	878	0	12	8	6	2	5
At 15s.	0	15	0	800	0	19	0	9½	3	9

The little dependance there is, in general, on the foil for the profit of sheep, is clearly evinced from the rent being exactly the same in the three first articles, while the

the profit varies from 4 *s.* 9 *d.* to 12 *s.* 8 *d.*; which is, upon the whole, very remarkable, and shews that general good husbandry, and a tolerable breed, are of more consequence than richness of land: but when it rises to the fertile marshes of *Lincolnshire*, with their very large breed, the case changes, as may be supposed.

As profit increases, the size of the flocks decreases; the fall is unbroken: This proves that the large flocks are generally a poor breed of sheep, or else the husbandry very bad; but the fatting system is plainly, from the whole course of the enquiry, the most profitable, and the smaller flocks include all these.

Profit, wool, and value of the fleece, are all connected, as one might suppose them to be; the three columns are in regular gradation.

It is a very important enquiry to discover that management of sheep which is most profitable on given soils; these minutes will not completely answer it, but they enable us to form a nearer idea than general notions.

In my observations on the *Dorsetshire* husbandry, I endeavoured to shew that their breeding

breeding fyftem was remarkably unprofitable, from their applying vaſt tracts of land to keeping a few ſheep; but as this inferiority did not ſo much proceed from a defect in breeding, in general, as from a want of turnips, &c. it is not ſo much to the purpoſe, as the inſtance of the beſt farmers in *Norfolk*, who have *changed* their management, and inſtead of conſtant breeding flocks, now keep annual fattening ones. They buy in wether lambs, ½ year old, in *Auguſt*; keep hardily through winter; to graſſes in ſummer, folding conſtantly; ſoon after *Michaelmas* to turnips, and fold fat from *Candlemas* to *May-day*; four to 1 acre of graſs, and ten to 1 acre of turnips. I have been the more particular in this repetition, as I conceive it is on all, except rich grazing ground, the moſt profitable ſheep management.

The firſt winter and the ſecond ſummer they are folded, which pays for their keeping, as they live in a hardy manner, and even in winter only eat the leavings of the fat ſtock at turnips, by which means that crop is eaten *clean*; never the caſe if only one ſtock feeds them. In the ſummer they have the clover and ray-graſs, which improve

prove them in flesh at the same time that they stand the fold, and being finished on turnips, there is the great advantage of selling at the most profitable time of the year. All these circumstances are of consequence. But this management further answers well, in proportioning the turnips and clover, so that all may be consumed by one stock if the farmer likes it; there should for this support of the sheep be about double the quantity of grass to that of turnips, which is just what one would wish, as it agrees with that beneficial course of,

1. Turnips
2. Barley
3. Clover 2 years
4. Wheat.

And to shew that there is a real profit on this application of these crops, I shall form a slight calculation of this sheep management on such soils, and under such circumstances, as those in the western parts of *Norfolk* where it is practised.

	£	s	d
100 sheep require 25 acres of clover; rent, &c. of it at 12 s. see vol. II. p. 15,	15	0	0
Tythe and town charges,	1	15	0
Seed,	5	0	0
Carry over,	21	15	0

Brought over, - £.21 15 0

Ten acres of turnips.

		£	s.	d.
Rent,	-	6	0	0
Tythe and rates,		0	10	0
4 Ploughings, at 2 s. 6 d.		5	0	0
Seed, harr. and sowing,		0	15	0
Manuring,	-	5	0	0
Hoeing,	-	3	0	0
		20	5	0
100 Wethers, suppose at 10 s.		50	0	0
Suppose a shepherd at 18 l. to 1000, the 10th is,	-	1	16	0
Total,	- -	93	16	0

Product.

		£	s.	d.
100 Wethers, fat in *April*, &c. at 22 s.	- -	110	0	0
Wool, at 2 s.	- -	10	0	0
Manure from feeding 10 acres turnips with them fat, at 25 s.		12	10	0
A winter and a summer's fold lean, at one square yard *per* sheep, is 7½ acres, worth 30 s.		11	5	0
Total,	- -	143	15	0
Expences,	-	93	16	0
Profit,	- -	50	0	0

This account I believe is realized on an average; the turnips and clover pay 1 l. 8 s. *per* acre profit; this is a degree of advantage, which will admit many deductions; for if those crops paid but 20s. or even 15s. it would be a much more beneficial application of them than many in use. They are considered as subordinate to corn; many farmers would not think themselves badly off, if they only payed their own expences, from their being sure means of getting fine corn crops.

This estimate is made with a view to the *Norfolk* breed; but if better sheep were taken, for instance *Dorsetshire* or *Wiltshire* wethers, I apprehend the profit would be more considerable.

In some places, where sheep are well understood, their time of buying in is *May*; but that is not so well; the price will be much higher, and the farmer will lose the advantage of winter feeding his ground, and at the same time suffer the loss of eating his turnips with only one stock; an object of real consequence, but not well understood in nine tenths of the kingdom.

That I am moderate in the rise from 10s. to 22s. appears from their buying these lambs about *Aylsham* at 10s. in *August*, and selling *the following April or May* at 18s. Whereas

whereas I reckon only 4s. more for keeping them a year longer; the *Aylſham* practice is uncommonly profitable, but it does not conſume the clover, which is neceſſary.

Reſpecting the rot; if the reader throws his eye over that column, he will at once ſee, that the accounts are ſo amazingly contradictory, that nothing is to be gathered from them. Every one knows, that moiſture is the cauſe, and that fine dry downs never rot; but

Is it water that falls in rains and ſtagnates?
That falls in rain and flows?
Floods from ſtreams?
Floods in ſummer or floods in winter?
Water from ſprings that ſtagnates?
Water from ſprings that flows?
Water from particular ſoils?

There are two or three pieces of intelligence, which inform us what will rot; but perhaps the moſt material point is to know what will *not* rot.

Mr. *Bakewell*'s account, and that at *Moreton*, ſeem to be the moſt explicit.

I ſhall in the next place review the accounts of folding, and quantities of food applied to keeping ſheep.

Places.	Fold.	Valued.	Sheep per acre.	Quantity folded.	Which be
Glendon	Fold all, even fatting sheep.	1s. 9d. per 100 a week.			
Tilton			1 in winter.		
Alfreton	Never.				
Tidswell	Ditto.				
Chesterfield	Ditto.				
Blythe	Ditto.				
Wombwell	Ditto.				
Bootham	Ditto.				
Leverington			1 of colefeed will keep 12 from Michaelmas to Christm.		
Runcton	All.				
Massingham	All, except at lambing; winter best.			600 fold 40 acres per anni	
Snettisham	All the year.		4 to an acre clover, 10 to an ac. turnips.		
Warham	All the year, ex. lambing.				
Aylsham	All the year.				
Earlham	Never.				
Woodbridge	All the year.				
Hastead	Never.				
Colchester	Ditto.				
Youngsberry	Only in summ.			230 an acre a week.	Wethers best.
Mr. Arbuthnot	All the year.	1s. 9d. ¼ per score per week		In a standing fold on straw for turnips, 134 and 30 lambs in six weeks, made 28 loads of dung, at 10s. from 5 loads and 40 truss of oat straw; eat 2 acres of turnips; clear profit by dung 2l. 2s. 6d. per acre.	
Cheam	In summer.		1 acre turnips, 100 shee. 11 days.	300 two acres in 3 weeks.	

…laces.	Fold.	Valued.	Sheep per acre.	Quantity folded.	Which fold best.
Car..lton					100 ewes equal to 140 wethers.
Ba..urn		Folding hired at 40 s. an acre.			Wethers so much better than ewes, that never fold the latter.
…e Thanet	All the year.		4 sheep to an ac. clover or trefoile.		8 sheep to a square perch.
…hurst	Never.				
…ld Place	Never.				
… on the …wns	Summer.		3 to an acre on the downs.	300 sheep 400 square yards.	Ewe fold best, as 3 to 2.
…Wight	All the year.				Wethers; they are kept by some merely for folding.
…ford	Never. All the year. Never.				
…ill	Summer.				Wethers; ewes will not bear in winter; & make more dung than ewes.
…orough	Only wethers all the year.				Wethers, ditto.
…ton	Ditto.	Fold of an ewe worth 1 s.	500 shee. require 200 acres grass, & 20 tons of hay.	100 wethers, 10 acres, twice in a place.	Ewes best in summer.
	Ditto.	1000 worth 15 s. a night.	2½ sheep per acre in gener.	1000 sheep an acre in a night once.	Ewes best from making more water.
…urn	Summer, wethers in winter.	1300 sheep, 30 l.		130 sheep 30 acres.	
…n Abbey	Summer.	1000, 30 l.	1 sheep to an acr. grass.	1000 thirty acres.	
…perton	Half the year.				
…b	Some in summ.				
…ton	Very few.				
…'s Down	All the year.			200 an acre in a week.	

Places.	Fold.	Valued.	Sheep per acre.	Quantity folded.	Which fold best.
B. Cannons	All the year.			200 an acre in 10 nights.	Equal.
Harleyford Mr. Burke Beconsfield	Very few, All the year. Only wethers.				
Average of such particulars as are reducible to numbers.		7*l*. 11*s*. per 100 sheep per ann.		100 sheep 14 acres *per* ann.	

These two averages are the medium of extremely various accounts, including some that hardly know what folding is, others that run their sheep quickly over a great breadth of land, and several that fold only in the summer. None of them nearly equals the profit made by Mr. *Arbuthnot*, by means of littering his sheep, which amounts to 22*l*. 19*s. per* 100 *per ann.* if that article is deducted, the average is no more than 4*l*. 9*s*. 4*d*. which shews that, upon the whole, this article of folding (principally from not continuing it through winter) is but poorly conducted.

The system of winter folding has been strangely neglected; at *Massingham* in *Norfolk*, it is reckoned much the best; and the slovens of *Dorsetshire* have found out, that the fold at *Michaelmas* is much better than in the heighth of summer; and yet the same blockheads leave their
yard-

yard-dung spread to a three months summer sun. But in *Wiltshire* they are wise enough to winter fold their ewes as well as wethers, and at lambing time, or in very bad weather, litter them with straw.

The management is upon the whole so bad, that it will be trusting to a surer guide, to follow some of the single articles of intelligence, where it is good, and supply what is wanting in one, by another.

At *Blakburn*, the hiring price of folding, is 40 *s*. an acre.

At *Findon*, 300 sheep, 400 square yards; this is 100—10 acres.

Youngsberry, 100 sheep, 20 acres.
Cheam, ditto 12
Moreton, ditto 10 twice in a place.
Massingham, ditto 7

As *Youngsberry* so much exceeds, I shall reduce it half, which will allow a double folding to equal the rest, as they certainly must be; the average of them then is nine acres and a half, which at the above price of 40 *s*. comes to 19 *l. per ann.* for 100 sheep. Against which calculation, I do not think there stand any good objections.

Another way of calculating it will be, to include the advantage of littering in winter.

Suppose them folded in the common manner half the year, paying,	-	-	£. 9	10	0
The other half year to consume in proportion to Mr. *Arbuthnot*'s experiment seven acres, which will last just 26 weeks; these at 2*l*. 2*s*. 6*d*. per acre, are,	-	-	-	14	17	6
Total profit by fold of 100 sheep *per ann.*	-	-	24	7	6

This, all things considered, is the system, at which every man should aim; and that he may equal the latter part of it, which appears the most difficult, cannot be doubted, since Mr. *Arbuthnot* bought his straw at the high price of 20*s*. the trussed load; whereas in nine tenths of the kingdom, it is to be had for less than half that price, and stubble, fern, &c. in many places got much cheaper. As to the health of the sheep, they are much better off on warm beds, well sheltered, than lying on the wet ground; but the common *Wiltshire* practice shews, that there is no objection on that account.

Respecting

Respecting the comparison between an ewe and a wether fold, opinions seem much divided; but if the univerſal practice be conſidered, where ſheep are well underſtood, of folding the latter in winter, while they do not venture it with ewes, the ſuperiority of ſuch a flock in this reſpect cannot, I think, be diſputed.

But this notion of not folding ewes in winter is totally inadmiſſible; common practice in *Norfolk*, *Wiltſhire*, &c. ſhews plainly, that it is an abſurdity; and individuals have proved it; Mr. *Burke* has conſtantly practiſed it at *Beconsfield*, contrary to the practice of that neighbourhood, and with uniform ſucceſs. Landlords ought therefore ſtrenuouſly to endeavour to change this practice; and if they can bring in the uſe of the ſtanding fold well littered, it will be ſo much the better.

LETTER XLIX.

THE next article I shall review is that of cows, in which will probably be found as many variations as in sheep; the averages of the circumstances concerning them, are much worthy of attention; not only to know the general fact, but also the means of remedying bad management. I must, as in the *Tour through the Northern Counties*, reduce weight of hay to acres, by the rule of 1 *C. wt.* for every 1 *s.* rent when no rent is named, one ton and ⅓ *per* acre.

Place.	Rent of Grass.			Sum. food acres.	Wint. food acres.	Wint. food loads.	Product.			Lett. for. lb. Butter per co.	Milk gal. p. cow.	Hay to 10 cows.	Maid to cow.	Breed.
	l.	*s.*	*d.*				*l.*	*s.*	*d.*					
1. Hoghton	1	5	0								3¼		25	
2. Blifworth	1	7	6	1	1¼	1½	6	0	0		5	10	20	L
3. Glendon	1	2	0	1			5	0	0		1½	15	10	L
4. Quenby	1	5	0	1	1¼	2	5	0	0		3			L
5. Tilton	0	16	0				5	0	0		3			L
6. Dispey	1	5	0				5	10	0		6½			L
7. Alfreton	1	5	0	1			7	0	0		3	0	10	L
8. Radburn	1	0	0	2			5	7	0		2			L
9. Tidswell	2	5	0	1							3			L
10. Chesterfield	1	0	0	1½			6	0	0		5	6		L
11. Lawton	1	0	0	1½			4	0	0		2½	6		L
12. Gateford	1	10	0	1¼			7	0	0		3			L
13. Blythe	1	5	0	1			6	6	0		3	5	10	M
14. Doncaster	2	10	0	1							4			S
15. Broadsworth				3							2			S

Place.	Rent of Grass. l.	s.	d.	Sum. feed acres.	Wint. feed acres.	Wint. food loads.	Product. l.	s.	d.	Lett for. l.	s.	d.	lb. Butter per co.	Fat. cal. p. cow	Hogs to 10 cows.	Maid to cows.	Breed.	
Wombwell	1	0	0				6	10	0					4	6		S	†Turnips
ootham	1	0	0	1½			4	0	0					2	2		[illegible]	
arwic	1	0	0	1½									6					* Clover
everington	1	0	0										7½	6				and ray.
unction	1	0	0	1¼			6	0	0				8	5	20	10	M	
ettisham	1	0	0				5	5	0				7½	3½		20		§By suck-
Varham	1	0	0							3	6	6	13½	5	20	12	M	ling.
Aylsham	1	0	0	2	0	1†				3	15	0		6	15	20	M	
arlham	2	0	0	1	0	0†				3	7	6			10		M	* Alder-
raken-Ash	1	0	0	1½			4	15	0				6½	6			M	neys.
legg	0	15		1*			5	9	0	4	4	0		5			M	
orton	1	0	0	2			4	10	0	4	0	0		5		13	M	‡Have the
adleigh	1	10	0	1½									8½				M	farm yard
estead	1	0	0	1			5	0	0					4	10		M	for hogs
ungsberry	1	10	0	2			5	0	0				5	3	15	10		into the
orden	1	5	0				4	0	0§									bargain.
eam	1	5	0				5	0	0§									
uddington	1	0	0	1			5	0	0§									*‡* And ½
eversham	1	0	0				7	0	0				10½	5	20	12		acre bar-
awkhurst	1	0	0											3½				ley straw
ffield-place	0	15	0											4			S	
r. Turner	1	1	0				5	0	0§									‡ And ½
e of Wight	1	0	0	1½						3	12	6	*7½	5		11		acre straw
tto	0	15	0	1½			5	5	0	3	10	0		3½	15		L	for litter,
resford	2	10	0	¼			6	0	0	3	0	0		2¾			S	which
lbury	0	15	0	1			5	0	0	3	0	0	6	3	6	20	M	makes
itchill	1	10	0	1	*					3	12	6‖	4	2½	S	15	L	5 loads of
orston	2	0	0		1*		5	12	6	3	11	6	5		1	11	L	rotten
. White					*	1¼‡												dung.
me	1	15	0			1	5	2	6	‖4	12	0	6	4		10	L	
bottsbury	2	0	0							5	5	0						‖& half ac.
apperton	1	0	0				6	0	0	4	0	0‡						after grass.
minster	2	10	0				6	10	0	4	10	0‡						
Chard	1	10	0	1						4	0	0						° And 1½
igh	1	10	0	1½‖		1°	7	15	0	5	15	0‡	6				S	acre straw.
unton	1	10	0	1¼		1½*	7	0	0	5	2	6	6	6		10	L	
llsham	1	5	0							4	0	0		5				* And 1
arlborough	3	0	0															acre straw
ngerford																		
nnington	2	0	0				4	10	0				4½	2	0		L	** Muuch
ensfield	1	10	0				5	5	0**				7	3			L	suckling.
ages,	1	6	[illegible]	1⅓	1½	1⅓	5	10	0	4	3	2	7	4	9	13		

From these averages it appears, that the mean rent of grass land is 1*l.* 6*s.* 8*d. per* acre, of which average grass a cow eats one acre and one third in summer, and as much hay in winter. Thus fed she gives four gallons *per diem* of milk, which makes 7*lb.* of butter a week, on a medium, of making cheese or not: something better than one hog is kept to every cow. Under these circumstances they let at 4*l.* 3*s.* 2*d.* and the whole product is 5*l.* 10*s.* consequently the mean profit of those who hire them is 1*l.* 6*s.* 10*d.* a head. How far these products make cows answer, will best appear from calculating their expences.

	£	s	d
Rent of two acres and two thirds of grass, at 1*l.* 6*s.* 8*d.*	3	11	0
Tythe and rates, suppose 4*s.* in the pound,	0	14	0
Mowing, &c. &c. one acre and one third of hay,	0	10	0
Suppose all assistance from straw only,	0	10	0
Total,	5	5	0

Which expence of five guineas is returned by 4*l.* 3*s.* 2*d.* let: but if the whole produce is reckoned, then the account will be,

		£. s. d.
As above, — —		5 5 0
A dairy-maid's wages and board 13 *l.* she takes care of 13; so this is — —		1 0 0
Wear and tear, &c. of dairy utensils, — — —		0 5 0
Firing, at least, —		0 7 6
Total, — —		6 17 6
Product, —		5 10 0
Loss, — —		1 7 6

That this account is exact, I do not pretend; all that is wanting here to be proved, is that cows thus conducted are undoubtedly unprofitable. I do not think the excess if any thing is great; for in many parts the dairy men have the keeping a mare and colt, and all the swine of the farm-yard; therefore let these be calculated, and then the estimate again examined; and I think no person will believe, that cows are among the profitable articles of the farmer.

Upon the journey in several places, I asked the reason of their keeping cows. On giving my reasons for thinking them disadvantageous, the general answer I received was their consuming that food,

which

which they could not apply to other uses: and in some places, this is partly satisfactory; but the number is extremely few: for an idea of this may be formed from the rent of the land applied to them on an average, which is 20 s. 8 d.; a circumstance, which alone shews that it might be applied to any thing; land of 20 s. an acre would fat an ox as well as feed cows. But where the grass of a farm is too poor for grazing, and at the same time too wet for sheep, which is the case with great tracts of country, then cows must be kept. Grazing admits of variations enough to allow all the sorts of food produced by a farm, to be applied in it. The good grass, all hay, straw for litter, turnips, &c. so that every man may thus manage if he has good grass land; and that it will prove much more profitable, than the system of cows here explained, cannot for a moment be doubted.

For cows to be an advantageous article, there are several requisites necessary, many of which are neither understood or thought of in nine tenths of this tract of country.

The most material point is the winter food; as to straw, they should have what they

they will eat and make into dung; for the manure gained will well pay for it; but hay is an article totally to be ſtruck off; ſtraw alone, when dry, and ſtraw with turnips, when they give milk, ſhould be the ſyſtem. This change would make a vaſt difference; and that it is quite practicable, appears from the conduct at *Aylſham* and *Earlham* in *Norfolk*, where turnips totally ſupply the place of hay. In *Suffolk*, they underſtand this point ſo well, that they will keep no cow that calves before *April*, if they can poſſibly help it, that ſtraw may be the only food till very late in the ſpring.

Another point is that of hogs, and this ought to be the grand profit of the dairy. Ciſterns to keep the waſh during ſummer, againſt it is wanted in winter, are abſolutely requiſite; and in the uſe of it, not given promiſcuouſly to ſtock hogs, that will live on turnips and the farm yard; but only to ſows with pigs, and weaned pigs, due regard being alſo had to feeding the hogs half and three fourths grown, and the ſows, on clover in ſummer, which is a link in this chain of management. With proper attention to this ſyſtem, the cows would

would pay, on a moderate computation, 20s. a head more than at prefent, which with faving all the hay, and fubftituting turnips in their room, would convert this article from a lofing into a profitable one.

The breed is another point of no flight importance; for if fmall mongrel breeds are found to exceed for the pail, others of near twice the fize, the faving would be prodigious, and there is good reafon to think this the cafe.

Having thus remarked what was neceffary on cows in general, from the average of all circumftances, throughout the whole Tour, I fhall in the next place divide the table according to product.

Product under 5 l.

Places.	Rent. l. s. d.	Product. l. s. d.	Lett at. l. s. d.	B.	M.	H.	Breed.
No. 11	1 0 0	4 0 0			2½	6	L
17	1 0 0	4 0 0			2	2	M
25	1 0 0	4 15 0		6½	6		M
27	1 0 0	4 10 0	4 0 0		5		M
31	1 5 0	4 0 0					
54	2 0 0	4 10 0		4½	2		L
Aver.	1 4 2	4 5 10	4 0 0	5½	3½	4	

THROUGH ENGLAND. 299

Product at 5l. and upwards, under 6l.

Places.	Rent.			Product.		Left at.		B.	M. H.		Breed.
	l.	s.	d.	s.	d.	l.	s. d.				
No. 3	1	2	0	5	0	0			1½	15	L
4	1	5	0	5	0	0			3		L
5	0	10	0	5	0	0			3		L
6	1	5	0	5	10	0			6½		L
8	1	0	0	5	7	0			2		L
21	1	0	0	5	5	0		7½	3½		M
26	0	15	0	5	9	0	4 4 0		5		M
29	1	0	0	5	0	0			4	10	M
30	1	10	0	5	0	0		5	3	15	
32	1	5	0	5	0	0					
33	1	0	0	5	0	0					
37	1	1	0	5	0	0					
39	0	15	0	5	5	0	3 10 0		3½	15	L
41	0	15	0	5	0	0	3 0 0	6	3	6	M
43	2	0	0	5	12	0	3 11 6	5		1	L
45	1	15	0	5	2	6	4 12 0	6	4		L
55	1	10	0	5	5	0		7	3		L
Averages	1	3	2	5	3	3	3 15 6	6	3½	10	

Product at 6l. and upwards, under 7l.

No. 2	1	7	0	6	0	0			5	10	L
10	1	0	0	6	0	0			5	0	L
13	1	5	0	6	6	0			3	5	M
16	1	0	0	6	10	0			4	6	S
20	1	0	0	6	0	0		8	8	20	M
40	2	10	0	6	0	0	3 0 0		2¾		S
47	1	0	0	6	0	0	4 0 0				
48	2	10	0	6	10	0	4 10 0				
Averages	1	9	0	6	3	3	3 16 8	8	4½	8	

Product at 7l. and upwards.

No. 7	1	5	0	7	0	0			3	0	L
12	1	10	0	7	0	0			3	6	L
34	1	0	0	7	0	0		10½	5	20	
50	1	10	0	7	15	0	5 5 0	6			S
51	1	10	0	7	0	0	5 2 6	5	6		L
Averages	1	7	0	7	3	0	5 8 9	7	4	8	

Recapitulation.

	Rent.			Product.			Lett at.			B.	M.	H
	l.	s.	d.	l.	s.	d.	l.	s.	d.			
Under 5 l.	1	4	2	4	5	10	4	0	0	$5\frac{1}{2}$	$3\frac{1}{2}$	4
5 l. to 6 l.	1	3	2	5	3	3	3	15	6	6	$5\frac{3}{4}$	10
6 l. to 7 l.	1	9	0	6	3	3	3	15	8	8	$4\frac{1}{2}$	8
7 l. upwards	1	7	0	7	3	0	5	8	9	7	4	8

From thefe averages it appears, that the product, though not *regularly* depending either on grafs, butter, milk or hogs, yet is there a *general* dependance for the average of the two firft and the two laft that is all to 6 *l.* and all above 6 *l.* then both grafs, butter, milk and hogs, would correfpond with product, and alfo the letting price; whereas in the table at prefent there are fome manifeft contradictions. Nothing in thefe mediums give us the leaft reafon to change our opinion, refpecting the conduct of this part of the farmer's ftock.

LETTER L.

TO discover the real price of provisions in every county, and to know the general averages of the whole kingdom, becomes every day a more interesting object; opinions on this point, instead of being enlightened in proportion as knowledge is gained, too often remain in suspence; the fixed rates of all sorts of eatables consumed by the poor, the most advantageous to them and the nation in general, is unknown, and highly disputable; nor can it ever be well understood, unless the real prices are brought to light. Before we can discover what *ought to be*, we must know what *is*. I had the satisfaction of laying before the public in my last Tour, exact information on this head, through a very considerable part of the kingdom.

I have, in this journey, made similar enquiries, and shall proceed to draw the particulars together in one view, that the result may be clearly understood.

Butchers

Butchers meat, butter, cheese, and bread, demand the most attention. I give the average of meats, and the distance of each place from *London*.

Places.	Distance.	Bread. d.	Butter. d.	Cheese. d.	Mutton. d.	Beef. d.	Veal. d.	Pork. d.	Average. d.
1. *Hempstead,*	22	1	7	4½	4	3¾	4	4	4
2. *Tring,*	30	1	7½	4½	4	4	4	4	4
3. *Blisworth,*	61	1	5	4½	3½	4	3½	3	3½
4. *Hazelbeech,*	77	1 *	5	3½	3½	3½	2½	3	3¼
5. *Glendon,*	78	¾ †	5	4½	4½	4	3‡	3‡	3½
6. *Quenby,*	90	1	6	3½	3½	3½	3½	3¼	3½
7. *Dishley,*	106	1 §	6½	3½	3½	3½	4	3½	3½
8. *Alfreton,*	135	¾ ‖	6	4	4	3½	3	3½	3½
9. *Radburn,*	122	1	6	4	3½	3½	3	3½	3¼
10. *Tiddswell,*	146	1	6	4	4	4	3½	3½	3¾
11. *Chesterfield,*	134	1	7	4	3½	3	3	3½	3¼
12. *Lawton,*	142	1	6½	4½	3½	3½	3¼	4	3½
13. *Broadsworth,*	173	1¼	7¼	3½	3½	3½	3	3½	3¼
14. *Wombwell,*	172	1 ¶	7	3½	3½	3	3½	3½	3¼
15. *Bootham,*	128	1	6	3	3½	3½	3	3	3¼
16. *Swinehead,*	98	1¼	4¾	4	3½	3½	3	3¼	3¼
17. *Leverington,*	90	1½	6½	4	3½	4	3	4	3½
18. *Runcton,*	100	1½	6	3	3½	3½	3	3½	3¼
19. *Snettisham,*	112	1½	6	4	3½	3½	3	3	3¼
20. *Warham,*	130	1½	6	3	3½	3½	3	3½	3¼
21. *Aylsham,*	120	1½	6½	4	3½	3½	3	3½	3¼
22. *Norwich,*	106	1¼	7	2½	3¾	3½	3	3½**	3½
23. *Hadleigh,*	60	1½	7¼	4	4	3½	3½	4½	3¾
24. *Youngsberry,*	24	1¼	8½	4	4	3¾	5	3	4
25. *Petersham,*	10	1¾	9	4½	4½	2½ ††	5	4¾	4¼
26. *Cuddington,*	13	1½	8½	3½	4	3½	5	4½	4¼
27. *Feversham,*	‡‡ 45	1¾	9	4½	4½	3½	5	4½	4¼

* Two parts wheat, and one rye. † Part barle[y]

‡ Not minuted; supplied therefore by the average of t[he] prices before and after.

‖ Oat cakes.

§ Not minuted; supplied from the *Quenby* price.

¶ Wheaten and oat; average.

** Not minuted; supplied from the preceding.

†† Coarse joints sold. ‡‡ The *London* prices.

Places.	Distance.	Bread. d.	Butter. d.	Cheese. d.	Mutton. d.	Beef. d.	Veal. d.	Pork. d.	Average. d.
28. *Rye,*	64	1¾	7	4½	4	4	4	4	4
29. *Sheffield Pl.*	40	1½	6	4	3¾	3¼	3¾	3	3½
30. *Walberton,*	55	2	8	4	4	4	4	3½	3¼
31. *Isle Wight,*	90	1¼	8	2½	3½	3½	4	3¾	3¾
32. *Critchill,*	100	2	6¼	1½	3½	3	3	3	3
33. *Moreton,*	115	1½	6¼	2	3½	3½	2½	3	3
34. *Taunton,*	137	1½	6	3¼	3	3	2	2¾	2¼
35. *B. Canons,*	80	2	6¼	3¾	3¼	2½		3	3
36. *Harleyford,*	29	2	7½	4	4	4	5	4	4¼
37. *Beconsfield,*	27	1¼	7¼	4¼	4	3	5	4	4
Averages,		1¼	6½	3¾	3½	3½	3½	3½	3½

Before I divide this table, I must be allowed to remark, that none of these prices are extravagant; and if we reflect that the course of the Tour runs much through the counties surrounding the capital, from whence we may conjecture that labour is high; if this is considered, these rates must not be thought high. Bread, the principal, is *low*; butter, though not an article of great importance, is moderate; cheese is by no means high; and the average of all meats at 3 *d.* ½, no one will conceive to be at all oppressive: but bread at 1 *d.* ¼ brings all the rest, supposing them high, to be moderate upon the whole.

To discover what influence the capital may have on these prices, we must divide according to distance.

THE FARMER's TOUR

Fifty miles around London.

	Bread. d.	Butter. d.	Cheese. d.	Average Meats. d.
No. 1.	1	7	$4\frac{1}{2}$	4
2.	1	$7\frac{1}{2}$	$4\frac{1}{2}$	4
24.	$1\frac{1}{4}$	$8\frac{1}{2}$	4	4
25.	$1\frac{1}{4}$	9	$4\frac{1}{2}$	$4\frac{1}{4}$
26.	$1\frac{1}{2}$	$8\frac{1}{2}$	$3\frac{1}{2}$	$4\frac{1}{4}$
27.	$1\frac{3}{4}$	9	$4\frac{1}{2}$	$4\frac{1}{4}$
29.	$1\frac{1}{2}$	6	4	$3\frac{1}{2}$
36.	2	$7\frac{1}{2}$	4	$4\frac{1}{4}$
37.	$1\frac{1}{4}$	$7\frac{1}{4}$	$4\frac{1}{4}$	4
Average,	$1\frac{1}{4}$	$7\frac{3}{4}$	$4\frac{1}{4}$	4

From 50 to 100 miles.

	Bread. d.	Butter. d.	Cheese. d.	Average Meats. d.
No. 3.	1	5	$4\frac{1}{2}$	$3\frac{1}{2}$
4.	1	5	$3\frac{1}{2}$	$3\frac{1}{4}$
5.	$\frac{3}{4}$	6	$4\frac{1}{2}$	$3\frac{1}{2}$
6.	1	6	$3\frac{3}{4}$	$3\frac{1}{2}$
16.	$1\frac{1}{4}$	$4\frac{3}{4}$	4	$3\frac{1}{4}$
17.	$1\frac{1}{2}$	$6\frac{1}{2}$	4	$3\frac{1}{2}$
18.	$1\frac{1}{2}$	6	3	$3\frac{1}{4}$
23.	$1\frac{1}{2}$	$7\frac{1}{4}$	4	$3\frac{3}{4}$
28.	$1\frac{3}{4}$	7	$4\frac{1}{2}$	4
30.	2	8	4	$3\frac{3}{4}$
31.	$1\frac{1}{4}$	8	$2\frac{1}{2}$	$3\frac{3}{4}$
32.	2	$6\frac{3}{4}$	$1\frac{1}{2}$	3
35.	2	$6\frac{1}{4}$	$3\frac{3}{4}$	3
Average,	$1\frac{1}{4}$	$6\frac{1}{4}$	$3\frac{1}{2}$	$3\frac{1}{2}$

From 100 *to* 150 *miles.*

	Bread. d.	*Butter.* d.	*Cheese.* d.	*Average Meats.* d.
No. 7.	1	6½	3½	3½
8.	¾	6	4	3½
9.	1	6	4	3¼
10.	1	6	4	3¾
11.	1	7	4	3¼
12.	1	6½	4½	3½
15.	1	6	3	3¼
19.	1½	6	4	3¼
20.	1½	6	3	3¼
21.	1½	6½	4	3¼
22.	1¼	7	2½	3½
33.	1½	6¼	2	3
34.	1½	6	3¼	2¾
Average,	1¼	6¼	3½	3¼

From 150 *to* 170 *miles.*

No. 13.	1¼	7¼	3½	3¼
14.	1	7	3½	3¼
Average,	1⅛	7⅛	3½	3¼

Recapitulation.

50 Miles,	1¼	7¾	4¼	4
50 to 100	1¼	6¼	3½	3½
100 to 150	1¼	6¼	3½	3¼
150 to 170	1⅛	7⅛	3½	3¼

It is here to be observed, that the result of scarcely any table can be more natural than this; the effect in each column is such as might be expected. Bread is uninfluenced in its price by the neighbourhood of the capital, arising from the ease with which wheat is transported, and from all places that have a regular demand in the way of trade, (for so wheat at *London* may be called) being better supplied than others with any commodity. This equality of the price of bread throughout *England*, is a proof of the excellent internal police of corn, which obtains, in this kingdom, from an aggregate of improvements and natural advantages, principally owing to the near neighbourhood of the sea, and to the country being intersected by numerous navigations.

Butter, on the contrary, rises greatly at the capital, which must always be the case with a product in which distant parts cannot partake in the supply; the neighbourhood of *London* producing the whole, it commands an high price. From 50 to 150 miles being equal, is not a great contradiction in this article, which is as much out of the reach of *London* at 50 (speaking in general)

general) as at 500 miles. From 150 to 170 miles, is only at two places in that manufacturing region, the *West Riding* of *York*.

Cheese is in general equal; this is consistent with the foregoing principles, being easily conveyed in large quantities. The small rise at *London* is owing to all being of the better sort.

Butcher's meat rises gradually and regularly with the approach to the capital; this is a consequence that might be expected, because the increase of demand has not a corresponding neighbouring increase of product, and must therefore be supplied from a distance, at a pretty heavy waste and

LETTER LI.

THERE are some other articles of a poor man's housekeeping which should not be looked over; the principal are his house-rent—firing—and the wear of his tools. To these I shall add, though of a different nature, the price of potatoes, as I think they are an object of some importance, and might be, with good management, much more.

Places.	House-rent.			Firing.			Tools.			Potatoes per peck.
	l.	s.	d.	l.	s.	d.	l.	s.	d.	d.
1. *Hempstead*,	2	5	0							
2. *Tring*,	2	2	0	1	10	0	0	15	0	
3. *Blisworth*,	1	0	0							
4. *Hazelbeech*,	1	10	0	2	0	0	0	5	0	4
5. *Glendon*,	1	10	0	2	0	0	0	5	0	3
6. *Quenby*,	1	0	0	1	10	0	0	7	6	
7. *Dishley*,	0	15	0	1	0	0				7
8. *Alfreton*,	1	10	0	0	10	0	0	5	0	3½
9. *Radburn*,	1	10	0	1	10	0	0	7	6	6
10. *Tiddswell*,	1	2	0	2	5	0				4½
11. *Chesterfield*,	2	10	0							4
12. *Lawton*,	1	0	0							
13. *Broadsworth*,	1	5	0	1	1	0				3½
14. *Wombwell*,	1	2	6	0	8	6				4
15. *Bootham*,	1	10	0	0	13	0	0	5	0	4
16. *Swinehead*,	3	10	0	1	5	0				3
17. *Leverington*,										2½
18. *Runston*,	2	0	0	1	10	0				4

Places.	House-rent.			Firing.			Tools.			Potatoes per peck.
	l.	s.	d.	l.	s.	d.	l.	s.	d.	d.
19. Snettisham,	2	0	0	0	10	0				4
20. Warham,	1	13	0	1	0	0	0	19	0	3
21. Aylsham,	2	0	0	0	0	0				
22. Earlham,	4	0	0	1	0	0				
23. Norwich,	2	10	0	2	0	0				6
24. Hadleigh,	2	0	0	1	10	0				4
25. Youngsberry,	2	0	0	0	0	0				3
26. Petersham,	5	0	0							
27. Cuddington,	3	10	0	2	0	0	0	5	0	7
28. Feversham,	2	15	0							
29. Rye,	3	0	0	3	0	0				8
30. Sheffield Pl.	2	5	0	3	0	0				8
31. Walberton,	2	0	0	2	0	0				
32. Siddlesham,	2	0	0	1	4	0				
33. Isle Wight,	2	10	0	1	0	0				
34. Critchill,	1	15	0	1	5	0				5¼
35. Moreton,	1	10	0	0	0	0				
36. Henlade,	1	10	0	1	0	0	0	10	0	6
37. B. Cannons,	1	15	0	1	10	0				6
38. Harleyford,	1	15	0							
39. Beconsfield,	2	5	0	1	10	0				8
Averages,	2	0	0	1	6	0	0	7	6	4¾

These prices are not extravagant, nor such as can oppress the poor. On the article firing, I should observe, that it explains more the expence of the really industrious part of the poor, who do expend something in firing, rather than the average of any neighbourhood; for there is scarcely any in the Tour, where great numbers among them, do not depend for this article totally on pilfering, breaking hedges, and cutting trees; and this so general, that if a real

average

average had been gained, I do not apprehend it would amount to 10 *s.* a year.

The price of potatoes, I think, is very high, confidering that the poor might, in their little gardens, raife them, for, perhaps, a tenth of it. This is a point much deferving attention: it is to be wifhed, that all perfons who have it in their power to render this root more common among them, would exert themfelves in it; for in thofe places where the rates of provifions are high, and the price of labour low, fubftitutes of this fort would prove of confequence; and extenfive experience fhews, that the potatoe is a very wholfome nourifhing food, if not totally depended on.

LETTER LII.

THE utility of discovering the price of labour in all parts of the kingdom, must be apparent to every one; it is the lower classes of the people, in whom the nation's strength materially consists; publick prosperity much depends on the balance of their *earnings* and *necessary expences*. The latter should not exceed the former, nor should their wages be so high, as to bring on an exemption from regular labour. In all these points, there certainly is a golden mean, how seldom so ever it is found; but the first step to any disquisitions on that head, consists in a clear decision of the present fact. Every circumstance that exists should be compared with its cause, and traced into its consequence; I am unequal to so arduous a task; I shall therefore content myself with plainly stating the case.

When there are other considerations for labour besides money, such as board, beer, &c. they must be valued, and I shall ollow the rules laid down in my *Northern Tour*.

    Board, 10 *d.* a day.
    Ale, 2 *d.*
    Small beer, 1 *d.*
    Milk, ¼ *d.*
    A dinner, 6 *d.*

The division of the year is,
    Harvest, five weeks.
    Hay-time, six weeks.
    Winter, 41 weeks.

Hay-time is not always of this duration, any more than harvest; but summer prices in most places rise pretty much on winter ones, though neither hay nor harvest are in hand.

I add, the rise in labour of late years.

Places.	Distance.	Pay per week. Har. s. d.	Hay. s. d.	Wint s. d.	Medium. s. d.	Rise of labour.
1. Hempstead	22	17 0	10 0	7 0	8 3	
2. Tring	30	14 0	10 0	7 0	8 0	
3. Blisworth	61	14 0	8 6	7 0	7 10	⅓ in 20 years.
4. Hazelbeach	77	11 0	11 0	6 6	6 1	Near ½ in 10
5. Glenden	78	11 0	11 6	6 0	7 1	years, more
6. Quenby	90	11 0	11 0	6 0	6 10	than ¼.
7. Diskley	106	12 0	8 0	5 6	6 4	⅓ in 20 years.
8. Alfreton	135	11 0	10 0	6 0	6 11	¼ in ditto.
9. Radburn	122	11 6	11 6	7 0	8 0	½ in ditto.
10. Tiddswell	146	11 0	9 0	6 0	7 0	
11. Chesterfield	134	14 0	14 0	7 0	8 0	⅓ in ditto.
12. Lawton	142	14 0	14 0	7 0	8 0	¼ in 10 years.
13. Broadsworth	173	9 0	6 0	6 0	6 3	
14. Wombwell	172	15 0	12 0	9 0	9 11	½ in 20 years.

Places.	Distance.	Pay per week.						Medium.		Rise of labour.
		Har.		Hay.		Wint				
		s.	d.	s.	d.	s.	d.	s.	d.	
5. Bootham	128	12	0	12	0	4	6	6	0	¼ in 20 years.
6. Summer-Cast.	140					5	0			½ in 10 ditto.
7. Swinehead	98	21	0	14	0	11	0	12	3	¼ in 20 ditto.
8. Leverington	90	16	0	11	0	6	0	7	6	
9. Run?on	100	13	0	10	0	8	0	8	8	¼ in 10 ditto.
0. Snettisham	112	14	0	11	6	7	0	8	2	
1. Warham	130	14	0	10	0	7	0	8	0	¼ in 20 years.
2. Aylsham	120	12	0	8	0	7	0	7	7	¼ in ditto.
3. Earlham	106	13	0	10	0	7	0	7	11	½ in ditto.
4. Hadleigh	60	13	0	10	0	7	0	7	11	
5. Youngsberry	24	12	6	9	0	7	0	7	9	
6. Petersham	10	20	0	13	0	9	6	10	10	
7. Cuddington	13	17	0	17	0	9	0	10	7	
8. Feversham	45	15	0	9	0	9	0	9	7	None.
9. Rye	64	16	6	12	0	9	0	10	0	
0. Sheffield Place	40	9	0	8	0	7	0	7	3	
1. Walberton	55	17	0	10	0	7	0	8	3	
2. Isle of Wight	90	15	0	10	0	7	9	8	8	¼ in 20 years.
3. Critchill	100	13	0	6	0	6	0	6	8	
4. Moreton	115	13	0	7	0	6	0	6	9	¼ in 20 years.
5. Leigh	135	8	0	6	0	5	0	5	5	None.
6. Taunton	137	10	0	7	0	7	0	7	7	
7. B. Cannons	80	5	8	5	0	5	0	5	0	
8. Harleyford	29	11	9	7	0	7	0	7	6	None in 20 ye.
9. Beconsfield	27	13	0	9	0	7	0	8	0	
Averages,		13	1	9	11	7	11	7	10	¼ in 18 years.

Upon these averages I may remark, that they are high enough for maintaining the labouring poor in that comfortable manner, in which they ought certainly to live; and I may add, also nearly to exclude parish assistance; the medium of the year wants but 2 *d.* of 8 *s.* a week. I do not think the farmer ought to complain of this price, while poor rates

rates are moderate; but where *they* are high, this average I may venture to fay will not eafily bear much increafe, unlefs his products rife proportionably.

The rife of labour a fourth in 18 years cannot be condemned, unlefs it was at the fame time proved, the general average of all the earth's products have not rifen in the fame time equal to that, and to the increafe of poor rates; if the rife is only mutual, the farmer has certainly no reafon to complain. How this matter ftands, is beyond the prefent enquiry; I therefore fhall not deviate into digreffion. But I fhall remark, that correct fpirited hufbandry, while products bear a fair price, will very well pay a high price of labour; thorough good farmers, who are ALIVE in their bufinefs, do not complain of the rates of labour, provided men can be got: and this I have remarked in numerous places. If it was a point of confequence enough to raife or deprefs hufbandry, what would become of the farmers in tracts, where on comparifon with others they pay double the rates of labour, and yet fell their products at the fame price? Yet this is the cafe in feveral counties.

However,

However, as to the fact of labour being raised, it will not admit a doubt, that it rises to a fourth in this period. What therefore are we to think of the short-sighted, ignorant assertions of a writer, who tells us, that " labourers wages at present are but ten pence a-day in some places; nor in any I believe more than twelve pence, in the common course of business;" and his authority will make you smile, the Earl of *Lincoln* paid but 1 s. 2 d. a day in the reign of *George* I. to the men who made his improvements at *Oatlands* *! Surely none could write such stuff, which it is impossible but a man of two ideas must *know to be false*, unless he was just dropped down from the moon, and began with abusing the landed interest, before he knew land from water. Such silly books, especially when they pretend to prove the kingdom undone, captivate weak minds, who are easily led to believe any assertions, which they wish to be true, through the malignant desire of finding themselves

not

---

* Considerations on the Policy, &c. of this kingdom.

not entirely mistaken. Instead of labour being no where more than 1 *s.* a day, I think I have shewn, and on somewhat better authority than the Earl of *Lincoln*'s *haste*, or *charity*, that labour is 1 *s.* 3 *d.* ½ *per* day on an average of this extensive tract of country; and so far is it from not being risen since queen *Anne*'s time, that it is risen *a fourth* in only 18 years.

Respecting the comparison between the mean price of labour, and the distance from *London*, the following table will shew the averages.

To 50 miles, - - £.0 8 7
From 50 to 100, - 0 7 10
    100 to 170, - - 0 7 4

The influence of the capital appears very strong and regular; for if this fall of price is not owing to distance from *London*, it will be very difficult to assign a cause for it.

In the next place, I shall review the other articles of labour, that of servants and women, and in valuing their board, &c. follow the estimate of,

    Board, 6 *d.* a day.
    A dinner, 4 *d.*
    Beer, ½ *d.*

Places.	1st Man.			2d Ditto.			Lads.			Da.Mai.			Other dit.			Women per week: Har.		Hay.		Wint	
	l.	s.	d.	l.	s.	d.	l.	s.	d.	l.	s.	d.	l.	s.	d.	s.	d.	s.	d.	s.	d.
1. Hempsted	9	0	0	5	0	0				4	15	0	4	15	0						
2. Tring	9	0	0	5	0	0										6	6	3	3		
3. Blisworth	8	0	0	5	0	0	3	0	0	5	0	0	5	0	0	7	0	3	3		
4. Hazelbeach	8	0	0	5	5	0	3	10	0	3	6	6	3	6	6	6	0	3	6		
5. Glendon	7	7	0	5	0	0	3	0	0	3	10	0	3	10	0	9	0	3	6		
6. Quenby	10	0	0	7	0	0	5	0	0	4	0	0	4	0	0	3	9	3	9		
7. Diss ey	8	10	0	7	0	0	4	0	0	3	15	0	3	15	0	4	0	3	0		
8. Alfreton	9	0	0	7	0	0	3	0	0	3	0	0	3	0	0	7	0	6	0		
9. Radburn	9	10	0	7	0	0	4	0	0	4	0	0	4	0	0	6	3	4	3	4	0
10. Tiddswell	9	0	0	7	0	0	5	0	0	4	0	0	4	0	0	6	0	3	0	3	0
11. Chesterfield	10	0	0	6	0	0	4	0	0	3	15	0	3	15	0	7	0	7	0	3	0
12. Lawton	9	0	0	8	0	0	6	0	0	3	10	0	3	0	0	5	0	3	3	2	0
13. Broadsworth	12	0	0	7	0	0	5	0	0	3	0	0	3	0	0	6	0	4	0	3	0
14. Wombwell	10	10	0	8	8	0	5	0	0	3	0	0	3	0	0	6	0	4	0	4	0
15. Bootham	9	10	0	8	10	0	5	0	0	3	10	0	3	10	0	4	0	4	0		
16. SummerCastle	10	10	0	8	8	0	5	5	0	3	0	0	2	10	0			4	0		
17. Swinehead	12	0	0	9	10	0	6	0	0	3	0	0	3	0	0	9	0	9	0		
18. Leverington	10	0	0				5	10	0	5	0	0				7	0	6	0	3	0
19. Runeton	12	0	0	9	0	0	4	0	0	4	10	0	3	0	0	6	3	6	3		
20. Snettisham	11	0	0	9	0	0	5	0	0	5	0	0	3	10	0	9	0	4	0	9	3
21. Warham	10	0	0	8	0	0	3	10	0	3	6	0	3	6	0						
22. Aylsham	7	12	0	5	12	0	2	10	0	3	10	0	3	2	0	6	6	0	6	0	3
23. Earlham	10	10	0	6	6	0	3	0	0	4	4	0	3	0	0						
24. Hadleigh	10	5	0	7	0	0	3	0	0	3	0	0	2	10	0						
25. Youngsberry	8	0	0	7	0	0	3	0	0	5	0	0	4	0	0	9	0	4	0	3	0
26. Petersham	8	8	0	8	8	0	3	10	0												
27. Cuddington	10	10	0	8	10	0	6	0	0	3	0	0	3	0	0	8	0	7	0	4	6
28. Feversham	11	0	0	9	0	0	6	0	0	3	0	0	3	0	0	6	0	6	0	4	0
29. Rye	10	0	0	7	7	0	3	0	0	3	0	0	3	0	0						
30. Sheffield-place	8	8	0	7	7	0	3	10	0	3	3	0	3	3	0						
31. Walberton	9	10	0				3	0	0	3	0	0	3	0	0						
32. Isle of Wight	8	18	6	6	6	0	2	10	0	4	4	0	3	0	0	5	3	3	3	6	3
33. Critchill	8	10	0	4	5	0	2	11	0	3	12	0	2	0	0						
34. Moreton	8	8	0	5	5	0	3	0	0	3	0	0	2	10	0						
35. Leigh	7	0	0	5	10	0	4	0	0	3	0	0	3	10	0	5	0	3	0		
36. B. Cannons	6	10	0	3	10	0															
37. Licconsfield	8	0	0	6	0	0	4	0	0	3	10	0				5	3	5	3		
Averages,	9	7	3	7	9	0	3	4	0	3	12	0	3	6	0	7	3	4	9	3	3

LETTER LIII.

HAVING concluded the review of labour and provisions feparately, it remains for me to compare them together; an object which appears to be of particular importance. The proportion between the rates of labour, and the prices of provisions, is the foundation of at leaft forty publications, and a fubject that has been treated by fome of the ableft writers on domeftic oeconomy in *England, France,* and *Holland.* One of the moft common axioms that have been laid down by thefe gentlemen, ever fince the firft undertakings of *Colbert,* in the reign of *Lewis* XIV. has been, that provifions muft be kept low, that the rates of labour may be the fame; all of them feeming to take for granted, that if the one was effected, the other muft follow of courfe. Had fuch an idea dropped by chance from the pen of one or two writers, though of reputation, it would not be a matter of confequence; but this is not the cafe; it
is

is the corner-stone of a vast fabric in modern politics; the whole manufacturing and trading interest of nations are said totally to depend on it; and the fall of some countries, with the rise of others, have been attributed to this cause: and these sentiments are adopted and published by numerous most respectable authors, who have enlightened almost every subject they have treated.

While opinions have such authority for their foundation, the most one can venture to do is to examine, if general maxims have not been laid down, without sufficiently attending to exceptions; an error too common in the greatest writers. The assertions that have been so generally hazarded, either tend strongly to evince, that the rates of labour depend on those of provisions, or they tend to nothing: if it is meant with relation, not to different districts of the same kingdom, but on comparison of one against another, the smallest knowledge is sufficient to shew, that other causes must be recurred to, because where provisions are of very little value, labour we are told is extremely dear, from the natural difficulty of inducing those to work,

work, who can live without it: not to speak of manufactures, an aggregate of labour flourishing most where provisions are dearest; whereas, if the latter regulated the price of the former, the cheapest countries of *Europe* ought to have the greatest fabricks, which is the direct reverse of truth.

For this reason, there is as much propriety in examining this argument by the variations of the different provinces of the same kingdom, as those of different nations.

No one can wonder at the idea in general of labour depending on provisions, because it is so natural, that it ought ever to be the fact. A labourer's earnings should be guided by his necessary expences; for if he earns double, treble, &c. he will no longer be a labourer, but a master, or merely idle. Thus, in the great distinctions of rates, not such as are any where to be found, but may be supposed, this dependance would become real; for if bread was to be 6 *d.* a pound, and meat 1 *s.* and cheese 9 *d.* and so forth, it is very evident, that labour must greatly rise, or the poor starve; but cases, which can have no existence, ought not to be the occasion of

such

such arguments. In the slighter deviations, which are really co-existing, but in different places, we must look for facts to guide us in such enquiry.

A modern author of real abilities*, starts on this subject an idea, which seems extremely just. He observes that the rates of labour cannot be decided by those of provisions; and as an instance, asks if a weaver could live upon air, whether he would sell his labour so much the cheaper? attributing the variations to the competition of demand; a notion in which he has been copied by more than one insignificant scribbler. But this is a new idea; if it is just, the old one of *provisions* being the guide, must be false. The point under consideration, when we are examining the circumstances relative to various prices of necessaries, is to prove how just the assertions of numerous authors are *on that subject*. We are to prove that labour *does not* depend on provisions; it is an after enquiry, to shew on what *it does* depend; and not so nearly connected with an undertaking of this sort.

Here

---

* Sir *James Stewart*, in his *Political Oeconomy*.

Here then appears the propriety of comparing the rates of labour with those of provisions; as the result may tend to correct errors of great consequence in themselves, and yet greater from the characters of the persons from whom they have proceeded.

That the idea of the rate of labour may be clear, I shall pursue the method followed in my *Northern Tour*, supposing a labourer to earn the average of the three seasons.

His wife to work in that of harvest and hay-time, and to have six weeks employment at the winter price of women.

His eldest son to be a *first man*.

His next, a *second*.

His third, a *lad*.

One daughter, a *dairy maid*.

Another a common *maid*.

Not, as I there observed, that this is a state of real families, but only a true way of representing the total of labour in one sum. But for the satisfaction of the reader, I shall add the average weekly pay of the men. In respect to the comparison with provisions I shall give the average of bread, butter, cheese, and meat, and also those articles separate.

Where

Where there are blanks that have prices in the *near neighbbourhood*, I ſhall ſupply them.

In caſe no winter employment of women, it will be left out in the calculation.

Places.	Bread.	Butter.	Cheeſe.	Meat.	Aver.	Total earnings.			Weekly Pay.	
	d.	d.	d.	d.	d.	l.	s.	d.	s.	d.
1. *Hempſtead*	1	7	4½	4	4	50	14	0	8	3
2. *Tring*	1	7½	4½	4	4¼	49	19	0	8	0
3. *Bliſworth*	1	5	4½	3½	3½	49	2	6	7	10
4. *Hazelbeach*	1	5	3½	3¼	3	45	6	6	6	1
5. *Glendon*	¾	6	4½	3½	3½	44	5	6	7	1
6. *Quenby*	1	6	3¾	3½	3½	50	8	3	6	10
7. *Diſhley*	1	6½	3½	3½	3½	45	8	6	6	4
8. *Alfreton*	¾	6	4	3½	3½	49	2	0	6	11
9. *Radburn*	1	6	4	3¼	3½	53	4	3	8	0
10. *Tiddſwell*	1	6	4	3¼	3½	50	1	0	7	0
11. *Cheſterfield*	1	7	4	3¼	3¾	54	6	0	8	0
12. *Lawton*	1	6½	4½	3½	3¼	54	12	6	8	0
13. *Broadſworth*	1¼	7¼	3½	3¼	3¾	50	9	0	6	3
14. *Wombwell*	1	7	3½	3¼	3½	59	18	0	9	11
15. *Bootham*	1	6	3	3¼	3¼	48	0	6	6	0
16. *Swinſhead*	1¼	4¾	4	3¼	3¼	70	9	0	12	3
17. *Leverington*	1½	6½	4	3½	3¼	57	7	6	7	6
18. *Runcton*	1½	6	3	3¼	3¼	59	11	9	8	8
19. *Snettiſham*	1½	6	4	3¼	3½	59	6	8	8	2
20. *Warham*	1½	6	3	3¼	3¼	52	2	4	8	0
21. *Aylſham*	1½	6½	4	3¼	3¾	46	15	6	7	7
22. *Earlham*	1¼	7	2½	3½	3½	51	16	0	7	11
23. *Hadleigh*	1½	7¼	4	3¼	4	49	7	0	7	11
24. *Youngsberry*	1¼	8½	4	4	4¼	51	10	6	7	9
25. *Peterſham*	1¾	9	4½	4¼	4¾	62	2	6	10	10
26. *Cuddington*	1½	8½	3½	4¼	4¼	64	5	0	10	7
27. *Feverſham*	1¾	9	4½	4¼	4¼	61	8	0	9	7
28. *Rye*	1¾	7	4½	4	4¼	53	0	6	10	0
29. *Sheffield Place*	1½	6	4	3½	3¾	44	11	0	7	3
30. *Walberton*	2	8	4	3¼	4¼	47	9	0	8	3
31. *Iſle Wight*	1¼	8	2½	3¾	3¾	51	0	9	8	8
32. *Critchill*	2	6¾	1½	3	3¼	38	15	0	6	8
33. *Moreton*	1½	6¾	2	3	3	39	16	0	6	9
34. *Henlade*	1½	6	3¼	2¼	3¼	44	14	0	7	7
35. *B. Cannons*	2	6½	3¾	3	3¾	33	4	0	5	0
36. *Beconsfield*	1¼	7¼	4¼	4	4	47	13	9	8	0

Here the reader sees the proportion between labour and provisions at every distinct place; but this is not sufficient for the comparison at large; we must for this end divide the table into classes, according to the average of all provisions.

Average price of 3 d. *per lb.*

Places.	Bread.	Butter.	Cheese.	Meat.	Tot. earn.			Weekly pay.	
	d.	d.	d.	d.	l.	s.	d.	s.	d.
No. 4	1	5	$3\frac{1}{2}$	$3\frac{1}{4}$	45	6	6	6	1
33	$1\frac{1}{2}$	$6\frac{1}{4}$	2	3	39	16	0	6	9
Averages	$1\frac{1}{4}$	$5\frac{1}{2}$	$2\frac{3}{4}$	$3\frac{1}{8}$	42	11	3	6	5

Average price of 3 d. $\frac{1}{4}$ *per lb.*

	Bread.	Butter.	Cheese.	Meat.	Tot. earn.			Weekly pay.	
No. 15	1	6	3	$3\frac{1}{2}$	48	0	6	6	0
16	$1\frac{1}{4}$	$4\frac{1}{4}$	4	$3\frac{1}{2}$	70	9	0	12	3
18	$1\frac{1}{4}$	6	3	$3\frac{1}{4}$	59	11	9	8	8
20	$1\frac{1}{2}$	6	3	$3\frac{1}{4}$	52	2	4	8	0
32	2	$6\frac{3}{4}$	$1\frac{1}{2}$	3	38	15	0	6	8
34	$1\frac{1}{2}$	6	$3\frac{1}{4}$	$2\frac{1}{2}$	44	14	0	7	7
Averages	$1\frac{1}{4}$	$5\frac{3}{4}$	3	3	52	12	1	8	2

THROUGH ENGLAND.

Average price of 3d. ½ per lb.

Places.	Bread. d.	Butter. d.	Cheese. d.	Meat. d.	Tot. earn. l. s. d.	Weekly Pay. s. d.
No. 3	1	5	4½	3½	49 2 6	7 10
5	¾	6	4½	3½	44 5 6	7 1
6	1	6	3½	3½	50 8 3	6 10
7	1	6½	3½	3½	45 8 6	6 4
8	¾	6	4	3½	49 2 0	6 11
9	1	6	4	3½	53 4 3	8 0
10	1	6	4	3½	50 1 0	7 0
14	1	7	3½	3½	59 18 0	9 11
19	1½	6	4	3¼	59 6 8	8 2
22	1¼	7	2½	3½	51 16 0	7 11
Averages	1	6	3¾	3½	51 5 3	6 9

Average price of 3d. ¾ per lb.

No. 11	1	7	4	3¾	54 6 0	8 0
12	1	6½	4½	3½	54 12 6	8 0
13	1¼	7½	3½	3½	50 9 0	6 3
17	1¼	6½	4	3½	57 7 6	7 6
21	1½	6½	4	3¾	46 15 6	7 7
29	1½	6	4	3½	44 11 0	7 3
31	1¼	8	2½	3½	51 0 9	8 8
35	2	6¼	3¼	3	33 4 0	5 0
Averages	1¼	6¼	3¾	3¼	49 0 9	7 3

Average price of 4d. per lb.

No. 1	1	7	4½	4	50 14 0	8 3
23	1½	7¼	4	3¾	49 7 0	7 11
36	1¼	7¼	4¼	4	47 13 9	8 0
Averages	1¼	7¼	4¼	4	49 4 11	8 0

Average price of 4d. ¼ per lb.

Places.	*Bread.*	*Butter.*	*Cheese.*	*Meat.*	*Tot. earn.*			*Weekly Pay.*	
	d.	*d.*	*d.*	*d.*	*l.*	*s.*	*d.*	*s.*	*d.*
No. 2	1	7½	4½	4	49	19	0	8	0
24	1¼	8½	4	4	51	10	6	7	9
26	1½	8½	3½	4¼	64	5	0	10	7
28	1¼	7	4½	4	53	0	6	10	0
30	2	8	4	3¾	47	9	0	8	3
Averages	1¼	7¾	4	4	53	4	8	8	11

Average price of 4d. ¾ per lb.

No. 25	1¾	9	4½	4¼	62	2	6	10	10
27	1¾	9	4½	4¼	61	8	0	9	7
Averages	1¾	9	4½	4¼	61	15	3	10	2

Recapitulation.

Aver. of 3 *d.*	1¼	5½	2¼	3⅛	42	11	3	6	5
Dit. of 3 *d.* ¼	1¼	5¾	3	3	52	12	1	8	2
Dit. of 3 *d.* ½	1	6	3¾	3½	51	5	3	6	9
Dit. of 3 *d.* ¾	1¼	6¾	3¼	3¼	49	0	9	7	3
Dit. of 4 *d.*	1¼	7⅛	4¼	4	49	4	11	8	0
Dit. of 4 *d.* ¼	1¼	7¼	4	4	53	4	8	8	11
Dit. of 4 *d.* ¾	1¾	9	4½	4¼	61	15	3	10	2

This account has not upon the whole near ſo many contradictions in it as the laſt I drew up on a ſimilar occaſion; but ſtill there are ſo many, that it will be difficult to attribute the variations to thoſe of proviſions. As to the laſt article of 4*d.* ¾, it by no means carries with it the ſame au-

thority

thority as the reft; it is drawn from only two places, one of them *Peterſham*, 10 miles from *London*, and in a diſtrict where twenty other cauſes conſpire to raiſe the rates of labour. The other *Feverſham*, a ſeaport on the *Thames*, that has ſuch inceſſant communication with *London*, that the prices of proviſions are regulated by her markets; full of hop grounds, fiſhermen and ſmugglers; in ſuch a ſpot, labour being high as well as proviſions is not at all characteriſtic of the union. The other parts of the table are not at all in uniſon. The average price of 3 $d.\frac{1}{2}$ earns within 12 $s.$ as much as 4 $d.\frac{1}{2}$, though 3 $d.\frac{1}{4}$ falls ſhort of it 40 $s.$ The riſe from 3 $d.$ to 3 $d.\frac{1}{4}$ is 10 $l.$; according to which there ought to be another *riſe* of 10 $l.$ from 3 $d.\frac{1}{4}$ to 3 $d.\frac{1}{2}$ but inſtead of that it *falls* 1 $l.$ 7 $s.$ and from 3 $d.\frac{1}{2}$ to 3 $d.\frac{3}{4}$ takes another fall of 45 $s.$ more, which is ſo contrary to all gradation, that it is impoſſible to ſuppoſe any can govern it; and when it begins to riſe, as it does from 3 $d.\frac{3}{4}$ to 4 $d.$, it is only 4 $s.$ 2 $d.$ in 50 $l.$ From thence to 4 $d.\frac{1}{2}$, inſtead of 4 $s.$ it is 4 $l.$ Every thing in the table is by the rule of contraries, except the loweſt, and the highest prices coinciding with those of provisions.

The weekly pay is not of so much consequence, because it is only one part of labour in many: this is more regular than the other, but is nevertheless full of contradictions. The rise from 3 $d.$ to 3 $d.$ ¼ is 1 $s.$ 9 $d.$, whereas from 3 $d.$ ¼ to 3 $d.$ ½ is a fall of 1 $s.$ 5 $d.$—4 $d.$ earns less than 3 $d.$ ¼; with several other variations, directly contrary to the rate of provisions.

The price of bread is so even, that I cannot compare labour with that alone, in the same comprehensive method; but it is worthy of noting, that in general the same inconsistencies would be found.

Earnings, at 1 $d.$ - £. 51 5 3
Average ditto, at 1 $d.$ ¼ - 49 6 0

Which is directly opposite to the price.

In a word, I must be allowed to suppose, that labour and provisions have no other connection than in very great variations, and not always in them; but in the intermediate spaces, the whole depends on other causes, or on chance. It is not difficult to suppose several that may have an influence.

The

The great cause is probably the proportion there may be between the demand, and the hands to supply it; for if many men are wanted, and few to be had, prices will rise though the people lived upon air. There are more variations in demand than may be at first thought of; all publick and parliamentary works affect a whole neighbourhood: great private undertakings do the same: improvements in husbandry, such inclosing, marling, claying, &c. Another great source of variation is, the manner in which our poor-laws are executed; if the poor are, through the justices biass, favoured greatly to the encouraging idleness, it will have the same effect in taking hands from the old quantum of work, as a fresh demand, and prices must in consequence rise. These and several other causes it is very clear would operate, without any dependance on the price of provisions.

It is the manufacturing interest in this kingdom, that has usually complained of the rates of provisions raising the price of their labour; or perhaps more the sentiments of various writers than of persons really concerned in our fabrics. But their

their complaints are certainly groundless: some of our manufactures have sunk, and others have risen. Has the former been the effect of dearness of provisions, or the latter of cheapness? Manufactures have declined in *Suffolk*, and flourished in *Yorkshire* and *Somersetshire*, and all the west; but *Suffolk* of all those is the cheapest. They decline in *Suffolk* and rise in *Norfolk*, though provisions be the same in both.

And let it be remembered, that while provisions are at a *regular* price, labour is *irregular*; great orders for goods, from abroad, raise the prices much, though provisions remain exactly the same.

All these circumstances would be different, if there were arbitrary laws of police to force men to work at rates decided by variations in the price of provisions. How far this is the case in *France* I am not clearly informed; but how they can now, and for some time last past, be rivalling us in manufactures from cheapness of provisions, I cannot understand, while it is very well known, that we should have exported much corn to them without any bounty, had the ports been open; which

is

is a plain proof, that wheat has been higher there than in *England*.

We are for ever *prohibiting* the exportation of wheat, and at the same time complaining, that other countries underfel our manufactures *through cheapness* of *provisions*. I speak not of the bounty, but mere exportation, which would at this day go on were it allowed; and is I think proof sufficient, that the commodity is much cheaper with us than in other countries, else most assuredly they would not pay freight, expences, and the merchants profit, besides our market price.

But supposing this was not the case, yet are we not to assert, that nations are on an equality, because a weaver in one receives a shilling, and in another has no more. There are many circumstances, which should be taken to account. Will a *Frenchman* work as much and as well in a given time for the same pay as an *Englishman?* Is a *Dutchman* and an *Englishman* exactly upon a par? Surely these questions are of essential consequence; but who will answer them? Is no account to be taken of numerous holydays in one country, few in another?

Are not all *neceffaries* to be confidered? The *French* manufacturer pays perhaps lefs for bread and drink than the *Britifh* one; but who pays moft in *perfonal* taxes, befides numerous others? Which, under the burthen of a numerous family, meets with moft eafe and relief? The *Frenchman* muft earn for all, and not keep from ftarving perhaps at laft, but not the *Englifhman*: a miferable oppreffed life muft have many days of neceffary relief from work; and much work badly done. Is nothing to be allowed for thefe articles?

But all that is *French* is to fill this country with terror. While the fuperior power of that kingdom threatened the liberties of *Europe*, fuch apprehenfions were political, and kept up a conftant vigilance to watch her motions. But as well might a *Greek* dread the power of the great king after *Alexander*'s expedition, or an *Englifhman* under *Cromwell* tremble at that of *Spain*, as any one in the prefent age fear the fuperior genius of *France*. Nations have their grandeur, but they have alfo their declenfion; and there is not in the records of hiftory an inftance of one flourishing to a moft formidable height, and then finking regularly for near fourfcore years, which has been the cafe with *France* fince the peace of *Nimeguen*, and afterwards enjoying a refurrection to dreaded power.

Let us not therefore be filled with vain fears and apprehenfions of every manufacture, every advantage, gained by *France*. We have nothing to dread from the power of the houfe of *Bourbon*; and thofe who pretend that the manufactures and trade of that kingdom are to deftroy ours, fpeak like merchants that have not an idea beyond their counting-houfe, inftead of taking a view of the progrefs of human affairs, and from the paft judging of the future. The manufactures of *France* have declined fince the laft century. Where are a fourth of the forty thoufand looms at *Lyons*, now to be found? Where are her twenty millions of inhabitants? Where is the revenue of *Lewis* XIV.? Where his four hundred thoufand men in arms refifting three fourths of *Europe*? Where the navy that rode triumphant in the *Englifh* channel? Where is the man fo blind as not

to

to see, that the power of *France* is sunk, that she has but the remains of her former fame to patch out a ragged reputation? Need I reverse the medal? Does this nation want to have her state explained? Let her go to the croaking politicians, who tell her of the " unprosperous situation of our publick affairs," and feast on ridiculous tales of her declension and ruin.*

---

* " To so wretched a state have policy, principle, and even understanding, arrived in this country, that we estimate the degrees of our national wisdom and strength, by the comparative folly and debility of our neighbours," says the author of the *Considerations on the Policy, &c. of this Kingdom*: the comparative estimation of the wisdom and folly, is the creature of his own brain; but as to the strength and debility, the case is very different, and nothing but the darkest ignorance can ever fix any but a comparative idea to them. What is national strength? Are riches, armies, navies, people, to be so considered? By what measure are their power to be ascertained, if not by the strength of our usual enemies? For what purpose have we armies, fleets, debts, taxes, &c. but to *defend ourselves against*, that is, *compare with* our neighbours? Of what use is that boundless *trade* and excessive manufacturing, which these writers are ever haranguing on, if not to enable us to equal the power of *France* and *Spain?* National strength is not worth a groat to *Britain* for any other use: It is the only rule and measure of our strength, and the only idea this nation ever entertained of it. If our enemies sink into debility, we have no longer a use for that enormous power which has burthened us with debts; provided other rivals do not arise on their ruins, to continue the competition. The interests of *foreign* commerce are requisite, merely with a view to *strength*; the ease and happiness of the kingdom depend not on it.

LETTER LIV.

HAVING made such deductions from the prices of provisions and labour, as their variations appeared to me to call for, I shall next compare both these objects with another which ought to be closely connected with them, the *poor rates*, that we may be able to decide how far such assistance is proportioned to the necessities they were intended to relieve.

Places.	Poor rates per £.		Aver. price Prov.	Weekly pay.		Total earnings.			Rise of Labour.	Rise of Rates.
	s.	d	d.	s.	d.	l.	s.	d.		
Hempstead,	1	3	4	8	3	50	14	0		
Winslow,	3	0								
Blisworth,	1	0	3¼	7	10	49	2	6		Double in 10 years.
Hazelbeech,	1	0	3	6	1	45	6	6		
Glendon,	1	0	3¼	7	1	44	5	6		
Kettering,	3	0								
Quenby,	2	6	3¼	6	10	50	8	3	¼	20 Years ago but 3 d.; 15 years ago only 9 l. now 140 l. to 150 l.; not more poor now than then; attributed to excessive tea drinking.
{*Tilton,*	1	0							¼ in 20 years.	The rates risen double in 20 years.

Places.	Poor rates per £. s.	d.	Aver. price prov. d.	Weekly pay. s.	d.	Total earnings. l.	s.	d.	Rise of Labour.	Rise of Rates.
9. *Melton* and *Hinkley*,	4	6								
10. *Dishley*,	2	0	3½	6	4	45	8	6	⅓ in 20 years	Above half in : years.
11. Several towns by ditto,	4	3								
12. *Alfreton*,	1	0	3½	6	11	49	2	0	¼ in 20	
13. *Radburn*,	0	9	3½	8	0	53	4	3	½ in 20	
14. *Tiddswell*,	1	6	3½	7	0	50	1	0		Doubled in 15 or (years.
15. *Chesterfield*,	2	0	3¼	8	0	54	6	4	⅓ in 20	Ditto.
16. *Blythe*,	1	0								20 Years ago 6 and 20 before th nothing.
17. *Broadsworth*,	0	8	3¼	6	3	50	9	0		
18. *Wembwell*,	2	0	3½	9	11	59	18	0	½ in 20	
19. *Bootham*,	3	0	3¼	6	0	48	0	6	⅓ in 20	
20. *Lincoln*,	2	6								
21. *Canwick*,	3	0								Not 2*s.* 20 y ago.
22. *Summer* Castle,	0	7½							⅓ in 10	¼ in 20 years.
23. *Long Sutton*,	1	2								N. B. A comm of 3500 acres salt marsh, wo let at 24*s.* acre.
24. *Leverington*,	1	0	3¼	7	6	57	7	6		
25. *Wisbeach*,	3	0								
26. *Walpole*,	0	10								In 1760, - 1730, - 1700, -
27. *Runcton*,	1	8	3¼	8	8	59	11	9	¼ in 10	
28. *Massingham*,	1	3								
29. *Snettisham*,	1	0	3½	8	2	59	6	8		20 Years ago, 30 years ago,
30. *Warham*,	0	8	3¼	8	0	52	2	4	1/7 in 20	20 Years ago,
31. *Aylsham*,	2	0	3¾	7	7	46	15	6	¼ in 20	⅓ in 20 years.
32. *Brammerton*,	2	0								Doubled in 20 yea
33. *Earlham*,	1	9	3½	7	11	51	16	0	⅙ in 20	Ditto.
34. *Bracon Ash*,	2	6								Ditto.
35. *Flegg* Hun.	1	0								20 Years ago but
36. *Halstead*,	3	0								
37. *Colchester*,	16	6								
Ditto,	6	6								

'lace.	Poor rates per £. s.	d.	Avcr. price prov. d.	Weekly pay. s.	d.	Total earnings. l.	s.	d.	Rise of Labour.	Rise of rates.
8. .xden, &c.	3	0								
9. ungsbury,	3	0	4¼	7	9	51	10	6		20 Years ago not 1 s. 6 d.
.o. iare,	1	0								*Ware* is just by *Youngsbury*; rates are there so much lower on account of a work house.
1 ieam,	2	6	4¼	10	7	64	5	0		
2 versham,	3	6	4¼	9	7	61	8	0	none	More than ½ in 20 years.
3 aksburn,	3	3								
ldisham,	3	9								
ttleburn,	5	0								
eston,	1	6								40 Years ago but 3 d.
e Thanet,	2	9								
bailey,	9	0								Totally owing to the great commons.
effield Pl.	4	6	3¼	7	3	44	11	0		Much owing to the commons in the parish.
alberton,	1	6	4¼	8	3	47	9	0		20 Years ago 9 d.
e Wight,	3	1								
itto,	3	0	3¼	8	8	51	0	9	$\frac{1}{7}$ in 20	7000 l. a year in the island.
resford,	1	6								35 Years ago but one pauper; now the rates amount to 80 l. a year.
lbury,	1	9								35 Years ago, none.
itchill,	2	6	3¼	6	8	38	15	0		20 Years ago, 10 d.
oreton,	1	0	3	6	9	39	16	0	$\frac{1}{6}$ in 20	20 Years ago, 6 d.
ame,	1	0								
ilton Ab.	2	0								
apperton,	1	3								
igh,	1	8							none	20 Years ago, 10 d.
aunton,	0	10	3¼	7	7	44	14	0		20 Years ago, 5 d. and 80 years nothing.
onnington,	4	0								20 Years ago, 6 d.
ewbury,	5	0*								* Called 7 s. but not so full of real rent.

Place.	Poor rates per £. s. d.	Aver. price prev. d.	Weekly pay, s. d.	Total earnings. l. s. d.	Rise of Labour.	Rise of rates.
64. Harleyford,	2 6				none	Were 4s. 9d. but lowered by a workhouse.
65. Beconsfield,	2 6	4	8 0	47 13 9		
Averages,	2 8				¼ in 18½	And 1-7 in 20 years.

N. B. There is some rise of labour every where except in those places against whom the word " none " is put; but those who gave me intelligence knew not the proportion.

Here it appears, that on the average of this Tour, poor rates are 2 *s.* 8 *d.* in the pound rent. This enormous tax, which amounts to near *a seventh* of the rental, has, we find, considerably more than doubled its amount in 20 years; at the same time that the prices of labour throughout the same tract of country, are a fourth higher than they were 18 years ago. It is impossible to account rationally for such an increase; that it has kept pace only with the necessities of the poor, is impossible, as I shall attempt to shew clearly by comparing these circumstances together.

But it will be necessary to divide this table according to rates, that we may see what connection there is between them and the prices of labour and provisions.

Rates under 1 s. in the pound.

Place.	Rates.		Provisions.	Weekly labour.		Total earnings.			Rise of labour in 20 years in the £.		Rise of rates in 20 years in the £.	
	s.	d.	d.	s.	d.	l.	s.	d.	s.	d.	s.	d.
No. 13.	0	9	3½	8	0	53	4	3	10	0		
17.	0	8	3¼	6	3	50	9	4				
22.	0	7½							8	0	5	0
26.	0	10									6	8
30.	0	8	3¼	8	0	52	2	4	2	10	10	0
61.	0	10	3¼	7	7	44	14	0			10	0
Average,	0	8¼	3½	7	5½	50	2	5	6	11	7	11

Rates at 1 s. in the pound.

Place.	Rates.		Provisions.	Weekly labour.		Total earnings.			Rise of labour		Rise of rates	
No. 3.	1	0	3½	7	10	49	2	6			15	0*
4.	1	0	3	6	1	45	6	6				
5.	1	0	3½	7	1	44	5	6				
8.	1	0							6	8	10	0
12.	1	0	3½	6	11	49	2	0	5	0		
16.	1	0									10	0
24.	1	0	3¼	7	6	57	7	6				
29.	1	0	3½	8	2	59	6	8			10	0
56.	1	0	3	6	9	36	16	0	3	4	10	0
Average,	1	0	3¼	7	2	48	15	2	5	0	11	0

Rates from 1 s. to 2 s. in the pound.

Place.	Rates.		Provisions.	Weekly labour.		Total earnings.			Rise of labour		Rise of rates	
No. 1.	1	3	4	8	3	50	14	0				
14.	1	6	3½	7	0	50	1	0			10	0
27.	1	8	3¼	8	8	59	11	9	7	6*		
33.	1	9	3½	7	11	51	16	0	3	4	10	0
50.	1	6	4¼	8	3	47	9	0			10	0
Average,	1	6	3¼	8	0	51	18	4	5	5	10	0

* Doubled in 10.

Rates from 2 s. to 3 s. in the pound.

Place.	Rates.		Provisions.	Weekly labour.		Total earnings.			Rise of labour in 20 years in the £.		Rise of rates in 20 years in the £.	
	s.	*d.*	*d.*	*s.*	*d.*	*l.*	*s.*	*d.*	*s.*	*d.*	*s.*	*d.*
No. 7.	2	6	3½	6	10	50	8	3	5	0	18	0
10.	2	0	3½	6	4	45	8	6	6	8	11	0
15.	2	0	3¾	8	0	54	6	4	6	8	10	0
18.	2	0	3½	9	11	59	18	0	10	0		
31.	2	0	3¾	7	7	46	15	6	5	0	5	0
41.	2	6	4¼	10	7	64	5	0				
55.	2	6	3¼	6	8	38	15	0			13	4
56.	2	6	4	8	0	47	13	9				
Average,	2	3	3¾	8	0	50	18	9	6	8	11	5

Rates from 3 s. to 4 s. 6 d. in the pound.

No. 19.	3	0	3¼	6	0	48	0	6	6	8		
39.	3	0	4¼	7	9	51	10	6			11	0
42.	3	6	4¾	9	7	61	8	0			11	0
52.	3	0	3¾	8	8	51	0	9	2	10		
49.	4	6	3¾	7	3	44	11	0				
Average,	3	4	3¾	7	10	51	6	1	4	9	11	0

Recapitulation.

Rates under 1 s.	0	8¾	3½	7	5	50	2	5	6	11	7	11
At 1 *s.*	1	0	3¼	7	2	48	15	2	5	0	11	0
1 *s.* to 2 *s.*	1	6	3¾	8	0	51	18	4	5	5	10	0
2 *s.* to 3 *s.*	2	3	3¾	8	0	50	18	9	6	8	11	5
3 *s.* to 4 *s.* 6 *d.*	3	4	3¾	7	10	51	6	1	4	9	11	0

In remarking the variations of this table, let us first turn to the lowest earnings of the labourer, for there we should naturally look for the highest poor rates; but instead of so plain a connection, they are, except one,

one, the lowest in the table. On the contrary, the highest earnings should be attended by the *lowest* rates, but so far is this from being the case, that there are two complete divisions in the table lower, which are as many as are *above* it.

Rates under 1 *s*. and from 2 *s*. to 3 *s*. are, within a few shillings, attended by the same earnings. It is the same with 1 *s*. to 2 *s*. and 3 *s*. to 4 *s*. 6 *d*.

The prices of provisions are so regular, that not many conclusions are to be drawn from them; however, one may see that there is no connection between them and rates, or, at least, extremely trifling, for the lowest price is attended by the lowest earnings; yet 3 ¼ is the same as 3 ¼; and 3 ¼ in one column, varies half as much from 3 ¼ in another, as from the *lowest* earnings to the *highest*.

If the labourer's weekly pay is taken for the guide, yet greater contradictions will be found.

The average total earnings at those places where rates rise to 1 *s*. in the pound, are 49 *l*. 8 *s*. 9 *d*.; whereas earnings are 51 *l*. 7 *s*. 8 *d*. where rates are from 1 *s*. to 4 *s*. 6 *d*.; from whence one would suppose, that the more you raise the price of labour, the higher will the poor's tax rife with it, which is contrary to all reafon. In the weekly pay it is the fame; the rates to 1 *s.* have 7 *s.* 3 *d.* ½ *per* week labour; but thofe from 1 *s.* to 4 *s.* 6 *d.* have 7 *s.* 11 *d.*

Further; the rife of labour ought uniformly to mark the lownefs of rates, and in this inftance here appears more connection than in feveral of the other columns, for the higheft rife of labour has been where rates are loweft; and the fmalleft rife has been where rates are higheft; but then the intermediate variations are quite wild: the fecond greateft rife of labour correfponds with the higheft rates, except one, which is diametrically oppofite to what it ought to be.

At 1 *s.* rates, the rife of labour is ¼; whereas from 2 *s.* to 3 *s.* it is a third, which is a great difference, and on the wrong fide; with feveral other contradictions of the fame kind.

Relative to provifions, the rife of labour fhould correfpond with the increafe of their prices, but no fuch dependance is found. The loweft price of provifions fhould be attended by the higheft rife of labour; but it is almoft directly contrary; and where

the

the price of provisions is equal, the variations in the rise of labour are great; the rise of a third, a fourth, and a fifth, are attended by the same rates of provisions.

The rise of poor rates ought to have an intimate connection with the prices of provisions; but nothing that chance could cast, can be further from the fact; the *lowest* price of provisions is attended by nearly the *highest* rise in rates, and in one column of the highest price, superior. The average price of 3 *d*. ½ *per lb.* is attended by 3 *s*. in the pound less rise of rates than 3 *d*. ¼. In a word, the whole column little else but contradictions.

Nor is there more reason in the variations of the *rise* of rates and the earnings, for the average total earnings of the three highest articles are 51 *l*. 7 *s*. 8 *d*.; the attending rise in poor rates 10 *s*. 9 *d*.; the average earnings of the lowest articles 49 *l*. 8 *s*. 9 *d*.; the corresponding rise of rates 9 *s*. 5 *d*. ¼. Thus, by the poor's earning 1 *l*. 18 *s*. 11 *d*. *per ann.* more in one place than in another, their tax *increases* instead of *lowering*.

It appears equally strong in the weekly pay; at the average earnings of

7 *s*. 11 *d*. the rise in rates is (in the pound,) - - £.0 10 9

Whereas, at 7 s. 3 d. ¼ per week,
the rise is only   -   £.0 9 5¼

From all which it is sufficiently clear, that the variations in those sums which the poor receive either in pay or rates, do not, in scarcely any case, depend on their necessities.. Increase poor rates, you pay most to those who want the assistance least. Raise the prices of labour, the effect is the same.

Has the rise in labour and poor rates been proportioned to the rise in the prices of provisions? This is a very important point, but would require more minute elucidation than the present pages will allow.

The rise of rates in 20 years,   ½ and ⅐
That of labour in 18 years, - ¼
The first is, *per cent.* - 64
The second, - - - 25

Relative to the progress of the prices of provisions, not being the immediate subject of these papers, I can only give a slight sketch from an author before me, who I shall trust to with the more readiness, as his professed aim is to magnify the miseries of the poor from high prices, so that if he is wrong, we may be tolerably safe that it is not in lessening them. He gives, among others,

others, two periods from 1706 to 1730; and from 1730 to 1760; these will serve the purpose nearly as well as if they came down later, because that period was to the full as much complained of, as any one since; and going so far back will be the more satisfactory, as it will give the reader an idea of prices, compared with the rise of poor rates in the period preceding the last 20 years, often mentioned in the foregoing tables. But, as I said before, I am now offering a digression of curiosity, and not professedly treating the subject—therefore the same minute attention to every year is not equally necessary.

From 1706 * to 1730, mutton
and beef *per* stone, - £.0 1 8
From 1730, to 1760, - 0 2 0

The rise, - - 0 0 4

Which is *per cent.* - - 20

From 1706, to 1730. Pork,* 0 2 0
1730, to 1760. Ditto, 0 2 6

The rise, - - 0 0 6

---

* *An Enquiry into the Prices of Wheat, Malt, &c.* 1768, Folio.

	£	s.	d.
Which is *per cent.* —			25
Mutton and beef, — —			20
Average of the three, —			22½
From 1706, to 1730. Wheat *per* quarter, —	1	15	0¼
1730, to 1760, —	1	9	5¼
The fall, — —	0	5	7¼
Which is *per cent.* — —			16½
From 1706, to 1730. Malt,	1	6	2¼
1730, to 1760. Ditto,	1	4	5½
The fall, — —	0	1	8¼
Which is *per cent.* — —			6½*

Now

---

* It would be no eafy matter to find a page in the *Confiderations on Policy, &c. of the Kingdom,* that contained not a falfhood or an abfurdity. Among an hundred others, he tells us that the medium price of corn, ordinarily, is 26 s. a quarter throughout *Europe.* The gentleman, however, gives not his authority; I fhall therefore to avoid fuch an impertinence, merely transcribe a paffage from the fpeech of *M. de Chalotais,* procureur general to the parliament of *Brittany;* a piece extremely interefting, which, in two pages, contains more good fenfe, than this author will ever produce in two hundred. It is tranflated by the writer of the *Three Tracts on the Corn trade,* a work which does him no flight honour.

" The

question is, the comparison
all in wheat of 16 ½, and in
against a rise of meat of 22 ½.
nows, that with respect to the
of the poor, wheat is of far
:quence than meat, insomuch,
it of 16 ½ *per cent.* cannot be
than equal to 22 ½ in meat; I
ed to think the difference much
ever, if we take it only at that
propor-

---

non price of wheat through *Europ;*
it is notorious that it is never below
he setier (that is, twenty four, the
) and that it scarcely ever rises above
; therefore the average price is twenty

of the Corn Tracts adds this note.
6 *d.* ½ the *London* quarter. Now it
e average price of wheat for the last
cen 33 *s.* 2 *d.* ½ AT WINDSOR, THAT
HE GENERAL MARKET OF EUROPE;
, for 91 years, it was 38 *s.* ⅜, that is,
he said general price; and that these
re more to be depended on than could
n, is proved, not only by the said
Europe, but also by the average price
1740 to 1764, being found, on en-
cen only six-pence a quarter less—and
f all the wheat bought at the victual-
London, Dover, Portsmouth, and *Ply*
last 20 years, ending *February* 18,
by an account laid before parliament,
6 *d.* ¼, that is, 10 *d.* above the *Wind-*
same time, and this last sum will
amount

proportion, the average of those different articles of food is balanced; the fall in malt is not great, but uniting with that of wheat, it makes the equality of the two periods the more certain.

From these *data* I cannot apprehend that one period (relative to the consumption *of the poor)* in these articles is dearer than the other. It is true wheat, &c. was high in particular years, and there were many clamours and much rioting; but particular years are not the enquiry, for a rise in labour

---

amount to about 2 ½ discount on the bills, but we cannot well call it less than 4 *per cent.* and then it will be found to have been 6 *d.* below the *Windsor*, and to agree with the *London* price."

Upon reading part of the *Considerations*, &c. I met with forty glaring errors in a few pages, and formed an idea of replying to it; before I got to the end of the pamphlet I found five hundred, and what is much more, such a spirit of true prejudice—such an itch of double dealing—so many assertions ventured at random, without a shadow of argument or proof—such bold conclusions, in numerous passages, drawn from rotten premises, that I did not want the help of that miserable buffoonery, which runs through it, against the landed interest, doubtless thought by the author sterling wit, to make me leave the performance to the neglect, which works of such a cast are sure to be buried in. Even the cant preaching against the vices of the times will not save it; for, unfortunately, his gravity moves our risibility, and his humour makes us sad; neither of them being unlike the poetry which he quotes, (and therefore, I suppose, admires) which compares the want of merit to *leather or prunella*.

labour or poor rates, is not for one, two, or three years, but for perpetuity; it is the average of many, therefore, that is alone to be regarded.

The two periods appear to be equal; but how different has it been with poors rates and labour? The price of the latter has been pretty regularly rising; in the laſt 18 years the increaſe is 2 5 *per cent.* at the ſame time that poor rates have increaſed 64 *per cent.*; and in the period preceding, in as rapid a manner, as appears from various of the foregoing minutes, both thoſe and labour extending in the periods minuted in the table in various inſtances throughout the ſame period, as theſe now quoted of the prices of proviſions.

But whether theſe compariſons are minutely exact, is not of conſequence at preſent, becauſe it is from this ſlight ſketch manifeſt, that the riſe of labour has more than kept pace with that of proviſions, at the ſame time that that of rates has far outſtripped it.

This is a point of no ſlight importance, and I purpoſe taking a more proper opportunity of fully elucidating it by regular compariſons between every article and period.

The

The distresses of the poor are in many mouths, and have been so constant a subject of late, as capitally to affect the greatest public measures; but I will venture to assert, that they are equally ill understood and misrepresented by the numerous writers who plume themselves on their humanity, because they plead for removing the distresses of the poor, by raising the price of labour, sinking that of provisions, and increasing poor rates. Thus a late writer employs several pages, tending to prove, that wheat should be 26 s. a quarter in *England*, because it is so, on an average, through the rest of *Europe*; the fact, if true, by no means produces the conclusion he draws from it; but the fact is as false as the conclusion is ridiculous.

That there are distresses among the poor, and such as ought to be alleviated, no one will dispute; but they proceed not from these causes. Their grand source is the application of that money to *superfluities*, which ought to be, and formerly was expended in *necessaries:* I shall for the present name only tea and sugar, because it is universal throughout this Tour, except, I think, in one single place. Wherever I came, every body agreed in their affertions on this head; whether they were for or againſt the poor in their arguments, made no difference; all united in the affertion, that the practice *twice a day* was conſtant, and that it was inconceivable how much it impoveriſhed them; in very many pariſhes they attributed their exorbitant rates folely to this luxury; in many pariſhes does it reign uncontrouled among thoſe very families that receive regular and large allowances from the rates.

This is no matter of trivial confequence; no tranſitory or local evil; it is univerſal and unceaſing; the amount of it great. It is the principal cauſe of high rates and labour, without a correſponding relief to the poor, and as ſuch, cannot be too ſeriouſly confidered; the ſlighteſt calculations, of which, I have had many given me in various parts of the kingdom, are ſufficient to ſhew, that this ſingle article coſts numerous families more than ſufficient to remove thoſe real diſtreſſes, which they will ſubmit to rather than lay aſide their tea. And an object, ſeemingly, of little account, but in reality, of infinite importance, is the cuſtom, coming in, of *men* making tea an article of their

their food, almoſt as much as women; labourers loſing their time to go and come to the tea table; nay, farmers ſervants even demanding tea, for their breakfaſt, with the maids! which has been actually the caſe in *Eaſt Kent*.

If the men come to loſe as much of their time at tea as the women, and injure their health by ſo bad a beverage, the poor, in general, will find themſelves far more diſtreſſed than ever.

If the *real* diſtreſſes of the poor are in queſtion—if their pay will not properly maintain them—if they are not cloathed in a warm and decent manner—well lodged—and nouriſhed plentifully with wholſome food—if the ſick man has not wherewithal for cure—or the hand of death leaves the widow and her orphans in diſtreſs—if unrelenting time brings grey hairs on the head of the induſtrious, without ſtrength for ſupport, or ſtore to reſort to—in the name of *God* force the purſes of the rich, if humanity does not open them, to relieve the wants of their fellow creatures—raiſe the price of labour—increaſe your rates—do whatever the neceſſity of the caſe requires; it is then Humanity that ſpeaks,

nor

nor is this a nation that will ever be deaf to her call. Had it ever entered my heart to arraign the police of the kingdom for adminiſtring comfort to poverty in diſtreſs, I ſhould well have deſerved the aſſaſſinating ſtrokes more than once levelled, but which I diſdain too much to feel.

The man who takes the charitable virtues of humanity for his theme, is ſure of being, at leaſt, unattacked on that head; conſequently, if he has any intereſted point to carry—any ſecret motive of his conduct, he has nothing to do but in the true hypocritical ſtrain, to interweave the concealed idea with the plauſible covering, and mark himſelf for an aſſertor of the rights of humanity, or a defender of the intereſts of the poor. I cannot but conceive that this muſt have been the caſe with ſeveral publications, in which humanity and charity are ſo intermixed with rates, labour, and proviſions, that the reader may naturally take them all for ſynonimous terms, and think the road to heaven is to diſpenſe liberally to the poor—no matter how, for what purpoſe, or in what manner.

But I beg to be excufed from fuch wholefale dealings, and to keep clear from jumbling fuch different matters into the fame account. What is the object in view? Is it merely to raife rates and labour, and fink provifions, indifcriminately, to all the poor, till they may live idle as well as induftrious? Or is it to reduce the neceffities of the poor to fuch a balance, with their means of procuring them, that they may be comfortable and happy who are or have been induftrious? If the latter is not the point, I am perfectly in the dark.

Now let us flightly examine the matter thus ftated: fuppofe the price of labour raifed, who will be the better? I reply, Not thofe who moft want it, and this from the facts of the prefent Tour; not a fourth of the rife will go to thofe whofe former low earnings moft demanded an increafe. Suppofe the poor rates to rife, will that remedy the evil? Not a jot; thofe (it is very plain) are difpenfed by no rules of want or propriety, but are given to them who earn the greateft wages inftead of the leaft. But the price of provifions may be funk?—True; but the fuppofition muft be over the whole kingdom, not on divifion according to neceffity,

ceffity, but a general average; and I think I have proved fufficiently clear, that the variations will be wild as the winds; thofe who can hardly live would have no relief, and others who earn plentifully would be eafed to idlenefs.—Thefe fuppofitions are not more capricious than the facts have appeared to be throughout three fourths of *England*.

Does not all this tend ftrongly to prove what I have remarked, more than once, before? that the poor laws of this kingdom are fo thoroughly defective, that let the poor be ever fo diftreffed, you cannot relieve them with tolerable equality: you muft fpend ten fhillings in mifchief, in order to lay out half a crown effectually.

But hitherto I have taken the corner ftone of the argument for granted; fuppofing that the poor are really diftreffed through neceffity—but the contrary I aver. That fome few may be fo, nobody can deny; but it would be the fame under the beft regulations that could poffibly be framed, for human laws can never exclude exceptions; but in fuch debates as this, we muft reafon only on the multitude.

Wants, I allow, are numerous; but what name are we to give to those that are voluntarily embraced, in order for indulgence in tea and sugar. I again repeat, that this is not in reference to a few individuals, it is to the point with the whole body of the poor. Rates are to rise enormously—labour to do the same—and the prices of provisions are to be sunk, contrary to all the laws of common sense; for what? Not to house, clothe, or support your poor—not to alleviate their sickness—support their old age—or fill their bellies with beef and pudding; but to enable them to drink tea. Labour has risen 25 *per cent.* in 18 years; and rates 64 *per cent.* in the same time, in order that the poor might drink tea twice, instead of once a day; in 20 years more we may look for such another rise; most assuredly it will be, that instead of twice, they may have their tea thrice a day. There is no clearer fact than that two persons, the wife and one daughter, for instance, drinking tea once a day, amounts, in a year, to a fourth of the price of all the wheat consumed by a family of five persons; twice a day, are half: so that those who leave off two tea-drinkings, can afford

afford to eat wheat at *double* the price (calculated at 6 *s.* a bushel.)

Under such circumstances, will any one complain of the price of wheat on account of the poor? and who but an ideot will reflect on a man, for not seeing the propriety of heavily taxing the kingdom, that the poor may have the greater plenty of tea and sugar; for as to the necessaries of life, all the rubbish that has been published concerning their high prices, are continued strings of falshoods and absurdities.

I am no enemy to the poor expending that money, which their industry earns, in whatever they please; let them drink Burgundy if they chuse; but let it not be with money raised by rates; and let not the fools in politics harangue on the necessity of raising the price of labour, that tea may supply the place of milk, or that wine should be substituted for beer: our ancestors taxed themselves with other views.

A very few facts well attended to, would open the eyes of those who do not voluntarily shut them. The price of labour has risen more than provisions — rates have increased enormously, and for no use but providing tea.—I have a pretty clear idea

idea of these two points, but they will admit of more decisive proofs than I have given here.

However, let the result be what it may, the futile clamours of weak men, who think that every favour the poor receive, is just so much profit to manufactures, should be silenced; let them publish facts instead of empty harangues on humanity and charity, to which virtues they most assuredly have the least pretence; since hypocrisy points out the cause which ignorance teaches them to mar by their bungling defence.—Little pretence have such to ridicule the whole landed interest, for not entering into the ridiculous absurdities of men who falsly pretend to be the friends of the *British* manufacturers.

There is another point in which the affairs of the poor of this kingdom may be viewed; which is necessary to mention, in order to keep the two great ideas of conduct distinct. When one part of a nation is possessed of every necessary, enjoys all the conveniences, comforts, and agreeableness of life, while so many are even buried in profusion; the other part are in poverty, possessing not sustenance of life without a regular

lar labour. On what account is all the wealth and ease to be thrown into one scale, and the other left so miserably empty? While such monstrous disproportion is, and must be, the case, why should ever a word drop from the rich injurious to the helpless interest of the poor! Let advantages roll to them in their fullest tide, it will be but a scanty stream; a small increase of wages, assistance from rates dispensed with a sparing hand, and more moderate prices of the provisions consumed at their humble board—Are these objects to raise the envy or the anger of the rich?

Surely not: and in this view, which looks no further than morality, religion, and the dictates of humanity lead, no other consideration ought to come in question with levelling some of that rugged distance between the classes of life. But here does it not raise our indignation to find that the men who are so loud in their clamours in favour of the poor, (under the thin-spun disguise of tenderness for their fellow creatures) are those who exhaust all their impotence in abusing the landed interest, *opposing* to it the trading and manufacturing interest, as the superior genius, in whose favour the poor ought to be so and so; drawing odious parallels between the pillars of the state; as if any could be carried off without infinite mischief; but when they touch on the state of the poor, let me to their confusion observe, that it is manufactures, and a desire for their prosperity, that has brought on all the misery which our poor suffers, and which now arranges policy on one side, and humanity on the other. Let the price of labour rise to its uttermost, who is it that complains? Not the " engrossers of all vices, landed men, farmers, and jobbers," as they are politely coupled by a supercilious coxcomb*, but the manufacturers and traders; it is they who have turned all the melancholy ditties of ruin to the state, from *loss of manufactures* by *high rates of labour*.

Name me the publication, in which land men and farmers are the complainants of the rates of labour. I will in return, for every one you produce, name forty in which the other set are noisy in their exclamations, on this head.

If

---

* Considerations on the Policy, Commerce, &c.

If you talk of the interests of trade and manufactures, every one but an ideot knows, that the lower classes must be kept poor, or they will never be industrious: I do not mean, that the poor in *England* are to be kept like the poor of *France*; but the state of the country considered, they must be (like all mankind) in poverty, or they will not work.

Let not those therefore, whose interest makes such policy requisite, abuse the landed interest for the miseries of the poor, which are wholly owing to manufactures and trade.

Sudbury in *Suffolk* is named; it is a poor miserable place undoubtedly: *Lavenham*, its next neighbour on one side, and *Colchester* on the other, are in the same predicament: poor rates from 7s. to 17s. in the pound are miserable marks that they have had the curse of manufactures among them. An instance that the trading system ever stands on crazy foundations. Let the writer name a tract, in which agriculture falls in ruins; even around the places above named, although husbandry is enormously burthened by the manufacturing poor, she flourishes as much, and around *Colchester* more than in nine tenths of *Britain*; so little truth is there in the vague assertions, that the local value of land depends on the neighbourhood of manufactures. The soil around *Lincoln*, which possesses not one fabric, lets higher than at *Islington*; nay, some of it twice as high.

Go to towns, where manufactures are the most flourishing, you will there find poor rates higher than any where else; except where they have nursed up great numbers of inhabitants, and then fled to leave them starving.

I subscribe as readily as any one to the importance of that general aggregate of industry, agriculture, manufactures, and commerce; but let not the professors of one most falsely suppose the other is to be sacrificed on her altars: but if ever unfortunate questions should be started, in which a preference must be given to one, none but a fool can imagine, that the landlords of this great empire, of above fourscore millions of acres, are to yield to the transitory sons of trade and manufacture.

I shall

I shall venture to hazard one more reflection. Carry to a fair account every advantage ever coming from the introduction of foreign trade and manufactures; not the export of our products of whatever kind, becaufe that is agriculture, and not the commerce we are fpeaking of here. Calculate the increafed value of land— the general brilliancy diffufed through life, from the circulation of immenfe wealth— the acquifition of *great* naval power, vaft armies — and unbounded treafures — of conquefts, and fo on.

Then turn to the other fide of the account, and minute the cheapnefs of money— the increafe of thofe expences, and that luxury, which the landlord would never have known — a debt of above 100 millions, the very child of trade;—taxes to the amount of 10 millions *per ann.*—poor rates in all their amount—a fituation juft as precarious as wealth — and if all thefe points, and a thoufand others, are well confidered, I am thoroughly perfuaded, that the landlords of this country have fuffered in their interefts more than to the amount of all the advantages they have gained from the increafe of money.

Let

Let us therefore have no more futile complaints of the high price of labour from manufacturers, or noisy calls for lower rates of provisions; that they may think (falsely though) to pocket so much the more money. Let us give no ear to such invidious insinuations as the press has too much teemed with, that the miseries of the poor are all owing to high prices of necessaries, which are kept up by land men, jobbers, and farmers. These low ideas, picked up one would suppose in the rakings of a manufacturer's kennel, can never elucidate points, which require the examination of facts.

To drop such ideas, and to recur to the real case under the recollection of the interests of agriculture, manufactures, and commerce,—and not acting from the dictates alone of that compassion, which should teach us to throw every thing into the scale of the poor, to bring it the nearer to a balance with the rich.—These in view, we cannot hesitate to determine, that the poor, generally speaking, have not a shadow of complaint. The rise of their labour is equal to that of provisions, the increase of rates enormous, and feemingly anfwered by no new expences, except unneceffary ones: of thefe the ufe of tea and fugar is the chief; and I fhall add, ought (were it only through humanity) to be ftopped; for many, many are the naked half ftarving children, that might be cloathed and fed with favings in this article.

I would not have the price of labour lowered; for no country can poffefs flourifhing manufactures, or commerce, or agriculture, whofe rates of labour are very low; but I would have induftry enforced among the poor; and the ufe of tea reftrained. Nothing has fuch good effects as workhoufes; of which there are numerous inftances in this Tour; but the great object is the erection of Hundred Houfes of induftry, which have now been long tried in *Suffolk* and *Norfolk* with the greateft fuccefs; and of which I have in the proper place given a full account.

But under the fuppofition, that diftreffes among them became fo great (no matter from what caufe) that labour and rates muft be rifen, and provifions be funk, ftill the relief will go, as I before fhewed, to those who want it least in nine cases out of ten: if ever therefore such ideas become active, they must be prepared for with a complete destruction of all former rates, prices, and variations, and an universal law take place to proportion labour every where to the average price of provisions, and keep it fluctuating with them; all other measures would be but palliatives, and do mischief rather than good.

LETTER LV.

I Am now come to a part of my undertaking, which I esteem of greater national importance than any other; it is the particulars of farms. From the average of a great number we may certainly be able to calculate with much truth the general state of the whole kingdom; respecting the application, product and value, of the soil; the live stock it carries, and the people it maintains; I have in another work been particular on this subject, and said what I thought was necessary to explain my idea of the matter; the less is therefore necessary to be urged here; but I shall observe, that this method of coming at the real state of the nation, respecting its agriculture, is the only one tolerably sure, and that is not open to an infinity of objections and errors. A book containing these particulars of all the farms in the kingdom, I should esteem the pocket book of a *British* minister; it would be as useful to *study*, as it would be tedious to *read*.

368 THE FARMER's TOUR

Places.	Rent per acre. l. s. d.	Total acres.	Grass.	Arab.	Wood	Rent. £.	Siz in
1. Hempstead	0 10 0	600	60	540		250	20
2. Ditto		200	20	180		100	
3. Ditto		120	20	100		80	
4. Ditto		160	10	150		70	
5. Tring	0 10 0	60	10	50		40	20
6. Ditto		600	100	500		300	
7. Blisworth	0 12 0	100	30	70		60	30
8. Glendon	0 10 0			71		50	60
9. Ditto		100	20	80		40	
10. Mr. Booth	1 0 0	350	274	76		350	
11. Quenby	0 10 0	150	115	35		102	80
12. Ditto		600	594	6		400	
13. Ditto		550	544	6		330	
14. Alfreton	1 0 0	100	50	50		100	50
15. Ditto		50	20	30		50	
16. Ditto		40	36	4		40	
17. Kendal		420	170	250		420	
18. Radburn	0 14 0			65		100	20
19. Ditto				80		240	
20. Blythe	0 10 0	403	56	350		82	
20. *		681	180	500		139	
21. Ditto		50	36	24		21	
22. Ditto		190	57	133		126	
23. Ditto		121	24	97		121	
24. Ditto		112	20	92		74	
25. Ditto		853	273	400	180	325	
26. Ditto		985	70	257	66+	192	
27. Mr. Mellish		764	120	244	400	240	
28. Mr. Wharton		800	600	200		500†	
29. Broadsworth	0 6 0	100	35	65		40	
30. Wombwell	0 16 0	280	210	70		260	20
31. Ditto		110	70	40		100	
32. Ditto		50	30	20		50	
33. Ditto		200	130	70		170	
34. Ditto		120	70	50		100	
35. Sir C. Wray	0 7 0	750	644	106		200	
36. Leverington	0 18 0	600	300	300		500	15
37. Ditto		300	240	60		200	
38. Ditto		200	166	34		200	
39. Ditto		130	100	30		100	
40. Ditto		42	42	0		40	
41. Runcton	0 14 0	180				105	20
42. Mr. Carr	0 8 0	1000	150	850		400†	
43. Snettisham	0 12 0	300	0	300		150	20
44. Burnham	0 10 6	1000	100	900		500	

THROUGH ENGLAND.

Places.	Rent per acre. l. s. d.	Total acres.	Grass.	Arab.	Wood	Rent. £.	Size Farms in general.	Med.
15 Warham	0 8 6	500	120	380		260	200 to 500	
16 Sir J. Turner		236	72	100	64	100†		
17 Aylsham	0 14 0	300	50	250		200	50 — 150	
18 Earlham	0 16 0	100	10	90		65	50 — 200	
19 Mr. Thompson		200	30	170		†160		
20 Mr. Bevor		530	400	130		400		
20 Mr. Rogers		175	20	150		105		
21 Clegg	0 15 0	350	50	300		260	50 — 500	120
52 Hadleigh	0 15 0	300	50	250		200	40 — 300	100
53 Hastead	0 14 6	160	40	120		108	20 — 130	80
54 Ditto		150	75	75		120		
55 Colchester	0 16 0	400	40	360		333	20 — 1000	
56 Youngsberry	0 12 0	300	30	270		180	30 — 300	125
57 Morden	0 12 0	120	10	110		70	50 — 500	140
58 Suddington	0 17 0	350	50	300		300		
59 Carshalton	0 10 0	2000	400	1600		1000†	30 — 600	100
60 Feversham	1 0 0	180	4	176		200	20 — 200	70
Ditto		160	4	156		100		
Mr. Reynolds	0 6 0	520	85	435		185		
Thanet	0 17 0	440	0	440		374†	to — 500	200
Rye	0 16 0	400	300	100		300	40 — 400	80
Hawkhurst	0 12 0	150	80	70		100		
Mr. Holroyd		836	450	66	320	418†		
Sheffield Place	0 10 0	318	106	148	64	140	40 — 130	
Lindon	0 7 6	600	300	300		20	to — 500	200
Walberton	1 0 0	550	200	350		550†	40 — 400	100
Mr. Turner	0 10 0	300	185	115		150		
Easton	0 10 0	436	54	374	8	200		
Isle Wight	1 0 0	100	0	100		100		
Ditto		80	0	80		60		
Ditto	0 10 0	400	40	300	60	200	20 — 200	60
Ditto		1000	600	400		500		
Alresford	0 8 0	650	0	650		160	60 — 300	130
Tilbury	0 10 6	280	30	250		90	to — 300	100
Mr. Mitford		130	12	118		65†		
Critchill	0 10 0	960	130	770		450	100 — 400	250
Ditto		300	41	259		150		
Moreton	0 12 0	1000	624	296	76	260	40 — 400	250
Mr. Frampton		800	362	263	170	400		
V. White		266	160	103	3	50		
Mr. Damer	0 11 0	1255	874	526		500	300 — 700	
Mr. Pleydell	0 10 0	902	627	255	20	500	150 — 250	
Milton Abbey	0 8 6	1800	1620	180	0	700	150 — 700	
Lord Milton		3000	1380	120	1500	1275†		
Mr. Hardy	0 5 0	11000	9400	1600		3000		

Vol. IV.   B b

370 THE FARMER's TOUR

Places.	Rent per acre.			Total acres.	Grass.	Arab.	Wood	Rent.	Size Farms in general.	
	l.	s.	d.					£.		
90. Henlade	1	0	0	138	96	42		138	20 — 200	
91. Donnington	0	15	0	150	20	130		100	30 — 300	
92. Mr. Clayton	0	15	0	550	80	120	360	400	40 — 300	
93. Mr. Burke	0	13	0	410	160	160	90	250	20 — 200	8
Totals,				51113	25467	21627	3975	24202		

† All rents marked thus † are supplied from the average of the county

Next I shall give the live stock of these farms, under the heads of draught cattle, cows, fatting beasts, young cattle, and sheep.

Farms No.	Drau.	Cows.	Fat.	Young.	Sheep.
1	16	6	0	4	300
2	10	6	0	0	200
3	6	2	0	0	60
4	8	3	0	2	80
5	3	2	0	0	100
6	17	8	0	4	300
7	6	5	0	0	50
8	8	8	10	10	130
9	6	6	0	2	100
10	10	15	0	0	500
11	6	10	9	0	160
12	8	6	100	0	600
13	4	4	110	0	600
14	8	9	4	6	60
15	4	4	2	6	30
16	1	12	0	2	0
17	16	9	4	16	120

Farms No.	Drau.	Cows.	Fat.	Young.	Sheep.
18	10	27	0	10	40
19	12	50	0	40	100
20	6	8	0	12	260
20*	8	8	0	16	400
21	2	3	0	6	0
22	6	6	0	12	100
23	8	6	0	6	0
24	8	4	0	6	0
25	16	10	0	20	500
26	8	6	0	10	500
27	12	10	0	0	600
28	37	12	50	243	250
29	5	2	0	8	40
30	8	6	60	4	80
31	8	4	16	4	60
32	4	2	0	2	0
33	8	6	40	4	60
34	6	5	6	4	20
35	8	6	0	15	300
36	15	0	80	35	500
37	8	0	20	20	300
38	4	0	20	0	300
39	4	0	15	5	150
40	0	0	12	0	120
41	10	4	0	22	70
42	30	2	20	0	800
43	14	10	10	10	100
44					700
45	30	20	12	0	500
47	12	20	20	30	100
48	5	8	0	0	
49	14	27	0	12	60

Farms No.	Drau.	Cows.	Fat.	Young.	Sheep.	
50	10‡	22	20	30	180	‡ And 90 more joist.
50*	10	0	0	0	0	
51	17	20	50	40	0	
52	16	2	0	18	0	
53	8	10	0	6	60	
54	6	20	0	5	50	† 16 of them oxen.
55	12	8	0	0	0	
56	8	8	0	20	200	
58	9	6	0	5	130	
59	15	20	0	30	200	¶ 8 of them oxen.
60	34	60	0	25	100	
61	12	4	0	4	0	
62	10	4	0	3	0	
63	10	11	0	30	250	
64	16	4	0	0	200	
65	19†	12	0	36	200	
66	¶12	8	6	24	100	
67	¶14	12	48	0	500	‡‡ 12 of them oxen.
68	18†‡	6	0	0	0	
69	26*	5	0	0	900	
70	24	0	50	0	350	* 16 of them oxen.
71	18§	10	0	0	100	
72	26§	12	0	4	150	
73	6	2	0	0	0	§ 12 oxen.
74	5	8	0	0	0	
75	18	20	0	0	200	
76	36*	24	0	40	1200	
77	16	6	0	0	1000	
78	12	16	0	10	120	
79	7	12	0	4	60	
80	16	50	0	20	800	
81	9					

THROUGH ENGLAND.

Farms.	Drau.	Cows.	Fat.	Young.	Sheep.
No. 82	10	60	0	40	300
83	8	60	0	40	500
84	6	40	0	44	
86	10	20	0	25	1340
87	16	30	0	60	1700
88	6	23	0	0	1430
89	76	200	40	300	13000
90	8	6	12	18	80
91	8	6	0	8	150
92	14	10	0	6	300
93	6	14	0	6	0
Totals,	1128	1268	886	1509	36220

Crops of these farms.

Farm	Wheat.	Barley.	Oats.	Peafe.	Beans.	Turnip.	Clover.	Fallow.
No. 1	100	100	100	40	40	100	0	80
2	50	25	25	10	10	40	0	20
3	20	20	0	10	10	20	0	20
4	30	40	10	10	0	40	0	20
5	25	0	0	5	5	10	0	0
6	100	50	40	50	50	100	60	40
7	20	0	10	0	20	0	0	20
8	20	20	10	5	0	6	0	10
9	20	6	8	10	0	5	0	30
10	0	20	20	0	0	25	14	0
11	5	10	0	4	0	0	0	0
14	20	10	16	0	4	3	4	20
15	4	2	6	1	0	2	2	6
17	50	20	30	5	5	16	20*	
18	12	6	7	10	10	0	0	20
19	20	0	30	10	10			10

* Sainfoine.

Farms.	Wheat.	Barley.	Oats.	Peafe.	Beans.	Turnip.	Clover.	Fallow.
No. 29	15	10	5	5	0	10	10	10
35	11	5	50	39	0	10	0	0
36	100	20	100	0	30	0	0	0
37	30	0	10	0	20	0	0	0
38	10	5	5	4	5	0	0	5
39	11	0	5	0	14	0	0	0
42	100	200	40	60	0	200	250	0
43	60	60	0	0	0	60	120	0
44	200	200	0	0	0	200	300	0
45	60	100	30	0	0	60	130	0
46	0	24	0	0	0	24	48	0
47	24	60	0	42	0	42	84	0
48	18	36	0	0	0	18	18	0
49	30	40	10	10	0	45	40	0
50	32	32	0	0	0	32	32	0
51	60	120	0	0	0	60	60	0
52	62	62	0	0	0	62	62	0
53	24	24	0	14	0	10	24	24
54	20	10	10	0	0	5	10	20
55	90	90	0	0	0	90	90	0
56	40	40	20	20	0	20	10	100
58	28	0	20	4	20	0	0	28
59	80	50	50	5	20	30	50	40
60	200	200	100	60	10	140	450	200
61	84	0	0	0	84	0	0	0
62	50	50	0	0	50	0	2	0
63	95	50	55	13	50	37	43	65
64	100	100	0	25	25	20	50	80
65	40	0	10	10	0	0	40	0
66	20	5	20	0	0	0	5	12
68	60	0	25	12	0	4	25	20
69	60	60	0	0	0	60	120	0
70	70	70	70	10	0	20	60	50
71	30	12	30	6	13	6	0	12
72	148	8	92	54	0	0	39	33

Farms.	Wheat.	Barley.	Oats.	Pease.	Beans.	Turnip.	Clover.	Fallow.
No. 73	50	0	20	0	14	6	0	10
74	20	0	10	0	10	0	20	20
75	75	30	45	0	0	6	30	75
76	120	120	20	10	0	40	60	60
77	8	100	100	20	0	50	20	80
78	35	35	35	0	0	0	105	35
79	24	16	18	6	0	6	20	20
80	90	160	60	20	0	5	160	60
81	42	80	10	9	0	0	40	0
83	40	80	20	0	0	30	100	0
84	63	0	16	0	0	0	24	0
85	35	40	40	34	0	40	192	0
86	40	40	40	0	0	0	125	0
87	30	30	30	0	0	0	90	0
89	200	400	300	0	0	300	400	0
90	12	10	0	1	5	0	10	4
91	40	40	15	0	0	15	20	0
92	40	40	0	0	0	20	20	0
93	40	25	16	24	0	30	25	0
Totals	3562	3328	1894	671	534	2180	3733	1359

Servants, &c. on these farms.

Farms.	Serv.	Maids.	Boys.	Lab.
No. 1	8	0	0	6
2	3	1	1	2
5	0	0	1	1
6	1	2	3	12
7	1	1	1	1
8	3	1	1	2
9	2	1	1	1
10	1	0	2	20

376   THE FARMER's TOUR

Farms.	Servan.	Maids.	Boys.	Lab.
No. 11	2	1	1	1
12	3	1	1	3
13	2	2	2	2
14	3	1	1	1
15	2	1	1	0
16	0	2	1	0
17	6	2	6	4
18	3	1	0	2
19	9	2	1	6
20*	3	1	0	1
21	0	1	1	0
22	1	1	2	1
23	1	2	1	1
24	1	2	2	2
25	3	4	4	4
26	1	1	2	2
28	5	0	0	15
29	2	1	0	2
30	3	2	1	3
31	2	1	1	1
32	0	1	1	1
33	2	1	0	2
34	2	1	1	2
35	0	0	0	6
36	2	0	0	6
37	2	0	1	1
38	0	0	1	1
39	1	0	0	0
41	2	2	1	2
43	3	0	1	4
45	4	0	2	2
47	2	2	1	4
48	1	1	1	1

THROUGH ENGLAND.

Farms.	Servan.	Maids.	Boys.	Lab.
No. 49	3	2	3	8
50*	2	0	0	12
52	4	2	1	4
53	1	1	1	3
54	2	2	1	3
56	3	2	2	4
59	6	1	4	9
60	1	0	0	20
61	5	2	1	4
62	5	2	1	4
64	6	0	4	8
65	2	1	1	3
68	2	2	1	6
69	7	2	2	5
70	0	0	0	20
71	0	0	0	5
72	5	2	5	5
73	1	0	0	2
74	1	0	1	1
75	8	3	2	6
76	15	3	5	6
77	8	1	4	3
78	3	2	1	3
79	2	0	1	2
80	3	2	0	10
82	5	2	2	6
83	3	0	1	8
86	3	0	1	8
87	2	2	2	10
89	1	2	1	200
90	1	1	1	1
91	1	1	2	2

Farms.	Servan.	Maids.	Boys.	Lab.
No. 92	0	0	3	8
93	1	0	2	6
Totals,	205	82	103	525

The following is the average farm of these fifty thousand acres.

Total acres *per* farm,	561
Ditto of grass,	*279
Ditto of arable,	237
Ditto of wood,	42
Rent 265*l*. 19*s*. 1*d*.	
Acres of wheat,	49
Ditto of barley,	46
Ditto of oats,	26
Ditto of pease,	9
Ditto of beans,	7
Ditto of turnips, cabbage, potatoes, and carrots,	30
Ditto of clover, &c.	53
Ditto of fallow,	19
Draught cattle,	12
Cows,	13
Fatting beasts,	9
Young cattle,	16
Sheep,	389
Servants,	2¼
Maids,	1
Boys,	1½
Labourers,	7

* The grass comprehends all the waste tracts included in each farm.

Here we see the average farm of more than fifty thousand acres divided into numerous variations, and comprehending all sorts of soils and circumstances. The proportions of each article to the other are as follow.

Rent, 9 *s.* 5 *d. per* acre.

The wood, the thirteenth of the farm, 13 $\frac{15}{41}$.

The wheat, the eleventh, 11 $\frac{22}{41}$.

Ditto the fourth of the arable, 4 $\frac{41}{48}$.

The barley, the twelfth of the farm, 12 $\frac{9}{46}$.

Ditto the fifth of the arable, 5 $\frac{7}{46}$.

The oats, the twenty first of the farm, 21 $\frac{15}{26}$.

Ditto the ninth of the arable, 9 $\frac{3}{26}$.

The pease, the sixty second of the farm, 62 $\frac{1}{5}$.

Ditto the twenty sixth of the arable, 26 $\frac{3}{5}$.

The beans, the eightieth of the farm.

Ditto the thirty third of the arable, 33 $\frac{6}{7}$.

The turnips, the eighteenth of the farm, 18 $\frac{21}{30}$.

Ditto the seventh of the arable, 7 $\frac{27}{30}$.

The clover, the tenth of the farm, 10 $\frac{11}{13}$.

Ditto the fourth of the arable, 4 $\frac{25}{53}$.

The fallow, the twenty ninth of the farm, 29 $\frac{10}{13}$.

Ditto

Ditto the twelfth of the arable, 12 $\frac{9}{13}$.

Draught cattle. Forty six acres, total *per* head. Ditto; of arable nineteen and an half.

Cows. Forty three acres, total *per* head. Ditto; of grafs twenty one and an half.

Fatting beasts. Sixty two acres, total *per* head. Ditto; of grafs thirty one.

Young cattle. Thirty five acres, total *per* head. Ditto; of grafs seventeen and an half.

Sheep. One acre and half, total *per* head ($1\frac{1}{3}\frac{1}{5}\frac{1}{2}$): Ditto; of grafs, one sheep and one third *per* acre.

Men servants. Two hundred and four acres *per* head.

Maids. Five hundred and sixty one *per* head.

Boys. Three hundred and seventy four acres *per* head.

Labourers. Eighty acres a head.

Ditto servants. Fifty six ditto.

Upon this general account, we may observe, that farms are throughout this tract of country large, for so the average one of 561 acres must be esteemed; this however chiefly arises from some enormous

mous ones, particularly in *Dorsetshire*; the proportion of the very great, and smaller ones is worth calculating.

Average of all that reach 1000
    acres, being nine farms,   *A.* 2561
Rent,   -   -   -   *£.* 903
Average of all under,   -   *A.* 342
Rent,   -   -   -   *£.* 195

From which it appears, that those nine vast farms are what principally caused the general average to be so high as 561; and it is observable, that the rent *per* acre of them is much lower than the average of the rest; indeed the largest include a considerable quantity of waste land.

    The proportion of 279 grass to 237 arable is extremely good; the surplus of the former we may suppose to be occasioned by the wastes being included; so that the equality is pretty exact. This is alone a mark of good husbandry; for the miserable farmers, who can scarcely keep out of gaol, are nine tenths of them found on farms consisting all of arable land. Half a farm being grass, is a mark that a tolerable stock of cattle is kept, upon which the ploughed fields much depend for manure.

    The

The same observation is applicable to the article *clover*, which occupies *a fourth* of the arable land; which is upon the whole so excellent a proportion, that I cannot but congratulate the reader on finding this considerable part of the kingdom in so good a management; half the farms grass, and a fourth of their arable under artificial grass, is upon the whole a system, which the most correct idea would correspond with, rather than to be expected really to exist.

Pease,	9
Beans,	7
Turnips, &c.	30
Clover, &c.	53
Fallow,	19
Total,	118

These arable crops with a fallow are all such as clean and ameliorate the lands, if the pulse and turnips are well hoed, as they mostly are. Half the arable being fallow, or fallow crops, is not amiss, for a farm so conducted cannot well be kept in bad order.

The number of draft cattle is moderate; not consistent with the very best husbandry, but at the same time contains no dangerous excess; good management would even make this portion necessary.

The stock of cows, fatting beasts, young cattle, and sheep, seem tolerably adapted to the quantity and value of the land; it cannot be esteemed a bad stock: I found this remark on the rent of the land, and the grass including waste tracts; but I shall not venture to assert, that this article could not be amended; the stock is rather inferior than equal to what it might be in proportion to the crops of the farm, but however has nothing reprehensive in it.

As to the labour, it is better proportioned to the farm than I should previously have expected; very near ten men and a boy and half are tolerably well adapted; not to the ideas of spirited and correct husbandry, but to those of good common management; being sufficient to shew, that the culture of this tract of country, if not excellent, is at least many removes from very bad systems. Considering so much being grass, and some wood,

wood, it is superior to the portion of labour of the average farm of my *Northern Tour*; as indeed this is in almost all respects.

Upon the whole, this average farm shews, that the general system of rural oeconomy is advantageous; no kingdom in these proportions can be badly cultivated. Certain tracts may be much superior, but in these general enquiries, we should rather dwell on what is, than on what might be.

LETTER LVI.

THE sums necessary for stocking farms, according to the custom of those places, where the matter is registered; is an object that must on no account be overlooked, as it will let us almost as much as any other article, into some curious particulars of the state of the nation's agriculture.

I shall divide the sums into six articles: *live stock, labour, implements, furniture, seed, sundries.*

Places.	Farms. Rent	Ac.	Stock. £.	Implements. £.	Furniture. £.	Labour. £.	Seed. £.	Sundries. £.	Total. £.
Hempstead	100								400
Tring	100								425
Blisworth	100		183	88	80	72	20	174	617
Glendon	100								750
Quenby	200								1000
Dishley	150								550
Alfreton	100								300
Radburn	100								400
Tiddswell	100								400
Chesterfield	100								400
Lawton	100		170	72	100	31	20	105	500
Gateford	100	200	507	118	150	97	37	165	1074
Ditto	100								350

Places.	Farms. Rent £.	Ac.	Stock £.	Implem. £.	Furni. £.	Labour £.	Seed £.	Sund. £.	Total £.
Blythe	125	200	225	79	60	86	47	340	837
Ditto	100								300
Broadsworth	60								250
Wembwell	100								500
Bootham	100								400
Carwick		300							550
Swinehead	100								1000
Leverington	300	300	1158	79	100	124	30	210	1898
Rundton	100								400
Snettisham	500								3000
Warham	300	550	865	241	100	132	130	545	2013
Aylsham		300							700
Earsham	100								300
Bracon Ash	100								300
Fleg Hundred	300								1500
South of Eccles	300								3000
Hadleigh	100								500
Halstead	100								400
Colchester	300								2000
Youngsberry	200								1200
Cuddington	300								2000
Feversham	100								300
Beaksburn	200								650
Sheffield Place	100								500
Walberton	400								1500
Northern part Isle Wight	200								1000
Southern Ditto	200								750
Alresford	200								1400
Gilbury	100								500
Critchill	500								2000
Moreton	300		605	132	150	120	91	178	1275
Came	500								3000
Leigh	100								300
Taunton	100								300
Donnington	100								500
Beconsfield	100								300
Averages per 100 l. a year,			273	70	70	56	28	146	540

This account turns out far better than I expected, and shews, that this part of the kingdom is by no means badly stocked; almost five rents and an half being an ample allowance, though not for the best management, yet for very good common husbandry, and is far superior to the same average drawn in my *Northern Tour*. The article *live stock* amounts to a considerable sum, which is ever a sign of good husbandry. *Furniture*, again, equals *implements*, at which I before expressed my surprise; but being found in two such journies to agree, one cannot refuse assent to that proportion; but I continue in thinking, that the latter ought much to exceed it.

The great importance of a farmer stocking his land well, which can be only done by possessing plenty of money, is strongly exemplified in several instances in the minutes of this Tour. In the article, live stock, it is of more especial consequence; Mr. *Bakewell* of *Dishley*'s farm, is a proof of this; and honest *William White*'s, at *Moreton*, another striking proof, that great numbers of cattle are the support of a farm.

LETTER LVII.

TYTHE is an article, which here demands attention: the true state of the kingdom's agriculture cannot be known, unless the compositions for the tenth are discovered, and some idea gained of the proportion between the parts where it is taken in kind, with those in which it is compounded.

Places.	Compounded or Gathered.	Wheat.	Barley.	Oats.	P. & B.	Turnip.	Clover.	Grass.
		s. d.	s. d.	s. d.	s. d.	s. d.		s. d.
Hempstead	Comp.							
Blisworth	3 s. 6 d. per acre							
Hazelbeech	Gathered							
Glendon	4 s. 6 d. per acre							
Quenby	Gathered							
Radburn	Comp.	5 0	5 0	2 6				1 2
Tiddswell	Mostly free							
Chesterfield	Comp.							
Doncaster	Gathered							
Broadsworth	Ditto							
Wombwell	Mostly gathered	5 0	5 0	3 0	3 0			
Bootham	2 s. 6 d. in £.							
Canwick	Comp. inclos. free	5 6	2 6	2 0				
Swinehead	All gathered							
Leverington	Gathered							

THROUGH ENGLAND.

Places.	Compounded or Gathered.	Wheat.	Barley.	Oats.	P.&B.	Turnip.	Clover.	Grass.
		s. d.	s. d.	s. d.	s. d.	s. d.	s. d.	s. d.
Runcton	Comp. 20 d. an acre							
Massingham	Comp.							
Snettisham	4 s. in £.							
Warham	2 s. an acre							
Aylsham	3 s. in £.							
Earlham	Comp.							
Bracon Ash	2 s. 9 d. in £.							
Fleg Hundred	3 s. per acre							
Hadleigh	4 s. per ditto							
Colchester	3 s. 6 d. per £.							
Youngsberry	Comp.	4 6	4 6	2 3		1 6	1 0	
Cheam	Gathered							
Feversham	Ditto							
Beaksburn	Ditto							
Sheffield Place	Comp.							
Walberton	Gathered							
Isle of Wight	3 s. 6 d. in £.							
Alresford	Gathered							
Gilbury	4 s. 6 d. in £.							
Critchill		4 0	4 0	4 0	4 0		2 0	
Came	2 s. 6 d. in £.							
Mapperton	2 s. in £.							
Leigh		4 0	3 0	2 6	2 6			
Donnington	Both; comp. 3 s. an acre							
Harleyford	Gathered							
Beconsfield	Gathered							
Averages,	3 s. 3 d. in the pound, and 3 s. 4 d. per acre	4 8	4 0	2 8	3 2	1 6	1 6	

Twenty-three places compounded; eighteen gathered.

C c 3

LETTER LVIII.

NEXT, you must allow me, Sir, to give a table of the value of the soil at the market price; being the years purchase at which land is sold. This is an object of no slight value in political arithmetic; for the rise of that price at various periods since the beginning of the last century, has been often produced as the grand proof of the great increase in value, which results from an increase of foreign commerce; and to shew how much indebted the landed interest is to trade. The argument was used strongly by *D'Avenant*, and has been repeated ten thousand times since; it is certainly a sensible one, but when adopted by weaker writers, has been pushed like most others too far; for the lands of *England* have risen in value not so much in direct proportion to the progress of our *foreign* commerce, as to the increased quantity of money in *Europe*, which has raised the price of all sorts of commodities, not only in in countries possessing foreign commerce, but also in those which have none; for let intercourse, *home* trade, and other circumstances be at ever so low an ebb, still money will preserve something of that level so ingeniously stated by Mr. *Hume*; and as an instance, that the rise in the value of land in *England* is not wholly owing to foreign commerce, I quote *Poland*, which possesses no foreign commerce, and yet the value of the lands in that country, I am informed on good authority, has risen very considerably in the last 170 years; and this should be sufficient to make those writers, who are ever haranguing on the advantages of commerce, *in opposition* to those resulting from agriculture, with such unguarded vehemence, more cautious in their general assertions. None but a fool or a madman can assert, that an extended commerce will not raise the value of land, but it does not therefore follow, that its effects should take place to the exclusion of all others: all our exported commodities of our own growth and products, such as wool, leather, tin, copper, &c. &c. would without any help from foreign commerce raise the value of land, by bringing a price proportioned to the quantity of money in *Europe*.

Places.	Rent.			Years Purc.	Land-tax, at 4 s. in the pound yields	
	l.	s.	d.		s.	d.
Hempstead	0	10	0	28		
Blisworth	0	12	0	32½		
Hazelbecch	0	17	0	31		
Quenby	0	16	0	32½		
Dishley	0	16	0	30		
Radburn	0	14	0	37½		
Tiddswell	0	16	0	30		
Lawton	0	8	0	35		
Blythe	0	10	0	40		
Doncaster	2	10	0	50		
Broadsworth	0	6	0	36		
Wombwell	0	16	0	40		
Bootham	0	10	0	30		
Canwick	0	7	6	35		
Summer Castle	0	8	0	32½		
Leverington	0	18	0	27½		
Massingham	0	8	0	28		
Warham	0	8	6	27½		
Earlham	0	16	0	27		
Bracon Ash	0	15	0	32		
Fleg Hundred	0	15	0	26½		
Hasteead	0	14	6	30		
Colchester	0	16	0	30		
Youngsberry	0	12	0	30		
Feversham	1	0	0	25		
Beaksburn	0	14	0	31		
Sheffield Place	0	10	0	29		
Walberton	1	0	0	32	1	9
Isle of Wight	0	12	0	31	3	3
Alresford	0	8	0	32		
Gilbury	0	10	6	30	2	0
Lymington					3	6
Critchill	0	10	0		1	3
Moreton	0	12	0	30	2	0
Came	0	11	0	30	1	0

Places.	Rent. l. s. d.	Years Purc.	Land-tax, at 4 s. in the pound yields s. d.
Milton Abbey	0 8 6		2 0
Mapperton	0 16 0		0 9
Henlade	1 0 0	24	1 8
Taunton			2 0
Donnington	0 15 0	30	2 6
Harleyford	0 15 0	30	2 8
Beconsfield	0 13 0	27½	
Averages,		31½	2 0

I have added the land tax, what is really paid in the pound, at a 4 s. cefs, at a few places, where I gained that information.

Thirty one and a half years purchafe is inferior to the average of the countries travelled in the *Northern Tour*; which might have been expected from the hufbandry being better, and the rent higher; when eftates are perfectly cultivated, and let at their full value, they will of courfe fell for fewer years purchafe, than when improvements are poffible or probable; it is wafte tracts that fell the higheft in this kingdom.

LETTER LIX.

MANURING is an article that demands some attention here, but the minutes in this Tour, of the application of various sorts, are so numerous, that it may be difficult to give so clear an idea of each kind, as one could wish; the only method that promises success, is to form a table for each, drawing all the intelligence into one view. The soils that in good husbandry do not require ample improvement of this sort, are so extremely rare, that we may pronounce this article to be one of the most important, if not the first, in husbandry; it is a subject on which the common farmers think in large, very justly; they are all sensible of the great consequence of manures, and if any spirit is exerted on their farms, it is much but this is a principal in it. The great matter in dispute, and a point it is of which we are wonderfully ignorant, is the variations in *manures*, which ought to take place in consequence of variations of *soil*; how far these minutes will throw light on any one article, can only be discovered by examining the several accounts of each, and this I shall attempt in the present letter, beginning with

LIME.

Mr. Booth. The soil a rich red loam.
Quantity. Six quarters.
Use. For turnips of visible use, and also to the barley after.
Quenby. The soil a rich clay.
Quantity. Ten or 12 quarters, at 50 *s.*
Use. It opens and mellows these rich clays greatly.
Duration. It lasts 8 or 9 years.
Dishley. The soil clayey or sandy loams.
Quantity. Ten quarters, at 1 *s.* 4 *d.* a quarter at the pit.
Use. For turnips or wheat, to which it does good; but more to the barley, clover, and wheat.
Alfreton. The soil a hazel loam on a stone bottom.
Use. On cold land for wheat.
Quantity. Two cart loads, at 6 *s.* a load.
Radburn. The soil rich clays.
Quantity. Two to three waggon loads, at

14 s. cost, and 15 s. carriage *per* load; total 3 *l.* 10 s. to 4 *l. per* acre.

Duration. Lasts good 7 or 8 years.

Chatsworth to *Tiddswell.* The soils limestone, and grit stone land; the lime does great service on the latter, but not on the former.

Quantity. Twelve horse-loads for wheat, at 6 d. each, besides carriage.

Tiddswell. The soil a light dry loam, on rocks of limestone or grit-stone.

Use. Improve moors from the ling; the lime without any tillage kills all the spontaneous growth, and brings up a fine growth of white clover, &c. It improves bog if only 2 or 3 feet deep, and lasts 20 years.

Quantity. On land quite covered with ling, 360 bushels *per* acre; on whiter land 160 to 280; the expence 1 d. ½ *per* bushel.

Chesterfield. Hazel loams and some clay.

Quantity. One hundred bushels, at 30 s.

Use. They lay it on for every thing.

Gateford. Sand, clay, and limestone land.

Quantity. A chaldron at 11 s. carriage included.

Use. For turnips they find it of very great use.

Duration. Three or four years.

Colonel St. Leger. Soil; a thin loam on limestone.

Use. Tried it on grafs-land in various quantities; of no use.

Tried lime from *Derbyshire*.
- No. 1. 180 bushels *per* acre, left in heaps, and then spread.
- 2. 180, spread out of the cart.
- 3. 32 Bushels, ditto.
- 4. Slightly dressed with rotten farm-yard dung.

No. 4. yielded half as much again as any; and No. 2. and 3. better than No. 1.

Blythe. The soil sand.

Quantity. A chaldron, at 16 *s.* including expences.

Use. Best when mixed with earth and dung.

Duration. Lasts good 2 years.

Wombwell. The soil a rich sandy loam.

Quantity. Six quarters *per* acre.

Use. Sow it on clover land wheat after it is come up: it kills all poppies and many other weeds; and destroys much twitch.

At *Bootham.* Mr. *Greetham* laid 4 or 5

chaldron an acre on one place; a less quantity in another place; and in a third, mixed dung and lime together. The result was, that the large quantity alone, beat all the rest. It was ten years ago, and he now sees, to a foot, in every crop where the lime was laid. The soil a black sand on gravel.

Canwick. The soil thin loam on limestone. Lime has been tried, but it did little good. They discover the nature of it by dropping it in water; if it is good, it comes out soft and greasy; if bad, it is gritty.

Sir Cecil Wray. The soil a good loamy sand. Half a field dressed with farm-yard compost, and half limed for wheat; sainfoine seed harrowed in in the spring. The half limed better than the other several years, by ¼ a load an acre.

Snettisham. Light sandy loam. Lime from chalk tried; it did good, but not comparable to marle.

Feversham. The soil a rich black loam.
Quantity. 160 Bushels, at 3 $d.$
Duration. Two or three years.

Use. Of very great use both on wet soils, and also on sands.

Witstubble. The soil rich vale sand, and light loam on chalk.

Quantity. 160 bushels.

Use. A great improvement.

Hawkhurst. Soil, clay, and sand.

Quantity. A waggon load an acre, at 1 *l.* 1 *s.* at the kiln.

Duration. Two crops.

Heffel. Soil black peat moor.

Quantity. One, or 1 ½ load an acre. A kiln of 6 loads costs 12 *l.*; generally 40 *s.* or 3 *l.* an acre.

Sheffield Place. Soil chiefly clay.

Quantity. 4 or 5 loads an acre, 30 bushels each, at 10 *s.* besides carriage.

Duration. Lasts 3 crops, wheat, oats, and clover.

Mapperton. Soil a rich loam, or clay.

Quantity. 20 Hogsheads, each 4 bushels, at 20 *d.* a hogshead.

Use. Always mix it with earth; reckoned the best husbandry.

Duration. 4 or 5 years.

Leigh. Soil, clay on gravel.

Quantity. 10 to 20 hogsheads, at 2 *s.* a hogshead.

Use. Mix it with earth.

Duration. Three crops.

Mr. *Clayton.* Tried lime, 80 bushels, in one field, an acre, against dung and woollen rags in another; the latter the greater produce, but the wheat much blighted; whereas the limed not at all.

Mr. *Burke.* Sowed 100 bushels an acre on pasture; the soil a gravelly loam; did no good.

These minutes on the use of lime are extremely various, but they prove some important points which much deserve notice. Relative to soil, we find that it agrees with almost all; not only with those that are rich and fertile, but likewise such as are poor; the sands of *Gateford*, and the forest ones of *Blythe* are such, and yet lime is beneficial, which is owing to its binding these loose soils.

At *Chatsworth* and *Canwick* it fails, the soil a thin loam on limestone.

On old pasture it seems inefficacious from Col. *St. Leger*'s and Mr. *Burke*'s intelligence.

On black moory peat land, the effect universally great.

The greatest effect is in the peak of

Derbyſhire, where it converts waſte ſoils into fine paſtures, without tillage; but the ſort is a ſtrong ſtone lime, and burns ſoft and ſoapy. It is alſo obſervable that the quantity is very great, riſing to 360 buſhels.

The *Wombwell* minutes ſhew, that it has a ſtrong effect in killing weeds.

From the benefit and the duration being ſo much greater in *Derbyſhire* than elſewhere, there is great reaſon to attribute much to *quantity*; in waſte ſoils eſpecially, too much can hardly be laid on, becauſe diſſolving the roots of the ſpontaneous growth require a moſt powerful application. Of their ſtrong ſtone lime, 360 buſhels are probably equal to 5 or 600 of chalk lime: but what are 5 or 6 quarters an acre—no uncommon portion! Experiments on the quantities of lime, proper for given ſoils, are much wanting.

MARLE.

Maſſingham. The ſoil ſand; and light ſandy loam.

Quantity. Seventy loads, uſually; but now 35 or 40, and then as much more in 3 or 4 years.

Duration. Twenty five years.

Mr. *Carr.* Has found that the bad ſorts

of marle effervefce with acids more than the good; but falling quickly in water, and turning it white, is the beft rule to judge by.

Snettifham. The foil a light fandy loam.

Quantity. Eighty loads an acre.

Sort. A fine fat, white marle.

Duration. From 14 to 20 years.

Warham. Soil, a light fandy loam.

Quantity. Sixty loads an acre, at expence of 30*s.*; after 1 5 6 years, 25 or 30 loads more, and then after 10 or 12 years they repeat it again.

Ufe. It lafts 15 or 16 years in perfection: they are convinced, that the benefit of repetitions is very great. Compofts of marle and dung they find excellent; fo that if they would ufe 10 loads an acre of dung, they will not fubftitute more than 12 of that compoft.

Aylfham. The foil a fandy loam.

Quantity. Twelve loads, as much as 5 horfes can draw.

Duration. Lafts 20 years.

Ufe. They always mix their yard dung with marle; the fort is chiefly a grey, foft, and foapy marle.

Earlham. They always form compofts of

of marle and farm yard dung, mixing them well together, and spreading for turnips. This practice they find great use in.

Mr. *Thompson.* Soil a loamy sand; the deeper it is dug he finds it the better; lays 40 to 70 loads an acre, but generally mixes with dung. It destroys weeds almost at once, particularly ketlocks and poppies. They were common in his fields, but have disappeared since the marling.

Fleg Hundred. The soil a rich mixed loam.

Use. They bring it from *Norwich* to *Yarmouth* by water, and then from 4 to 8 miles by land; the whole expence 7*s*. 4*d. per* cart load.

Mr. *Acton.* Light good loam.

Quantity. Fifty to 90 loads of clayey marle, that effervesces strongly in acids.

Use. The greatest effect is clearing the land of weeds.

Colchester. The soil a sandy gravel and brick earth.

Quantity. Seven waggon loads an acre. It comes from *Kent* by shipping.

They give 7s. to 9s. a load for it, and carry it even to 10 miles.

Use. Does the best, and lasts the longest on stiff soils.

Duration. On stiff land 30 or 40 years; on sands and gravels 15.

Youngsberry. Clays, and stoney loams.

Quantity. Twenty loads an acre of chalk.

Duration. Six or 7 years.

Use. It does best on the heavy soils.

Morden. The soil clay, and strong loam.

Quantity. Twelve loads, at 4d. and 3s. 8d. carriage.

Use. Generally mix with dung and earth, call it chalk.

Duration. Six or 7 years.

Cheam. The soil a chalky loam.

Quantity. Twelve loads an acre.

Use. They reckon it does best on strong land; it mellows and makes it *kindlier*.

Duration. Six or 7 years.

Cuddington. The soil clay.

Quantity. Twenty loads.

Use. Not as an enricher, but to make the clay work more mellow.

Carshalton. The soil a light loam on chalk.

Quantity. Thirty loads; the expence 20s.
but

but the farmer finds one horse and two small carts.

Use. It is a hard chalk, that makes the land mellow, and cleans it from weeds; land that bears wild sorril wants chalk.

Duration. Forty years.

Hawkhurst. The soil, sand and clay.

Sort. Red, grey, blue, and yellow; blue they reckon best.

Quantity. Two hundred and fifty or 300 loads an acre, 8 bushels each, 5 *s. per* 100 load digging; four pair of oxen, and a horse and 2 or 3 boys for drivers, 4 carts, each 2 oxen and 1 horse carry 100 loads a day.

Duration. Lasts from 5 to 8 years.

Use. On light sandy soils it brings great crops, but not on wet ones; it binds such so close, that the water cannot get off.

Sheffield Place. Soil chiefly clay.

Quantity. Three hundred loads an acre, each 20 bushels.

Duration. Seven or 8 years.

Walberton. The soil a rich mellow loam.

Quantity. Forty loads, each 30 bushels.

Duration. Twenty years.

Isle of Wight. The soil a sandy loam.

Quantity. Thirty loads, each 40 bushels; 5 miles, price 1 s. carriage 6 s.

Duration. Twelve years.

Use. It is a hard chalk, does best on stiff land.

Isle of Wight. Some of their lands always the better for it.

Ditto. Soil a stoney loam.

Quantity. Fourteen to 20 waggon loads an acre, as much as 5 or 6 horses can draw, which is 3 tons: 3 d. cost 5 s. carriage.

Duration. Forty or 50 years.

Gilbury. The soil a heavy loam on gravel.

Use. They think that both chalk and clayey marle will be attended with no effect, if laid on land that has before been under chalked, until the first quantity is quite worn out. A farmer supposed marle to enrich land more than chalk, (N. B. the chalk is marle) but he preferred chalked land, because it might be worked on all occasions, and with less strength; marle land, if at all clayey, becoming mortar with a little wet, and brick with a little sun.

Milbourn. Soil a light loam on chalk.

Quantity. Eighty loads, each a ton.
Duration. Twenty years.
Use. On new broken up land, kills the roots of the furz, and could get no crops on it without it.
Beconsfield. Soils various, clays and loams.
Quantity. Fifteen to 20 loads.
Use. Mellows and makes it plough the better; and after grubbing up a wood, the land muſt be chalked to ſweeten it.

In theſe minutes I have found it neceſſary to rank what is called *chalk* under the head marle, becauſe I found on trial all their chalks to be real marle, and ſome of them remarkably ſtrong.

It appears very evidently that marle agrees with both ſtiff and light ſoils; the great ſucceſs attending it in *Norfolk*, ſhews how well it anſwers on very light ſandy loams, and on ſands: but numerous minutes, where it is tried on both heavy and light land, prove it beſt on the former: this is the caſe at *Colcheſter*, *Youngsberry*, *Cheam*, and the *Iſle of Wight*; and at theſe and others they remark a ſtrong effect in its *mellowing* the land, and making it *work* better; by which we are to underſtand, that it renders wet lands drier, and stiff ones more friable; so that both may be ploughed earlier in the spring, and one earth have the effect in pulverization of several. It also appears to clean the soil of weeds; but from whence this effect arises is difficult to conjecture, as it possesses, on comparison with lime, a very weak dissolvent quality.

A question not clearly understood in relation to this manure, is its enriching quality. Is it a fertilizer, or possessed of no other effect than giving tenacity to sand, and friability to clay? I think, from the experience of various *poor* sands marled in *Norfolk*, that it is a great fertilizer: it is difficult to comprehend how mere adhesion of parts, naturally poor, can produce such great crops: but the virtues of marle are not to be known by the common trials: Mr. *Carr*'s experiments, which shew that marle with the greatest effervescence with acids, is oftentimes the worst, are strongly to the point: and I have several times found a great effervescence in some sorts, not much esteemed by the farmers: let me further add, that *falling in water, effervescing in acids, effervescing in water, and*

destroying

deſtroying the acidity of vinegar, are all diſtinct qualities; marle poſſeſſing one, is no proof that it has the other. I have ſome ſorts now by me, which effervesce ſtrongly with acids; but will not fall in water: others that *effervesce*, but not *fall* in water: and mere clay, which in ſome parts of *Norfolk* is preferred to marle, has none of theſe qualities.

The duration of the effect appears in theſe minutes to depend much on quantity; on ſand in *Norfolk* it laſts twice as long as on loams in *Surry*, &c. That the ſame quantity will laſt on a ſtiff ſoil longer than a looſe one, may eaſily be conceived; and is plainly the caſe in ſeveral places. It is well known, that a dreſſing of yard dung laſts the longeſt on a ſtiff true tile clay.

The expence, at which marle is gained in ſome places, is aſtoniſhing. About *Yarmouth*, in *Norfolk*, they uſe it at 7*s*. 4*d*. a cart load. About *Colcheſter*, &c. they have it from *Kent*, it coſts them at the heap 7*s*. to 9*s*. a waggon load, and they carry it ſo far as 10 miles: this is prodigious! ſeven waggon loads an acre. Farmers, who practiſe this in common, would never do it if it was not a fertilizer.

The practice at *Warham* shews evidently the benefit of repetitions; experience has carried them to the third time, with advantage.

I have not met with any trials of the efficacy of regaining it, when subsided by ploughing deeper. That the marle does not lose its common qualities, I know from trying some ploughed up 16 inches deep in a field of Mr. *Arbuthnot*'s, at *Morden*; it effervesced in vinegar, and also in water; but did not fall in the latter. Benefit would probably arise from it, but the new quantity of staple gained would require a proportionate quantity of marle, according to the reasoning used in the latter on deep ploughing; and also proportionate additions of other manure; so that it is to be questioned, whether deep ploughing would ever be adviseable on this account *only*.

CRAG.

Woodbridge. The soil all sand.

Quantity. Ten or 12 loads; it is a body of powdered shells, but has no effervescence with acids; nor does it dissolve in water.

Use. It enriches the soil far more than any marle; lasts for ever; but they renew
it

it by forming composts of crag and yard dung.

This manure is of a very extraordinary nature: it is a shell marle, consisting of nothing but shells, whole, or powdered; the colours red and white; it is dry, not being the least soapy; it has not any effervescence in acids; and does not fall in water, from all which circumstances its virtues might be doubted; but all those effects produced in *Norfolk* by 60, 80, or 100 loads of their marle, are gained in *Suffolk* by 10 or 12 of this; and the effect is, I think, much stronger: respecting duration, crag lasts much longer, which they have discovered from an idea (a false one I suppose) that land once cragged will not bear any other repetitions than those of composts with dung; and accordingly they have many fields, in which it has lasted with only such additions, 50, 60, and to 100 years. With crag, the nature of the poor sands in that country are quite changed, and gain an adhesion, which they retain, as the farmers there say, for ever: it is also a very great fertilizer, as appears from the great and sudden increase in the crops after it.

CLAY.

Colonel Coney. The soil a sandy loam.

Quantity. Eighty loads an acre, at 2 *l.* 10 *s.* expences.

Use. Sown first with turnips, 2 *l.* 12 *s.* 6 *d.* an acre, wheat 4½ quarters, turnips, 40 *s.* barley 5 quarters; answers greatly.

Burnham to Wells. The soil a light sandy loam.

Quantity. Eighty loads an acre; they value clay more than marle.

Duration. Fourteen years, then they add a little more.

Fleg Hundred. The soil a rich light mixed loam.

Quantity. Forty loads.

Duration. Twenty years.

From these minutes we find, that clay is justly held in estimation in a country that understands, and has experienced, marle more than most in the kingdom: it is preferred to marle, where both are to be had. This gives no slight reason to suppose, there is something in Mr. *Carr*'s assertion, that his best marles are not those, whose effervescence with acids is the strongest; and confirms one in the idea, that chemists
are

are not the people to go to for the true practical knowledge of manures.

SEA OUZE.

Sir *John Turner.* Uses it instead of marle, and finds it to answer better: the soil a light sandy loam.

Sampford Hundred in Suffolk. Form composts of it with farm yard dung, which they mix well, and spread on clover land for wheat.

Sea ouze is to be had in very many places that totally slight the acquisition: I remarked large quantities quite blue with rotten weed at *Gilbury,* but none used. The effect at *Warham* on old marled lands, which wanted a renewal, is very great, and so much beyond laying on fresh quantities of marle, that Sir *John Turner's* tenant carries it from a distance to fields, in which are excellent marle pits; the land acquires a new fertility, equal, if not exceeding that of the first marling.

In *Sampford* hundred they are also such excellent husbandmen, that a practice common among them of this sort, must be good; they find infinite advantage from forming composts of sea ouze and their farm yard dung, under the expence of *double* carting both.

SEA WEED.

Minster, in the *Isle of Thanet*. They mix it with dung and earth till it is rotten, and lay 50 loads an acre; reckon it a very rich manure; never use it alone.

Isle of Wight. They bring it into their farm yards, and mix it with dung to carry on to their bean lands; without mixing, they say it won't do.

The same observation on the neglect of manures in so many farmers is applicable here also. This weed, which is so valuable in the *Isle of Thanet*, and which even the *Isle of Wight* men, their next neighbours, practise, the farmers at *Gilbury* insist will never rot; and nine tenths of the other farmers on the sea coasts of *England*, utterly neglect. But sea weed is an excellent manure, and cannot be prized too highly. The practice of both the islands appears to be excellent, for overcoming its resistance of putrefaction; making litter of it in the farm yard must be quite effectual in that respect, and at the same time produce a most rich compost.

BURNT CLAY.

Mr. *Bevor*. A hard strong clay, burnt; but calcined almost to bricks, which were broken and spread; the benefit very little.

Mr. *Turner*. Burns refuse earth, turfed, to ashes, for which he gives 1s. the 40 bushels; lays 20 loads an acre, chiefly on to clover and grass; the dressing lasts good 6 years.

There is no contradiction in these two articles; the first burns mere clay; but the latter only the surface of waste, refuse spots that have gained something of a turf, consequently the ashes are partly vegetable ones: and I shall remark that Mr. *Turner*'s practice is in many situations an excellent one; converting waste spots, which would be difficult to improve, into opportunities of gaining large quantities of excellent manure. As to burning clay, we much want experiments to ascertain the effect; hitherto the world has received little more than assertions and conjectures.

TOWN MANURE.

Blisworth. Can have it at 2s. at *Northampton*, 5 miles, but will not.

Gateford. From *Workfop*, at 2s. 6d. to 3s. 12 to the acre, last 3 crops.

Warham. Buy at *Wells* at 1 s. Sir *John Turner* remembers all that dung thrown into the harbour of *Wells*, which now brings 8 quarters of corn an acre in the inclosures around the town.

Earlham. *Norwich* manures at 1 s. and find they answer greatly.

Bracon Ash. They bring manures from *Norwich*, though 7, 8, and 10 miles distant.

Fleg Hundred. Buy at *Yarmouth* at 2 s.

Colchester. Much sold from this place at 5 s. a waggon load; they lay 7 or 8 on an acre.

Cheam. Bring it from *London*, at 2 s. and 10 s. carriage, as much as 4 horses can draw; lay 8 loads an acre.

Cuddington. From *London* lay 10 loads an acre at 7 s. a load, carriage included.

Chichester. Manure sells at 4 s. or 5 s. a load.

Isle of Wight. From *Portsmouth* at 3 s. a cart load, *freight* and cost.

Gilbury. From *Portsmouth* by shipping, 2 s. a load, and 1 s. freight. From *Southampton* 2 s. and 1 s. 6 d. freight. Lay 30 loads an acre; which last 8 years.

The value of town manure, which in general confifts of all forts of dungs, mixed with the fweepings of houfes, the fullage of ftreets, and afhes, is well underftood in moft places. The farmers have not always a juft notion how many miles it will anfwer to go for it; but near moft towns it is bought by fome in the neighbourhood. Around *London* they are at a very confiderable expence to get it, and with reafon, for the value of it is great; it is an improvement on the farm yard compoft, being compofed of richer materials, and at the fame time not fo expenfive as to make it neceffary to ufe it as a top dreffing.

PARING and BURNING.

Quenby. The foil a rich clay.

Ufe. Break up old grafs; the turnips they fow on it always great; alfo the barley, and then the oats.

Expence. 1 *l.* 4 *s.*

Difhley. The foil clayey, and fandy loams.

Ufe. On cold land for turnips.

Expence. 1 *l.* 1 *s.*

Alfreton. The foil a hazel loam, on a ftone bottom.

Ufe. For turnips or wheat, and fure of a great crop of either.

Expence. 19 *s.*

Tiddſwell. The ſoil thin loams, on lime and grit-ſtone.

Expence. 1 *l.*

Lawton. The ſoil thin loam, on lime and grit-ſtone.

Uſe. Sow either turnips or wheat after it. No manure exceeds it.

Expence. 18 *s.* 6 *d.*

Colonel St. Leger. His ſoil a thin loam on lime ſtone.

Uſe. Has practiſed it with the utmoſt ſucceſs for ſeveral years; has been practiſed regularly for many ages on lime ſtone ſoils in the neighbourhood, not 4 inches thick: He is very clear, that it does not in the leaſt diminiſh the ſtaple of the ſoil.

Wombwell. The ſoil a rich ſandy loam; reckoned a fine improvement.

Expence. 17 *s.*

Canwick. The ſoil a thin loam on lime ſtone.

Uſe. Pare old heath land for turnips, which enſures great crops.

Expence. 1 *l.* 1 *s.*

Alresford. Thin loam on chalk.

Expence. 1 *l.* 1 *s.*

Uſe. For breaking up old ſainfoine.

Paring and burning ſhould certainly be ranked as a manure; for it is one of the richeſt kinds. In theſe minutes it appears to great advantage, as indeed it alſo does in every part of the kingdom where uſed. But as of late years ſome people have entertained ideas very contrary to it, ſome explanation is neceſſary.

In the firſt volume, this miſtake is enquired into, under Col. *St. Leger*'s article; that gentleman very juſtly remarked, that the reaſon the practice was condemned, was the farmers, on the credit of a paring, taking ſo many ſucceſſive crops as to exhauſt the ſoil; but he found uniformly from his own practice, that it does not in the leaſt diminiſh the ſurface.

It is aſtoniſhing, how gentlemen can argue againſt this practice, from its leſſening the ſtaple, when they muſt know, that in ſeveral counties land not four inches thick has, in the memory of old men, been burnt four or five times, and the huſbandry common on it for ages. The truth is, you burn not the ſoil, but the vegetables in it, and in diminiſhing the ſtaple, reduce only thoſe, which would be the caſe was the ſoil ploughed without it. The queſtion therefore

therefore is, shall I *burn* or *rot* the vegetable matter? That it is nothing more, appears from the impossibility of paring and burning land before it has got a complete turf. The power of the ashes forces such great succeeding crops, that a new turf, when laid to grafs, is sure to be gained soon, provided, as before remarked, the farmer does not run out the land.

The value of the manuring may be guessed from the ashes, which generally amount to 5 or 600 bushels an acre; what dressing of other ashes can be given in such quantities? 500 of wood ashes at 6 *d.* are 12 *l.* 10 *s.* of coal ashes at 3 *d.*—6 *l.* 5 *s.* whereas the expence of these is not a sixth.

	£	s.	d.
At *Quenby*, –	1	4	0
Disbley, – –	1	1	0
Alfreton, – –	0	19	0
Tiddfwell, – –	1	0	0
Lawton, – –	0	18	6
Wombwell, – –	0	17	0
Canwick, – –	1	1	0
Alresford, –	1	1	0
Average,	£ 1	0	2

COAL ASHES.

Tring. Soil, loams stoney and on chalk; sown over clover in *March*.

Quantity. Twenty bushels.

Sir *Cecil Wray.* The soil a loam on lime stone.

Use. Tried for two years on sainfoine, but did not the least good.

Youngsberry. Clays, and stoney loams.

Quantity. Twenty bushels an acre.

Use. Chiefly on clover, and find the improvement great.

David Barclay. Soil, a good brick earth loam.

Quantity. 160 bushels, at 3 *d.* ½, expence inclusive, an acre, were compared on grass land with 16 loads an acre of rotten dung. Before the manuring, the product half a load hay an acre; the ashed part, 1 ¼, and the dunged ¼; much white clover in the former, none in the latter.

Mr. *Clayton.* Soil, clay, and loams.

Quantity. Twelve to 20 bushels, at 6 *d.*

Use. The effect very great on clover and sainfoine; on the latter better than peat ashes.

Beconsfield. Various clays and loams.

Quantity. Forty bushels. 6 *s.* for 50, and 14 *s.* carriage.

Use. Sow them on clover, and answer better than any other manure.

The soils, on which these ashes have been tried, are so various (mere sands excepted) that they do not seem to be a manure peculiar to any in particular. The quantities *per* acre vary much.

	Bushels.	Prices.
Tring,	20	
Youngsberry,	20	
David Barclay,	160	3½ *d.*
Mr. *Clayton,*	16	6
Beconsfield,	40	5

Much the greatest effect is at *David Barclay*'s, who uses by far the greatest quantity. May we not from hence conclude, that these ashes are generally used in too small quantities? I viewed *David Barclay*'s grass, and can testify that the superiority, to 16 loads of rotten dung more than a year after the manuring, is extremely great; the one a good verdure for the season, the other, comparatively stubble. The soil a rich brick earth loam.

It is remarkable, that with Sir *Cecil Wray* they were of no service to sainfoine, a crop they are so generally used for, and on which so small a quantity as 16 bushels, with Mr. *Clayton*, have superior effects to peat ashes.

Clover, sainfoine, and natural grafs, are the only crops they are used for.

WOOD ASHES.

Mr. *Arbuthnot*, tried them on various arable fields, 25 bushels at 3 *d. per* acre, without any effect. On grafs their use great.

The distinction here made between grafs and arable land, should always be remembered; for the use of a manure being with the same person great in one case, and trivial in the other, is decisive of their effect; we may from these trials conjecture, that wood and coal ashes should be applied for the same purpose.

SOOT.

Hampstead. The soil loams, stoney, &c.
Use. Sown over wheat in *March.*
Quantity. Thirty or forty bushels.
Tring. Sown over wheat in *March.*
Quantity. Twenty bushels.

Earlham.
Soil. A loamy sand.
Quantity. Thirty bushels, at 6 *d.*
Use. Lay it on grafs land, and also on wheat in spring. It does great service

for one crop, and sometimes for the succeeding one.

About *Colchester*. Much sown on their pastures, at 6 *d.* a bushel.

Mr. *Arbuthnot*.

Quantity. Thirty bushels an acre, at 7 *d.* and 1 *d.* sowing, besides carriage.

Use. Excellent on grass land, and on wheat if sown early in *February*. Compared with coal ashes 40 bushels of each; at first the soot made the greatest appearance; but no difference in the crop of hay.

Cheam. The soil a chalky loam.

Quantity. Twenty bushels an acre, at 6 *d.*

Use. On sainfoine and clover.

Newbury. Soils various.

Quantity. Twelve bushels, at 8 *d.*

Use. Sow it on the green wheat in the spring.

Beconsfield. Various clays and loams.

Quantity. Thirty or forty bushels, at 5 *d.* or 6 *d.*

Use. Sow it on the wheat in *March*; it forces straw much, but apt to cause the blight.

From these particulars it appears, that soot is used to much advantage on arable as well as grafs: the only application mentioned, however, is the fowing it on wheat in the fpring; a ufe that may be determined advantageous to the wheat crop, but not to thofe which follow. On clover and graffes the application is alfo common.

The following are the quantities.

	Bufh.	Price. d.
Hempftead, - -	35	
Tring, - -	20	
Earlham, - -	30	6
Mr. *Arbuthnot,* -	30	7
Cheam, - -	20	6
Newbury, - -	12	8
Beconsfield, - -	35	6
Average, - -	26	6½

Thefe quantities appear to be very fmall; too trifling to have any but a flight effect on the firft crop; thefe minutes do not give one a great idea of its virtues, which I apprehend to be totally owing to the quantities being too fmall. Coal afhes, with Mr. *Arbuthnot,* equalled foot, which is remarkable.

It is not worth while to manure at a lefs expence than 40 *s.* an acre, and in feveral parts of *England,* where they are excellent farmers,

farmers, that is the price of dressing with purchased dung; not thinking a less quantity effectual: The advantage is, that such a manuring lasts 3 or 4 years; whereas 10 s. or 20 s. in a top dressing, scarcely ever lasts more than one crop.

PEAT ASHES.

Cheam. Soil a chalky loam.
Quantity. 16 Bushels, at 6 d. and bring it 12 miles; reckon it better than soot.
Hungerford.
Quantity. 10 to 20 bushels, at 5 d. or 6 d.
Use. Chiefly on clover, and does some good to the following wheat; sometimes on green wheat in the spring.
Newbury. Soils various.
Quantity. 10 Bushels, at 6 d.
Use. Only on clover in *March:* the red ash the best.
Duration. Only the clover crop, but that is encreased by it, as 3 to 2.
Mr. *Clayton.* Soil, clay and loams.
Quantity. 10 Bushels.
Use. Sows it on clover, which doubles its produce.

The effects here mentioned of peat ashes, are very astonishing; so small a quantity as 10 bushels

10 bushels doubling the product of clover, or increasing it even as 3 to 2, are such powerful effects, that I can only express my wonder at them: the expence of 5 *s.* an acre in manure, to be attended with such surprizing advantages, is a degree of profit not equalled in any other method I ever heard of, and determines me, at *North Mims,* about 30 miles from *Marlow,* (the neareſt place on the *Thames* at which I can have theſe aſhes) to ſend my waggon thither next ſeaſon for a load, by which means I ſhall have it in my power to try the effects of them on theſe ſoils; they will at that expence, be much cheaper than coal-aſhes from *London,* as I can bring 100 buſhels at a time, or enough for 10 acres of land.

It ſeems very remiſs in farmers not to ſearch for ſo valuable a commodity as peat in all their low grounds, eſpecially bottoms between ſteep hills; or in flat meadows on the banks of rivers.

SOAP ASHES.

Colonel *St. Leger.* Spread 40 buſhels *per* acre on grafs on limeſtone clay; 1 *l.* 1 *s.* 6 *d.* expence; of not the leaſt uſe. Harrowed in with barley; juſt viſible.

—60 bushels an acre with turnips; the effect good.

Mr. *Bevor.* Uses them on grass-land with such success, 20 loads an acre, that land let at 5 *s.* was advanced to a guinea by them.

Mr. *Poole.* Soil, good loam.

Quantity. 4 loads an acre, 32 bushels each, at 3 *d.*—1 load an acre in drills, with hopper.

Use. Prefers them to all other manures for turnips.

Soap ashes possessing much fertility, is a fact that is here sufficiently proved, and yet it is very contrary to any idea one could form of them in theory. To preserve the salts of ashes, we are justly directed to keep them quite dry; but in the soap-boiler's hands they are so washed, that if water can carry their salts off, they should be left worthless; but the fact speaks against such reasoning, for in Mr. *Bevor*'s trials, the advantages attending their use, equal those of the finest manures; and both Colonel *St. Leger* and Mr. *Poole* find them excellent for turnips. It is however observable, that the quantities used are much larger than of any dry ashes.

	Bushels.
Colonel *St. Leger*, -	60
Mr. *Bevor*, (at 30 bushels a load)	600
Mr. *Poole*, - - -	128

And their proving successful when laid on in great quantities, is a confirmation of my former reasoning, that the manure being laid on in great bulk, is, singly, a matter of consequence.

MALT DUST.

Warham. Sow it on their barley lands, at 3 *d.* a bushel.

Earlham. Soil, a loamy sand.

Quantity. 40 Bushels an acre, at 4 *d.*

Use. Sow it on wheat in the spring.

Flegg Hundred. The soil a light rich mixed loam.

Quantity. Four quarters an acre.

Use. Sow it on clover, and find great benefit.

Youngsberry. The soil clay or stoney loam.

Quantity. Three or 4 quarters *per* acre, at 7 *s.* or 8 *s.* a quarter.

David Barclay.

Quantity. Four quarters, at 7 *s.* for barley; and answered well.

Mr. *Arbuthnot.* 50 Bushels an acre, tried on arable, against 20 sacks of coal-ashes, and turned out much superior.

Beconsfield. Various clays and loams.
Quantity. Thirty bushels, at 5 *d.*
Use. For turnips.

These accounts of malt-dust are all favourable; but it is a manure rather confined in its use, being difficult to get, and the price seems very great.

	Bush.	Price *a.*
Earlham,	40	4
Flegg Hundred,	32	
Youngsberry,	28	11
David Barclay,	32	10½
Mr. *Arbuthnot,*	50	
Beconsfield,	30	5
Average,	35	

The price near *London* is owing to their being used as food for cows. Suppose the price 6 *d.*; 40 *s.* would then buy 80 bushels; a quantity I should apprehend, that would be attended with very beneficial effects. By Mr. *Arbuthnot*'s trial they are plainly superior to coal ashes.

SALT.

Snettisham. The soil good loamy land.
Quantity. A ton, at 3 *l.* 5 *s.* and 10 *s.* expences, to three acres.

Use. Tried for wheat, and promised so greatly, that the farmers have bought some ship loads.

Mr. *Pett*, of the *Isle of Thanet*. Tried it, one bushel to 10 perches, against coal-ashes, 40 bushels an acre: the ashes beat the salt greatly, which, however, did some good to the barley, but destroyed the clover.

The quantities here used are extremely various; the *Norfolk* ton may be called about 30 bushels, but Mr. *Pett*'s is only 16, and yet that quantity destroyed his clover; 40 bushels of coal ashes exceeding the salt, and at the same time being beyond comparison cheaper, is decisive against it. The trials in *Norfolk* are yet in their infancy, and not at all explicit; but on sand in a very dry season, the salt might be of service, by attracting moisture from the atmosphere. Experiments to decide the merit of salt are much wanting; in those I formed in *Suffolk* it was uniformly unsuccessful, and often did mischief.

O I L.

James Stovin, Esq. On a rich sandy soil. One acre manured with 12 loads rotten dung, at 3*l.* 12*s.*; one ditto with

Dr.

Dr. *Hunter*'s oil compost, 15 s. 6 d.; all circumstances similar; sown with barley.

	Q.	B.	P.
The first produced,	5	5	0
The second,	4	3	2
Superiority,	1	1	2
At 20 s.	£.1	3	9
Saving in manure,	2	16	6
Superiority,	4	0	3

Second year sown with rye; the dunged half much the best.

This experiment is one of the most astonishing I remember to have heard. The oil compost does no slight honour to the worthy author of the *Georgical Essays*; but that so small a portion should exceed 12 loads of rotten dung, I must own, surpasses one's comprehension; as to its declining the second crop, it is not a matter of surprize. This manure calls for numerous trials to decide its merit, for it bids fair much to exceed all other top dressings.

That uncommon virtue is in oil, we see clearly from the great effect of all oleaginous manures, such as oil-cake, and the dung

dung of beasts fattened with oil-cake, rotten dungs, &c. and it certainly deserves no slight attention to examine, if the oil itself cannot be used with success; rendering it miscible with water appears to answer the end at once. I shall try some small experiments on oil, in various shapes, this spring, on my soils, which may enable me to discover how far it is valuable.

OIL-CAKE.

Mr. *Carr*. His soil a light sandy loam; tried 140 *l*.'s worth, but received very little benefit; then tried fatting beasts with it, and the dung proved excellent.

Snettisham. Light sandy loam.

Quantity. One ton, at 3 *l*. 10 *s*. to 4 *l*. 10 *s*. does 3 acres, broke in pieces no larger than walnuts, by mills.

Use. Attended with very great benefit.

Duration. Lasts only one crop.

Burnham to *Wells.* The soil a light sandy loam.

Quantity. Half a ton.

Warham. Soil a light sandy loam.

Quantity. A ton and ¼, at 3 *l*. 3 *s*. to 4 *l*. a ton, will do 3 acres; brought from *Ireland* and *Holland*, but the *Dutch* cakes the beſt, from their not preſſing them ſo much.

Uſe. For wheat; but laſts ſtrong only for one crop, but a help to the following turnips.

David Barclay. Clayey ſoil.

Quantity. Two quarters of rape oil-cake duſt, at 15 *s.* a quarter.

Uſe. Sown on barley; the effect remarkably great; 5 quarters of barley an acre, which is more than ever known on the land.

These trials, except Mr. *Carr*'s, are ſtrong in favour of the manure; his experiment muſt therefore have been an exception owing to a peculiar ſeaſon; the other minutes ſhew the effect to be ſo great, that the benefit is deciſive, and I ſhould remark, that it confirms the theory which gave birth to the oil compoſt.

BONE-DUST.

Colonel *St. Leger.* Spread 35 buſhels *per* acre on a limeſtone clay, at 11 *d.* a buſhel; much inferior to yard dung at ſame expence.

Part of an arable field manured with a compoſt of bone-duſt and horn-ſhavings, 40 buſhels *per* acre, at 11 *d.*; the other part 12 loads

12 loads yard dung. The latter fuperior the firft crop; the former, the fecond.

Although thefe trials are not decifive, the one being rather in contradiction to the other, yet they feem to prove bone-duft a good manure; I need not remark that it is an oily one.—The price is however high. The duft, I apprehend, muft be much more advantageous than large bones themfelves, as ufed in *Hertfordſhire*.

CUTLERS BONES.

Colonel *St. Leger*. Spread on a limeftone clay, 35 bufhels, at 11 d.; the effect quite imperceptible.

The obfervation on bone-duft is here confirmed; 35 bufhels an acre proving ufelefs, fhew, that they fhould be reduced to duft before they are fpread.

HARTSHORN SHAVINGS.

Colonel *St. Leger*. Spread on a limeftone clay, 35 bufhels, at 11 d. inferior to dung at the fame expence.

TANNERS BARK.

Rev. Mr. *Hall*. His foil cold and fpringy. 100 loads four years old, mixed with fome yard dung and lime, turned once, and when rotten, fpread on 8 acres wheat.

wheat. It much ameliorated the land, and prevented a too great adhesion. Mr. *Hall* thinks the virtues of the bark small; better for *opening* than enriching.

The bark being mixed with dung and lime in this experiment, we cannot decide how much of the benefit is to be attributed to it, but in all probability Mr. *Hall*'s observation is just, that the virtue of the bark is rather that of mellowing the land, than fertilizing it. I have tried it on grass-land alone without the least effect.

WOOLLEN RAGS.

Newbury. Use them with success; are very serviceable *to their lighter lands.*

Mr. *Clayton.* Finds them more beneficial on wet cold land, than on hot dry soils.

Woollen rags are a manure commonly used around *London*; but the farmers lay them in too promiscuous a manner on all soils, and are of very different opinions as to the land most proper. The two minutes here inserted, are in direct opposition: we want to be accurately informed, by minute comparative experiments made in the same season, of the benefit resulting from rags on various soils. Those who urge that they

they are proper only on wet foils, offer, for a reafon, the quality of keeping the land open; the bits of rags preventing a great adhefion. They affert that clay land will never *bind*, however unfavourable the feafon may be. On the contrary, the advocates for fpreading them on a dry fandy foil, quote the ftrong attraction of moifture known in woollen rags; which, fay they, muft be highly beneficial for fands and other dry foils; but muft, in the fame proportion, be pernicious in clays. When reafons are in this manner offered on both fides the queftion; the beft way is to give credit to neither, but reft the point totally on experiments; unfortunately fuch are wanting.

SHEEPS TROTTERS.

David Barclay. His foil a ftoney loam.

Quantity. Six quarters an acre of them, at 7 *s.*; 2 *l.* 11 *s.* with carriage; tried againft 10 quarters of rabbit dung, at 2 *s.*; 1 *l.* 10 *s.* with carriage, and alfo the fold.

Products.	*Bufh.*
Trotters,	25
Fold,	20
Rabbit dung,	15

Mr. *Arbuthnot*. Soils ſtrong and light loam.
Quantity. Five quarters, at 9 *s.* beſides carriage.
Uſe. For wheat, and alſo madder: they were not attended by any advantage, which he attributes to their going through the glue-makers hands.
Cheam. The ſoil a chalky loam.
Quantity. Three quarters an acre, at 8 *s.*
Uſe. Sow them with wheat ſeed; but do not think them ſo good as the ſame value in dung.
Cuddington. Soil a hazel loam on chalk.
Quantity. Eight quarters, at 6 *s.*
Duration. Two crops.

Trotters do not make any great figure in theſe minutes, proportioned to their price; Even with Mr. *Barclay*, rabbits dung and the fold are, at leaſt, equal to them, expence conſidered; and the idea common, at the other places, of yard dung being ſuperior, gives us no reaſon to recommend them as a manure, where other ſorts are to be had.

BUCK-WHEAT.

Mr. *Bevor*, Has ſown it on ſtrong land as a preparation for wheat. Part fed with

with cattle, and what remained, ploughed in the end of *July*; the wheat 5 quarters an acre.

Mr. *Sturt*, Tried it as a preparation for wheat, and beat all others.

The use of this crop, as a manure, depends wholly on the soil; first, in getting a great bulk of it, and then in its opening quality of making the soil loose, hollow, and puffy; an effect very desirable in those whose faults is their adhesion; but on others, such as sand, that wants adhesion, it cannot be proper; yet herein I speak from reason alone.

RABBITS DUNG.

Mr. *Arbuthnot.* Clay, and strong loams.
Quantity. Twenty-five sacks, at 1 *s.* 2 *d.*
Use. Sows it over the green wheat in March; the advantage very great.
Beconsfield. Various clays and loams.
Use. Sow it for turnips, and is better than malt-dust.

Rabbit dung can only be had near great cities; the use of it, therefore, is confined. I believe it is a very just maxim in husbandry, that all dungs are excellent manures; they are of that mucilaginous oily nature, that universally agrees with every kind of land. We are often in doubt about other sorts of dressing—lime, salt, malt-dust, ashes, &c. these are not always beneficial; but the case is very different with dungs. As to rabbit dung, if laid on in sufficient quantities, there can be no doubt of its excellence; 25 sacks are a much better dressing than ever given of pigeons; but why not lay it on at the expence of 3*l*. an acre, which would bestow *a quantity* to the soil, approaching town manures and yard dung; the duration, as well as the immediate effect, would, in all probability, be answerable.

POULTRY DUNG.

Mr. *Arbuthnot*. Soil, a clayey loam.

Compared with rabbits dung and wood-ashes, in *November* on wheat, 18 sacks an acre of each. It much exceeded the others; then the rabbit dung; the ashes worst.

PIGEON'S DUNG.

Mr. *Booth*. The soil a rich red loam.
Quantity. Two cart loads.
Application. Sown on poor wheat in the spring; it is very strong, but lasts only 2 crops.
Quenby. The soil a rich clay.

Use. With draining it completely kills rushes.

Lawton. The soil, loam on lime and gritstone, spread on their barley lands.

Quantity. Three quarters, at 8 s. a quarter.

Wombwell. The soil a rich sandy loam.

Quantity. From 3 to 5 quarters, at 8 s. a quarter; they reckon 5 equal to any common dressing of dung in a wet season.

Use. For wheat or turnips.

Youngsberry. The soil clay or stoney loam.

Quantity. Twenty bushels an acre.

Use. On barley, and they find that it beats all other manures.

Mr. *Burke* tried pigeons dung, rabbit dung, and yard dung, in quantities proportioned to their price: the pigeons dung best—next the rabbit—then the yard.

These particulars are, upon the whole, very satisfactory. Pigeons dung evidently appears an excellent dressing, and at an expence not great. The *Wombwell* intelligence, that 40 bushels are equal to any common dressing of dung, is particularly to the point. Mr. *Burke*'s comparison, and the *Youngsberry* article speak the same: one observation I shall make, is the advantage

age of this dung *always* being kept in the proper manner; that is, collecting in a close house, unexposed to the sun, air, winds, or rain, which is *never* equally effected with any other sort of manure; it is taken from the house, thrown into the carts, and directly spread on the land. The great force of this dung may be an essential quality of it; but I cannot help attributing part of it to this cause; it is at least a hint to imitate the conduct in other dungs, and to keep them in the same manner; could it be effected even with that of horses and beasts, it would probably be so much the better.

QUANTITY OF DUNG RAISED BY A GIVEN QUANTITY OF LITTER, OR NUMBER OF CATTLE.

Mr. *Moody.* Forty-five fat oxen, in fatting, littered with 20 waggon loads of stubble, raise 200 loads, each 3 tons, of rotten dung, worth 7 *s.* 6 *d.* a load.

Every load of hay and litter given to beasts, fatting on oil-cake, yields 7 loads of dung, each 1 ¼ ton, exclusive of the weight of the cake.

On a comparison between the oil-cake dung, and common farm-yard dung, 12 loads

loads an acre of the former, much exceeded 24 of the latter.

Mr. *Arbuthnot.* 134 Sheep and 30 lambs, penned 6 weeks in a standing fold, and littered with 5 loads and 40 truss straw, made 28 large loads of dung. Fed morning and evening in the fold with turnips. Eat 2 acres of turnips.

	£	s	d
Value dung, - -	10	0	0
Straw, at 20*s*. - -	5	15	0
Profit, - -	4	5	0
Per acre for turnips,	2	2	6
And *per* score *per* week,	0	1	9¾

William White. 36 cows and 4 horses tied up, eat 50 tons of hay, and have 20 acres of straw for litter; make 200 loads of dung quite in rotten order for the land.

FARM YARD.

Tring. Litter well with wheat stubble, and stack hay at home.

Blisworth. Litter with straw and stubble.

Quenby. Litter with rushes, rubbish, weeds, and stubble, but stack about the fields.

Dishley. Don't cut stubble, and stack about the fields.

Mr. *Bakewell.* Winters all sorts of horned cattle in the house, tied up; they are not littered, but kept quite clean by sweeping. He prefers, in raising manure, the dung arising from cattle that eat a given quantity of straw, to any manure to be gained from such quantity of straw by littering.

Whole farm, - 440 acres.
Corn, - - 40

Food of cattle besides straw, 400
On which he keeps all the year,
    400 Large sheep,
     60 Horses,
    150 Beasts; which is better than 1 sheep *per* acre, and 1 head of cattle to 2 acres.

Alfreton. Litter with stubble, but stack hay about the fields.

Radburn. Know nothing of chopping stubbles, and stack their hay about the fields.

Tiddswell. Ditto.

Lawton. No littering with stubble.

Gateford. No chopping, but confine their cattle to the yard.

Colonel *St. Leger.* Carries earth into his yard for littering upon, with stubble.

Canwick. Litter with stubble, and stack hay at home.

Snettisham. Do not chop their stubbles, but stack their hay at home.

Warham. Do not chop their stubbles.

Aylsham. Harrow them and litter the yard.

Bracon Ash. The best farmers chop their stubbles, and stack their hay at home.

Mr. *Bevor.* Chops his stubbles; clears the lanes of rushes, fern, &c. and rakes and saves all his leaves for littering; expence 6 *d.* a load. His yard dung he forms into composts with ditch earth, &c. and is attentive to keep the carts off the hills, to prevent treading, which injures the fermentation. The compost better, quantity for quantity, than dung alone.

Flegg Hundred. Chop their stubbles for littering, and stack their hay at home.

Woodbridge. Chop all their stubbles for littering, and stack their hay at home. They form all their yard dung into composts, with crag or virgin mould, turning them over twice or thrice.

Bramford. Ditto, and form it all into composts with chalk.

Colchester. Litter with all their stubble, and stack their hay at home.

Youngsberry. Ditto.
Feversham. Ditto.
Beaksburn. Ditto.
Addisham. Ditto; and cart earth to the yard to litter on, and throw the stable dunghills on to.
Sheffield Place. Litter with stubble and fern; but stack hay about the fields.
Isle of Wight. Do not chop, but stack their hay at home; they do not confine their cattle all winter to the yard.
Alresford. Confine their cattle, and stack their hay at home; but do not chop the stubbles.
Moreton. No chopping, and stack the hay about the fields.
Leigh. Ditto.
Newbury. Do not chop, but stack their hay at home.
Mr. *Bevor.* Saves all the drainings of his farm yard, with which he waters his worst grafs, and thereby soon converts it into the best.

I have thrown the articles, *cattle* and *farm yard*, together, because they are particularly connected; and I have to remark on them, that the true system of management,

ment, so as to raise the most and best dung, is very little understood throughout the kingdom; for which reason I shall venture a few observations, which may throw the subject with the general run of cultivators into that clear light, in which it is viewed by the best.

The first grand object is to confine the cattle close in the farm yards all the winter months. We find, that in numerous places they are suffered to run out in the fields; with which view the hay is stacked about them; this is a most execrable custom, and absolutely destructive of good husbandry. I have heard but one reason that even *seems* to have any weight; which is the good of the cattle requiring it. Mr. *Bakewell*'s never practising it, with much the most valuable cattle in this kingdom, should eternally silence this mistake. As to the cattle eating up the old grass left at autumn, and doing well on their straw thereby, I again reply, that the practice of the best farmers is against it; but the mischief they do by poaching is much greater than such benefit amounts to; and grass, which is of value withered, surely was of greater value when green and fit to be be eaten: so that this plea is merely a pretence, to defend bad husbandry.

But by confining them all winter, there is the great advantage of making considerable quantities of dung: the refuse litter is mixed with the dung and urine of the cattle, and forms a compost of the richest sort; but when the cattle are most of the time in the fields, both are lost; for it is the collection of dung into one body, that yields the advantage, not a thin and unequal scattering about the fields.

If they are not confined the whole winter, so much farm yard compost will not be raised as there ought; the farmer, like so many throughout this Tour, will not chop his wheat stubbles for litter; whereas, by confining them constantly, they will make any quantity of litter into manure.

In the farm yard management there are two methods, which deserve consideration; one, to let the cattle run loose about the area, and have their hay, straw or other food in racks and cribs; the other, to tye them up in sheds or houses: the latter is Mr. *Bakewell*'s universal method with all cattle; and that generally practised in fattening on turnips, oil cake, &c. I prefer it to the other much, because their food of whatever

ever fort will go infinitely further, and their dung turned to better account.

In the latter refpect are likewife two modes of conduct: Mr. *Bakewell* never litters but has contrived his ftandings for cattle fo that they lie clear of their dung; and he prefers the dung arifing from a given quantity of ftraw eat by cattle, to any larger quantity that can be gained by littering. I apprehend this reafoning is perfectly good, where ftubble, fern, &c. are to be had for litter; becaufe then the object is to keep as many cattle as poffible; but if nothing of that fort is to be had, the cafe will be found more doubtful.

It fhould be confidered, that the mere dung of the cattle is fo rich, or rather the quantity is fo comparatively fmall, that a farmer muft either ufe it very fparingly, or he will manure but a few acres in a whole year. Mr. *Bakewell* keeps his dung two or three years; this is confiftent with his other practice, and he prefers it for ufe, not when it is like black butter, but the moifture of it gone off, and the body of it become powder like fnuff: that fuch dung will be very ftrong, I have not a doubt; but at the fame time, the quantity will be so diminished, that it will nearly resemble a rich top dressing of soot, which has a moderate effect for only one crop; whereas the great mischief, as I have already remarked of those dressings, is the smallness of the quantity: manure to be of considerable service must be laid on in large bodies; it will then last. But if the essence of dung is the object, and you let fly the virtue of a whole dung-hill from a snuff-box, most assuredly the loss of quantity will produce a loss of crop.

A large body of compost, though not of the richest sort, occasions a fermentation in the soil, by completing under the mould the last putrefaction: this is of vast consequence in binding soils, or such as you want to pulverise.

Sow forty shillings worth of soot over a turnip fallow in *May*, and at the same time lay on the same value in farm yard compost; plough the ground twice or thrice for the turnips; at *Midsummer* view the land; the dunged part will be like a hot bed, and garden mould, but the soot will have had no effect.

For these reasons, which might be much extended, I am no friend to making the farm

farm yard compoſt ſo rich, that the quantity *per* acre muſt be ſmall; (let me remark however that I am throughout this enquiry ſpeaking of the application only to *arable* land) make all ſtraw, &c. whatever cattle will eat, go as far as poſſible; but on every account litter them well, that the compoſt may conſiſt of rotten vegetables, as well as mere dung and urine; and if earth or marle is added, more of the urine will be retained.

This ſeems to be a point of particular importance; the value of the urine appears clearly enough in Mr. *Bevor*'s practice; it muſt therefore be of particular conſequence to preſerve it: the general method is to make a preſent of it to the neareſt ditch or horſe pond; but manage how you will, the yard muſt overflow with rains and ſnow; the object is therefore to ſtop the ſtream as often as you can to filtre it thro' your compoſt and earth; by running over, or being thrown on to an abſorbent earth, a very good manure would be created.

The general practice, which I ſhall venture to recommend is, what I conceive for the preceding reaſons to be an improvement of Mr. *Bakewell*'s ſyſtem. Tye up all your cattle both lean and fat, litter them well with stubble, &c. In the middle of the area form a layer of marle, chalk, turf, or virgin earth, about a yard thick; clean out all the cattle; lean, fat, horses, cows, hogs, &c. into small carts or barrows, and pile up the dung on the earth, until you get eight or ten feet high; then form a fresh layer at bottom by the side of the first, and go on in the same manner: from time to time, pump up the drainings of the yard on to the compost, stir it over once before it is used; mixing it well together; and you will find that putrefaction will advance very quick. In this method, the dung lies in the smallest compass possible, consequently, the sun, wind, and rains, have the less power over it, and do it the least mischief; but when it is spread over the whole yard, much of the virtue is so lost. I recommend this plan with the greater readiness, because I have practised it this winter with what I think so much success, that I am fully determined never to pursue any other method.

I should not chuse to have the compost richer than would allow me to use 50 loads, each a cubical yard, *per* acre.

The great value of compoſts is clearly ſeen in the practice of the farmers in *Norfolk*, the beſt cultivated parts of *Suffolk* and *Eſſex*; in thoſe tracts where their huſbandry vies with perfection, they one and all unite in this, forming their yard dung into heaps with marle, chalk, ſea ouze, crag, or earth: and in *Eaſt Kent* and the *Iſle of Thanet*, cart earth into their farm yards; and put ſo much to their compoſts as to lay on 40, 50, and even 80 loads an acre. As the expence is the ſame in both caſes, mine, I think, is preferable; becauſe the body of marle or earth, being in the farm yard, has the advantage of retaining much of the urine.

The experiments of Mr. *Moody* and Mr. *Arbuthnot* prove how well it anſwers to buy litter with a view to the dung; in feeding oxen with oil cakes, one load of ſtraw makes ſeven of dung, each one ton and an half; and in feeding ſheep with turnips one truſſed load made more than four and a half large loads, worth 7 s. 6 d. each. With Mr. *White*, 20 acres of ſtraw, ſuppoſe 30 loads, made 200 of rotten dung in littering cows, which are ſix and a half for one.

From whence it appears, that litter may safely be purchased at a very high price, rather than be without it: an argument which should surely be convincing with the slovens, who have it in their wheat stubbles, and yet will not be at the trouble of chopping and carting it home.

LETTER

LETTER LX.

THERE now only remains for me to give you a little table of the state of the soil throughout *England*, supposing this Tour the general average. This is an enquiry of more than amusement; for, as I remarked on another occasion, there is a use in proportioning the particulars of any considerable part of the kingdom to the whole, that the real and comparative state may be clearly known.

It is not of consequence to know whether such parts of the kingdom, as are included in the particulars of farms, make just thirty two millions of acres, but I shall take that supposition.

STATE, RENTAL, *and* VALUE *of the* SOIL.

Acres in all,	32,000,000
Arable land,	13,518,716
Grass,	15,736,185
Wood,	* 2,395,721

---

* N. B. These three sums do not make 32,000,000 by 349,378, which is occasioned by the parts of 561 not being complete; they form gardens, yards, ponds, or other pieces not included.

Number of farms, - 57,040
Rental, at 14*s*. - £. 22,400,000
Value of the soil, at 31 ½ years
 purchase, - - £. 705,600,000

STOCK IN HUSBANDRY.

	Number.	Rate.			Value.
		l.	*s.*	*d.*	£.
Draught cattle	684,491	10	0	0	6,844,910
Cows	741,532	7	0	0	5,190,724
Fatting beasts	513,369	12	0	0	6,160,428
Young cattle	912,656	4	0	0	3,650,624
Sheep	22,188,948	0	15	0	16,641,711
Swine	†1,711,200	0	12	0	1,026,720
Poultry	§				171,120
Totals,	26,752,196				39,686,237
Total of live stock, according to the proportion in stocking farms, 273 *l.* to 100 *l.* a year,					61,152,000

 The difference between these two sums require some remarks; the latter being the sum used to stock, is generally below the truth; because farmers seldom stock themselves with all they want at first; but then, in some of the minutes, I was informed rather of what good farmers bought, than the average of good, bad, and indifferent, which perhaps might bring it to the truth.
            In

---

 † At 30 *per* farm conjectured.
 § Ditto at 3 *l.*

In respect to the estimation, the numbers of cattle, swine excepted, are the real numbers on the farms, but the value *per* head is a supposition; the total being inferior to the other, gives reason to apprehend, that the rates *per* head are too low; but I shall not raise them by conjecture, but rather adhere to the other method of ascertaining the fact.

DEAD STOCK.

Implements, at 70*l. per* 100*l.* a year,	£. 15,680,000
Furniture, ditto,	15,680,000
Total,	31,360,000

SUNDRIES,

Including feed, labour, &c. £. 51,520,000

Recapitulation.

Live stock,	61,152,000
Dead ditto,	31,360,000
Sundries,	51,520,000
Total,	144,032,000

'This total is the aggregate of the averages of the articles separately taken: the single one of stock in general by the same account will make it 120,960,000 *l.*

Pro-

Probably the average of these accounts would be near the truth; and if the valuation of live stock *per* head be taken, instead of the 61 millions, the account then will be near it.

Live stock, - -	£. 39,686,237
Dead ditto, - -	31,360,000
Sundries, - -	51,520,000
Total, -	130,566,237

PRODUCT OF THE SOIL.

Arable Crops.

Crops.	Acres.	Product per acre. Quarters.	Total prod. Quarters.	Per qu. s.	Value. £.
Wheat	2,795,008	3 0	8,385,024	40	16,770,048
Barley	2,623,885	4 0	10,495,540	20	10,495,540
Oats	1,483,065	4 6	7,044,558	16	5,635,645
Pease	513,369	2 7	1,475,935	26	1,918,714
Beans	399,287	4 1	1,647,058	26	2,141,174
		l. s. d.			
Turnips	1,711,228	2 2 5*			3,629,228
Clover	3,201,425	5 4 0†			16,647,410
Totals,	12,707,268		29,048,115		57,237,759

* The average price of the Tour.

† Ditto: this may appear too high; but, if the hay is taken as a guide, it cannot be estimated at less, the average first cut being 1 ton 13 C. wt. and a half, and the second 22 C. wt. in all 3 tons 15 C. wt. and a half, which are certainly worth 5 l. 4 s.

CATTLE.

	Rate per head.			Number.	Total.
	l.	s.	d.		£.
Cows	5	10	0	741,532	4,078,426
Sheep	0	11	8	22,188,948	12,943,551
Fatting beasts	5	0	0†	513,369	2,566,845
Young cattle	1	0	0†	912,656	912,656
Swine	0	15	0†	†1,711,200	1,283,400
Poultry					†171,120
Totals,				26,067,705	21,955,998

WOOD.

There are 2,395,721 acres of copse in these farms; we may venture to calculate the product at 25 s. an acre, without fear of being above the truth. It is 2,994,651 l.

Recapitulation.

Arable crops,	-	-	£. 57,237,759
Cattle,	-	-	21,955,998
Wood,	-	-	2,994,651
Total,	-		£. 82,188,408

EXPENDITURE OF HUSBANDRY.

Rent,	-	-	£. 22,400,000
Tythe, at the average composition of 3 s. 4 d. per acre, is 5,333,333 l. but as this does not include the gathering, we must call it,		-	7,000,000
Carry over,		-	29,400,000

† Conjectured: the profit by poultry supposed to equal their value,

THE FARMER's TOUR

	£
Brought over,	29,400,000
Poor rates, at the average of 2s. 8d.	2,986,666
All other rates, suppose 9d.	420,000
The number of servants is 156,860, and their wages, at the average of 8l. 8s.	1,317,624
Their board, at 9l.	1,411,740
The number of maids 57,040, their wages, at the average of 3l. 9s.	196,738
Their board, at 5l.	285,200
The number of boys 85,560; and their wages, at the average of 3l. 4s.	273,792
Their board, at 6l. 10s.	556,140
The number of regular labourers is 399,280; their pay, at the average of 7s. 10d. per week,	7,958,964
Extra labour, suppose a fourth,	1,989,741
The number of horses 684,491, their expence, at the average of 9l. 4s.	6,297,317
Wear and tear, at 7l. a horse,	4,791,437
Reparation of half the buildings, suppose at 5l. a farm,	142,600

Seed.

Wheat, 2,795,008 acres, at two and a half bushels per acre, 873,440 quarters, at 40s.	1,746,880
Carry over,	59,774,839

Brought over, —	£. 59,774,839
Barley, 2,623,885 acres, at three and a half bushels, are 1,147,949 quarters, at 20 *s*.	1,147,949
Oats, 1,483,065 acres, at four bushels and a quarter, are 787,878 quarters, at 16 *s*.	630,301
Pease and beans, 912,656 acres, at three and a half bushels, are 399,287 quarters, at 26 *s*. — —	519,072
Clover, 3,201,425 acres, at 5 *s*.	800,356
Turnips, 1,711,228, at 1 *s*.	85,561
Interest of 130,560,000 *l*. stock in husbandry, at 4 *per cent*.	5,222,400
Total, —	68,240,478
Products, —	82,188,408
Expenditure, —	68,240,478
Profit of husbandry, according to this account, —	13,947,930

As the stock in husbandry is upwards of 130,000,000 *l*. by this average, it shews, that the general profit is 14 *per cent*.

I forbear making further reflections, as it is drawn not from the whole kingdom, but only a part of it.

POPULATION.

Number of farmers,	57,040
Ditto of labourers,	399,280
Number of houses and families,	456,320
Total, at 6 to a family,	2,737,920

This state supposes, that all the servants hired by farmers are from one another's children, and those of labourers.

Upon this subject of population, I shall just observe, that from the minutest enquiries I have been able to make throughout this Tour, I find no reason to change the opinion I ventured in my Northern journey, that *England*, so far from having lost above a million of people since the revolution, had probably much increased her numbers: I have not even met with any arguments in conversation to support this idea, which seemed the least conclusive; one I shall not pass over. A gentleman of considerable fortune in *Dorsetshire* assured me, that twenty years ago he could almost command any number of labourers for works, that required many hands at once; and instanced the making a large lake, in which work he procured an hundred men easier than he could

could get twenty now. This furprized me very much; but knowing that hufbandry had been much improved in *Dorfetfhire* during the period mentioned, and that all other general improvements kept pace with it, both of a private and publick nature, I confidered the cafe, and muft own, that it appears clearly to me, inftead of being a proof of a declining population, that it is ftrong in favour of the idea of an increafing one. When a gentleman could eafily command an hundred men, the neighbourhood on the very face of the fuppofition muft have been an idle one: the induftry of a regular employment could not have fpread among the lower claffes: the country being moftly a fheep walk, and the hufbandry miferably bad, the cottagers were poorly employed, and depended much on fome paltry common rights, or fome other fupport than induftry, being at the fame time few in number.

In fuch a fituation, a gentleman commands a great proportion of them unemployed with that regularity, which is effential to fixing them. He commands an hundred men. Why? Not becaufe the country is populous; but becaufe it knows not how

to

to employ the few hands it possesses; for men that spend much of their time in idleness are easy to be had, especially by a gentleman, and to work in a great number, for a time.

But a greater industry comes into the country, agriculture improves, arts increase, and the territory carries a new face; an hundred men no longer appear on the signal; twenty cannot be had. Not because they are not in being, but because they are better employed. They were before to be gained, because idle: they cannot now be had, because industrious. Now they are regularly employed and industrious the year through; which employment is of much more consequence to them, than any by fits and starts. They are not to be had, except by great pay, which is a case seen in every county in *England*. While matters are in such a train, the people may have double their numbers, and men to a gentleman scarcer than ever.

A strong proof that this reasoning is just, is the difficulty to get men even in the most populous counties; where, if any great publick or private work is wanting to be executed, men in sufficient numbers are
never

never to be gained, unlefs by raifing wages.

To render this more familiar, and to fhew, that a country may increafe prodigioufly in population, without the plenty of men at command, which are found in idle periods, let us fuppofe a tract contains an hundred farmers, twenty manufacturers, and ten gentlemen of private fortune: the regular employers of a thoufand labourers of all forts. Now this population may gradually increafe by regular increafe of the bufinefs already among them, even to any amount; but if one of the gentlemen ftarts beyond his ufual expence, and wants thirty, forty, or fifty labourers to float a valley, who can fuppofe that he will be able to get them at the former prices? The old mafters will never readily fpare their regular hands, to have the trouble of finding new ones; but by raifing wages the gentleman breaks through this obftacle, and forces the mafters to take care of themfelves from elfewhere. Is it not from hence evident, that the cafe of his fupplying himfelf does not in the leaft depend on the tract of country being very populous, but merely on the proportion,

proportion, which the regular employment bears to the number of people. That number may be trebbled, and yet his difficulty be precisely as great.

From the general result of this journey, I may here add, that the kingdom carries all those marks of sound health, wealth, and strength, of which I made mention in my *Northern Tour*, and offers every appearance of being in a most flourishing situation. The soil well cultivated, industry active, the people easy, rich and happy.

I will not go to *'Change-Alley* for information, until I am convinced, that these signs are deceitful; and I must own, when I see ten millions of people with one voice thanking heaven for the enjoyment of all the blessings of which humanity is capable; when I behold this spectacle, I shall not easily be persuaded, that the interests of this great empire are in the shuffling hands of the bulls and bears of *Cornhill*.*

---

* The result of my enquiries, both in this Tour and the Northern one, is nearly similar in the reason it gives for supposing the kingdom, on the whole, to be in a flourishing situation; but every one of the facts brought in proof are diametrically contradicted by a late anonymous writer, (*Considerations on the Policy*,

Policy, Commerce, and Circumstances of this Kingdom, 8vo. 1771) at which I am not much displeased; for, if I am not in direct opposition to all his assertions, I am very confident I must be far enough from plain truth: for of all the works of this sort, which I have read, I do not recollect one of an equal number of pages, that contains a tenth of the falsehoods abounding in that book—the mere effect of a virulent prejudice against landed men, and the landed interest, in favour singly of merchants and manufacturers. Had more art been used to disguise this manifest prejudice, the work would have done more mischief, and required a particular reply; but as it is, a few notes are a sufficient antidote to all the poison.

There have been writers, who reckon manufactures and commerce somewhat more beneficial than agriculture, but generally recommended all three. This marvellous politician, however, stamps all agriculture, and the landed interest, with the title of *cow-keepers*, which clumsey piece of wit he repeats for its poignancy. I pass over his general argument, which is founded on mere falshood, without even the varnish of sophistry, and come to the chapter, which he politely dedicates to abusing me.

But he appears to be so ill informed, as to ground all his opinions on the state of the corn-trade within the twelve last years. Let the impartial reader turn to the pieces I laid before the public, and judge if this is not a mere, unpalliated, direct falshood: just as well might it be said, that I grounded it on the last nonsense this writer uttered in conversation.

Next he directly arraigns me for wanting fifteen millions of waste acres to be cultivated; and his reasons are, that we shall want ship timber, fire wood, and sheep. This is too ridiculous to require a comment. Leaving them waste will certainly make mutton very cheap!

He depreciates the employment of manufacturers, in favour of wheel-wrights and black-smiths. I only quote this: to enter into a revision, in order to refute a man, who assures me gravely, that, so far from being at *North Mims*, I am really at *York*, would be absurd:

absurd: one might order such a fellow to the horse-pond, but never altercate the matter.

He asserts, that the demand for our corn is surer than for our cloth, which is contrary to all experience. This assertion he fully answers in various other passages, in which he represents our manufactures *gone to ruin*, BECAUSE our corn *sells so well*.

Next comes as special a piece of criticism as can easily be produced. In my *Farmer's Letters*, p. 53, I shewed, that the export of corn in 68 years was above 36,000,000 *l*. made by freight near 40 millions. Page 66, I observe as follows: *So far indeed has the bounty been from raising the price of corn at home, that, as I have before proved, it has constantly lowered it; and* HERE *lies a vast saving to the nation, which is not considered by those who plead against the measure;* SINCE *the bounty, wheat, on an average, has been* 9 *s*. 3 *d. a quarter cheaper than before, if reckoned at the mean fineness of quality, and the* Winchester *measure in quantity. Now the saving of this single article, in* 68 *years, amounts to upwards of* 100 *millions* Sterling. *The gain therefore to the nation, arising from the bounty, amounts clearly to* 140 *millions.* Afterwards I repeat this last circumstance.

Now let me ask the reader, in what manner, shall I say a candid man?—no, any one, whose sole principle was not imposing on the world the most manifest untruths for the clearest facts, would chuse to refute these sentiments. Would he not endeavour to shew, either that the value of the corn and freight did not amount to 40 millions, or that the sinking of price did not amount to 100 millions? Something of this sort surely might be expected! But no such matter with this gentleman. The following is his reply.

But the most extraordinary part of this writer's wonderful productions is that, in which he gives his calculations of the benefits derived to this kingdom from the exportation of corn. The following are his words: " I "have already shewn, that the nation has in fact " profited by the annual exportation of rather more " than 420,000 quarters of corn, of all sorts, above " the sum of 140 millions, in less than 70 years."

By comparing my estimation of profits to this kingdom, with that of Mr. *Young's* exorbitant ones, it will appear with what accuracy he calculated our 70 years gains from trade therein.

By his account, the profits have been, £. 140,000,000
By mine, - - - 41,160,000

Difference, - - 98,840,000

Let it rest with Mr. Young to satisfy the public, whether his misrepresentation of a matter of such importance, as 98,840,000*l.* is owing to ignorance or design.

It rests with Mr. *Young*, and he is totally at rest, notwithstanding the imputations of ignorance and *design*. But what says the reader to such square accounts? — to quoting and branding one passage, and being quite silent about the other, which is explanatory of it? With whom now does it rest to fly for refuge to ignorance and design? If he says my argument was false, I reply, that is not at present the question, but merely the existence of that argument. If he asserts, that he read only one passage, I answer, that it belongs only to so very candid a man to call upon a writer for a public retraction of a passage, incomplete in one page, which is fully explained in another. So little reason has this pretended politician to talk of *explaining my mysteries to my conviction and confusion.*—A blessed predicament he must be in, who wants such a commentator!

APPENDIX.

Vol. I. page 182.

At the word improbable.

SIR *Robert* has informed me, by letter, of the result of this crop. His bailiff wrote him in *January*, that they had been of infinite service in the hard frost in feeding beasts, while the turnips could not be got at. The extreme unfavourable season for cabbages all over *England* affected this crop, so that they did not come to their usual size; but even under this circumstance, the product was greater than ever known from any other cabbage; the weights being from 25*lb.* to 50*lb.* each; and the average 30*lb.* or SIXTY FIVE TONS *per* acre, at a yard square, which was the distance. This product, in an unfavourable season, needs no eulogy.

Page 237.

Paring and burning.

	£	s	d
The expence here is,			
Paring,	0	9	0
Burning,	0	6	0
250 Kids of whins, at 1 *s.* *per* hundred,	0	2	6
Spreading the ashes,	0	1	0
	0	18	6

APPENDIX. 471

Page 284.

on such principles.

After the paring and burning, and sowing turnips on one very shallow ploughing, the Colonel strongly recommends the spiky roller going over the land two or three times, as the ground is generally very hard; it loosens it, and the harrows then raise a fine mould, for the fibres of the plants the quicker to get through to the ashes.

Page 342.

at remember to have seen.

Mr. *Wharton* has favoured me with the result by letter. A piece 52 yards long, by 11 broad, yielded 81 bushels, besides some that the pigs eat, on once or twice breaking into the field; call it therefore 85 bushels. This is 719 bushels to the acre, which, at the *Doncaster* price of 1*s.* a bushel, come to 35*l.* 19*s.*; and Mr. *Wharton* is clearly of opinion, that all his rich sands, with the like management, would produce equal crops.

Vol. II. page 119.

Two acres and an half of these cabbages kept 5 oxen, of from 40 to 50 stone (14 *lb.*) stall-feeding 5 weeks; the value of which Mr. *Rogers* reckons at 2*s.* 6*d. per* week; this is in the whole 3*l.* 2*s.* 6*d.* or 1*l.* 5*s.* an acre; a very poor produce; but the sort is not the *great Scotch*.

Page 122.

after the word hereabouts.

Mr. *Fellowes* has been so obliging as to communicate, by letter, the product of this wheat.

The quantity of land, sixty rods and an half; the product, 1 quarter, 1 peck of very good wheat, and 2 pecks of drofs, which is fomething more than 2 quarters 5 bufhels an acre of good wheat.

Page 123.

the beft crop.

December 25th, two fquare perches of thefe cabbages were weighed, and alfo two of the turnips.

	T.	C.	lb.
The cabbages, 3 C. wt. 107 lb. ½, or per acre,	15	16	88
The turnips, 6 C. wt. 69 lb. ¼, or	26	9	92

But neither the tops nor roots were cut off. Carrots weighed at the fame time, came to 2 C. wt. 23 lb. ¼, or *per* acre, 8 tons 16 C. wt. and 108 lb.

Page 195.

Mr. *Acton* has fince been fo kind as to advife me, by letter, of the product of this year's crop of carrots. The quantity of land, not exactly an acre, but 1 acre 10 perches, yielded 17 cart loads of roots, and 8 loads of tops, each load 48 bufhels; this is 816 bufhels of roots; but a fixteenth muft be deducted for the 10 perches, there then remains 765. At 6 d. a bufhel thefe come to 19 l. 2 s. 6 d.; at 8 d. to 25 l. 10 s.; at 1 s. to 38 l. 5 s. They were taken up and houfed in *November*. The ufe to which they have been applied, is, feeding deer, horfes, and hogs; all which thrive to admiration on them. This crop has been vifibly much inferior to feveral others of former years; confequently the intelligence
this

this gentleman gave me of his crops rising to 960 bushels, is fully confirmed.

The cabbages he planted, proved of a very bad sort; none of the true *Scotch* kind, except a plant or two for seed, differently procured. Four cows were fed on them from *December* 10th to the 19th, both inclusive, being ten days; they eat 33 square perch, which, at 2 *s.* a week *per* cow, come to 2 *l.* 16 *s.* 10 *d.* ¼ *per* acre. The cream and the butter were both exceedingly good; did not taste of the cabbages in the least. His expression is, *I never tasted better, and every body that have tasted of it said the same.*

Vol. II. page 199. After the word *luxuriance*,

Experiment, No. 11.

Makin's draining plough, for which the Society gave a bounty of fifty pounds, Mr. *Afton* has purchased, and tried very accurately; it did, in his park, from *ten* to *twelve* score perch in a day, that is, from 7 in the morning to half past 2, from 18 to 20 inches deep, and, in general, pretty clean. The *crumbs* will fall in a little, but are easily taken out. For this cleaning and filling up, he gives 1 *s.* a score, without beer. It requires 6 horses, and 3 men are necessary to attend it. The soil where it worked a good mould on a strong clay. Arable land Mr. *Afton* recommends to be laid down to clover, or clover and ray-grass before it is drained, which is certainly a very just thought, for the plough going 4 or 5 times in a place, it must necessarily do the work the neater, and with more ease to the horses.

The drains are filled with bushes, and then with straw.

APPENDIX.

As I was at *Bradfield* in *Suffolk* when I received from this gentleman the above account, he further advised me, that at *Lawshall* near *Bradfield*, some tenants of his had one of the ploughs, made by a wheelwright at that place, who had improved it. I went thither to view it; the alterations are, *first*, the moveable mould-board, instead of being drawn up by hand, which is troublesome in dirty work, winds up by a jack, which is certainly a great improvement—it rises gradually and accurately, and contracts or expands at pleasure. *Secondly*, The wheels are only 4 feet high, which, if I recollect right, are much lower than those which Mr. *Makins* made; this does not by any means appear an improvement.

Mr. *Smith* (one of Mr. *Acton*'s tenants) informed me, that he valued the drawing one furrow, to make way for the plough, at 6 *d*. a day's work.

In the common method of making the drains he ploughs four furrows, which is 1 *d*. ¾ a score, and then digs one spit 18 inches deep, for which he pays 1 *s*. 6 *d*. a score.

From these several particulars we may draw up a pretty exact comparison between the plough and the spade.

The plough.

	£.	s.	d.
Six horses, at 1 *s*. 6 *d*.	0	9	0
Three men, at 1 *s*. 2 *d*.	0	3	6
We may allow for the expence of the plough,	0	1	6
This I do not apprehend too much for a machine that costs 10 *l*. 10 *s*. the price, improved.			
Drawing furrows,	0	0	6
Filling and cleaning,	0	11	0
Total for 11 score,	1	5	6
Which is *per* score,	0	2	3¼

The spade.

	£	s	d
Four furrows,	0	0	1¼
Digging,	0	1	6
Filling. This, in proportion to 1 *s.* for filling and cleaning, may be reckoned at	0	0	8
Total *per* score,	0	2	3½

Here I should observe, that Mr. *Smith*, abovementioned, fills with haulm, that is, wheat stubble, and does it by the day, at a much cheaper rate than here reckoned, but that makes no alteration, since this is a mere comparison; the drains *dug*, are filled as cheap as those *ploughed*, nor do I think the proportion of 8 *d.* for filling, to 1 *s.* for filling and cleaning, an unfair one.

Upon the face of this account it appears, that the plough is the most expensive method, nor do I see any exaggeration in it. It may be said that the farmer's horses do not cost him 1 *s.* 6 *d.* each a day; in answer to this, I reply, what do they cost him? Nothing is so fallacious as supposing that a man's horses cost but little if he does not hire; if keeping, shoeing, wear of harness, interest of money, decline of value, renewal of stock, &c. are taken into account, I believe 1 *s.* 6 *d.* will be found no extravagant idea; if it is said, the horses stand still often, that only makes the expence so much greater when they *are* used. Suppose a team costs 100 *l.* a year, and work 100 days in a year, it is 20 *s.* a day; but if they work only 80 days, the price *per* day, rises, as the sum total of time falls. 1 *s.* 6 *d.* a day is about 24 *l.* a year; some have observed that this is too high, but it supposes that the horse works every day in the year, which is never the case, consequently it is a mode-a moderate price. Some farmers never work their horses for months together, through œconomy; but two and two making four, is not plainer than the mistake; they only raise the expence of ploughing, &c. from 4*s.* to 7*s.* by this means. If the horse lived upon air when he did not work, the idea would be just. But all good farmers feed their horses with some regularity, whether they work or not; the poor man who starves his team on straw, to save hay and oats, may think himself a gainer, but if hard work comes in the spring, the land will be weakly and poorly ploughed, nor will his day's work, in quantity, nearly equal his neighbour's, unless he over-works and ruins his beast.

Upon the whole, I adhere to the charge of 1*s.* 6*d.* a day, as a *low one*. As to the 1*s. per* man, it cannot be lower, but in many places must be higher.

The result of the comparison is, that the spade is not only cheaper, but goes, at the above expence, deeper, and has the great advantage of being applicable to all soils, and every state of the land—to little as well as to great inclosures —in the power of little as well as great farmers. In this account I state nothing but a calculation drawn from facts; being much more a friend to the plough, as an ingenious contrivance, than prejudiced against it; but the real and fair truth should always be known, and no new machine is ever produced, without many exaggerations, for I have heard accounts totally contrary to the truth which now appears from persons who attended the trial before the committee of agriculture at *London*.—But this must ever be the case with trials that last only an hour or two, or more likely, ten minutes; I have been present at some of these committee trials, and am clearly of opinion, that not one in ten is worth a groat; for what analogy is there between the trial of an instrument

APPENDIX. 477

instrument in turning a furrow or two, or performing any other operations by a stop watch, and the usual execution during a common day's work? Will horses or men work for a whole day, as they do for a few minutes? and perhaps under the immediate direction of the inventor.

A draining plough, that would greatly reduce the expence of cutting them, would be a most useful contrivance; but I apprehend one necessary circumstance attending it, is to perform the work at one cut; and another very material point, is to rise out of the earth, or stop without damage, if it meets with a root or great stone.

* * * *

Since this was written, I have read in the second volume of Mr. *Dossie's Memoirs*, page 331, that Mr. *Makin's plough cut 1400 feet of trench in one hour, without the horses going a greater pace than they are able to hold in a whole day's work; that in land of moderate tenacity and resistance, it can be wrought with four horses, under the direction and guidance of a man and a boy.* This is just the result I should look for from a committee experiment of one hour. It requires six horses, unless worked in sand, which wants no draining:—instead of a man and boy, three men are necessary;—and as to the 1400 feet in an hour, which amounts to 678 perch in a day of eight hours, Mr. *Afton's* experiments above mentioned assert only 220 perch; so the Society's plough did more than *thrice* as much. How are we to reconcile this, but by a general idea that stop-watch experiments are not worth sixpence an hundred?

Vol. II. page 211.

In several parts of the preceding minutes, particularly in *Suffolk*, mention is made of cows often giving eight gallons of milk *per* day; this fact

fact is thought very improbable in some other parts of the kingdom; this induced me, on all occasions that offered, to make minute enquiries into the product of cows. I can pledge myself for the accuracy of the following account.

Three cows (one of them a heifer after her first calf) the property of the Rev. Mr. *Aspin*, of *Cockfield* in *Suffolk*, yielded from *June* to *December*, 1770, SIX HUNDRED AND EIGHTY-THREE pounds of butter, the old ones giving for some time in the height of the season, each EIGHT GALLONS of milk a day. The benefit received in pigs amounted to 3*l.* and the three calves were sold at a fortnight old for 10*s.* 6*d.* each.

	£	s	d
683 *lb.* at 7*d.* (the selling price of the neighbourhood)	19	18	0
Pigs,	3	0	0
Calves,	1	11	6
Total,	24	9	6
In this country they reckon a heifer in her first year as half a cow; at two and a half this is *per* cow,	9	15	10

These cows were kept on only three acres of grass without any change of pasture till after mowing time; in the winter chiefly on straw, with very little hay.

These particulars are very valuable; they prove that I have not dealt in romance, when I have spoken of the *Suffolk* breed; and they shew, that this poor looking, mongrel breed, is greatly preferable for the pail to the large *Holderness* cow, one of which would have consumed all the food of the above three cows, without returning half the produce; or to the fine *Lancashire* breed, which sells at such enormous prices. Those, who are curious in cattle, should make these necessary distinctions; for according to the

general

general notions of a breeding stock, we may safely pronounce, that the finer your breed is, the more mischief you do to the dairy; a consideration that should perhaps check the rage of *breeding* so common at present in some counties*.

I cannot here omit observing, that Mr. *Aspin*'s husbandry is excellent: he does full justice to the course; 1. Turnips, 2. Barley, 3. Clover, 4. Wheat. His soil a fine kindly light loam on gravel. The turnips exceeding fine, being the large globular sort that grows above ground, and roots only by the tap. For the barley he ploughs but once, which method he finds far more advantageous than giving more earths, the land breaking up in a fine mouldering order. One year he stirred thrice, but his crop suffered much by it. This is owing to the loss of an early season; for barley must be sown while the land is *quite* dry; if it is stirred early in the spring, a very little rain will cause long delays, so that the seed will not be in the ground till too late; and with all crops, nothing is more important than an early sowing.

The barley and the wheat yields each five quarters *per* acre.

The clover is fed with *Scotch* black cattle, and fatting wethers, which is an application that

---

* This is not an improper place to introduce the following certificates, with which I was favoured at *Lincoln* by the Mayor and one of the Aldermen.

Lincoln, July 31, 1770.

This is to certify, that a cow, now the property of *John Davies*, of *Lincoln*, gives 5 gallons of milk at a meal, for some time after her first calving.

John Davies, alderman.

Also, two cows, the property of *Henry* and *Phil. Bullen*, *Lincoln*, give upwards of five gallons each, at a meal, for some time after calving.

Phil. Bullen, mayor.

N. B. *Winchester* measure.

turns out very profitable; for the beasts being purchased lean in *November*, kept on straw in the winter, and a few turnips in spring, and then finished in the clover, are generally sold within a trifle at double the cost; coming to from 36 to 50 stone (14 *lb.*) The wether lambs are bought in *September*, and sold that time twelvemonth at treble their cost. This system is, upon the whole, one of the most beneficial that I have any where met with.

This winter, Mr. *Aspin* had a small piece of great *Scotch* cabbages for an experiment to try the effect on milch cows. They were fed for some time on cabbages alone, and the butter and cream proved incomparably good; without the least taste; equal to the best hay butter.

Vol. II. page 211.

The Revd. Mr. *Curteen*, of *Bradfield St. Clair*, has for some years tried a hand-mill for grinding wheat, invented by *William Brand*, the ingenious mechanic mentioned in Vol. II. p. 212. See the annexed plate.

References.

From	1 to 2	—	2 feet	11 inches.
	2 to 3	—	2	2
	3 to 4	—	3	6
	5 to 6	—	1	4
	7 to 8	—	2	3
	9 to 10	—	0	10
	9 to 11	—	0	9
	12 to 13	—	0	11
	15 to 16	—	1	3
	12 to 17	—	0	5
	18 to 19	—	1	3
	19 to 20	—	1	3
Length	of 14	—	1	5
	21 diameter		0	3

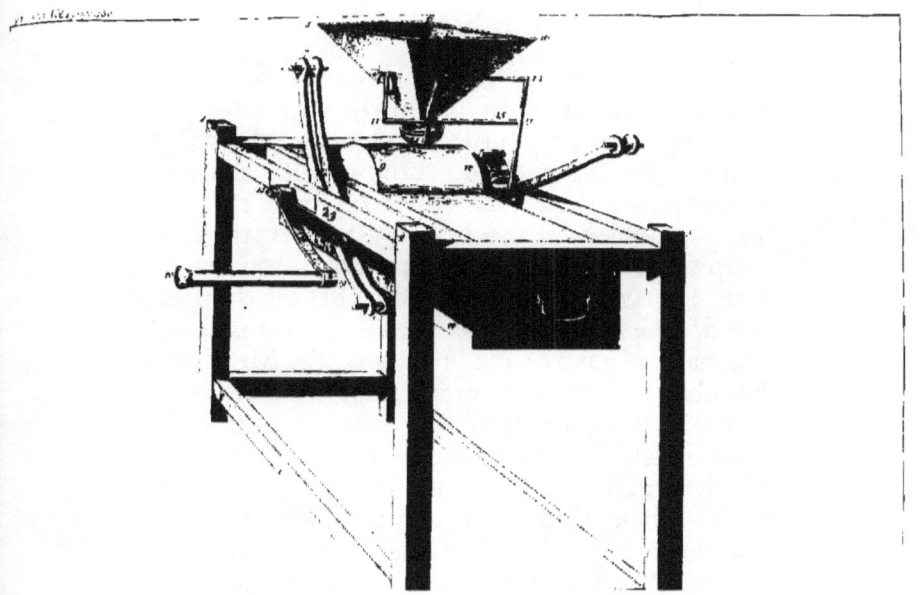

APPENDIX.

The corn is put into the hopper 6, out of which it is let very gradually by a moveable iron, fixed at 17 and 12, but moveable at 13 and 14, by the iron 22, turning with the axis of the mill; the little cogs in it strike the iron 13, 14, which by the iron 13, 12, lets the corn drop from the hopper: 21 is a small iron bason, 2 or 3 inches below the point of the hopper, out of which it falls into the mill. This is one of the material parts of the invention; for Mr. *Brand* has observed, that the great fault in these mills is the weight of the corn in the hopper lying immediately on the grinding part of the body of the mill; which clogs it, and makes the work much harder; the meal falls into the drawer 22.

The handle of the winch, 20, that turns the mill; 18 the axletree which runs through the beam 23 to the double irons 7, 8. The axle does not go strait to the beam 24, but only to the first iron of the 7, 8; this is with intention to lengthen the lever, and ease the work.

Respecting the execution, Mr. *Curteen* and myself tried it very accurately; we ground ¼ of a peck of wheat in 7 minutes, the meal of which filled the quarter peck measure, and ⅛ over; whence it appears, that when a sack of wheat is sent to a miller, he should return 7 bushels.

Mr. *Curteen* was however of opinion, that if 2 men work a whole day, 15 minutes would be a proper allowance: as we did not work at all hard. I think this is rather too much; however, to allow it fully, this is a peck in an hour, and, if we call a day 10 hours, it is 10 pecks a day. Two men, on an average of seasons, may be called 2 *s.* 6 *d.*; this is exactly 1 *s.* a bushel.

A miller

A miller in this country in pay 3 *d.* ; toll, and avowed deductions, takes about 6 *d.* a bushel. Mr. *Curteen* is very clearly of opinion, that the 1 *s.* a bushel answers in mere expence ; for a general complaint here, as well as elsewhere, is the unbounded knavery of these rascals, not only in direct stealing, but also in changing the corn, giving bad for good, grinding white pease, &c. and playing a thousand tricks of the same sort.

The mill, which appears most to be wanting, is one to be turned by a jack-ass or a little horse ; but then it must be on the horizontal principle, not the perpendicular one ; the common hand coffee-mill, which turns round on the top, offers a hint ; if the handle was a very long lever, even a man would have a great force.

Vol. III. page 41.

Since this article was written, Mr. *Crow* has advised me of the products of several acres of madder, taken up in the autumn of 1770.

Page 38, I mention his not thinking it impossible to gain 30 *C. wt.* on one acre ; he now finds that idea exceeded ; for he has taken up one acre, from which no plants were ever drawn, that weighs dry 1 *T.* 12 *C. wt.* 1 *Q.* 24 *lb.* The minutes of this product, with a sample of the madder, he sent to the *Society for the Encouragement of Arts, Manufactures and Commerce,* as a candidate for their premium *for the greatest quantity raised on one acre,* and obtained the gold medal of the Society.

Adjoining to this acre, Mr. *Crowe* had another, for an experiment of comparison ; the preceeding one had no plants drawn from it ; this had two hundred thousand plants drawn from it the two first

APPENDIX.

first summers; which circumstance was the only difference, the soil, culture, &c. were perfectly alike. The product of this acre was 19 C. wt.

	T.	C.	Q.	lb.
Undrawn,	1	12	1	24
Drawn,	0	19	0	0
Superiority,	0	13	1	24

No comparison can be more decisive; the difference at 4 *l*. 10 *s*. is near 60 *l*. from whence we may clearly determine, that plants should never be drawn but on the most urgent necessity, unless they are sold like these at 10 *s. per* thousand; then the practice is profitable, for here they came to 100 *l*. whereas the damage is only 60 *l*. From this proportion we are able to draw a very material piece of knowledge for valuing madder crops; which is, that for every 10 *l*. you receive for plants, you reduce 6 *l*. from the product of the crop, which in such cases may be allowed accordingly. Mr. *Crowe*'s idea therefore of using winter plants to save this great damage to the growing crops, appears to be perfectly just.

On another piece, containing one acre and 20 perches, the soil a light sandy loam, planted with winter plants, dug up at only two years old, he had 17 *C. wt.* dry and clean madder, besides 172,000 winter plants. This crop is amazingly great, and shews the importance of the light sandy soils for this vegetable, in the strongest light.

Mr. *Crowe* further informs me, that there are 12 acres planted about *Feversham* last *Michaelmas*, and 30 more ready for spring planting.

APPENDIX.

Let us in the next place take the account of these crops, as of the others, at p. 40.

		£	s.	d.
1 T. 12 C. wt. 1 Q. 24 lb. at 4 l. 10 s. per C. wt.	-	146	2	1
Expences, (with 4 l. 4 s. added for drying)	-	43	17	6
Profit,	-	102	4	7
Which is *per* acre *per ann.*	-	34	1	6

Another.

		£	s.	d.
19 C. wt. at 4 l. 10 s.	-	85	10	0
13 C. wt. 1 Q. 24 lb. at ditto, being the loss by drawing,	-	60	12	1
Total,	-	146	2	1
Expences,	-	43	17	6
Profit,	-	102	4	7
Per acre *per ann.*	-	34	1	6

Another.

		£	s.	d.
14 C. wt. 3 Q. 14 lb. at 4 l. 10 s.		66	18	9

Expences.

	£	s.	d.
Tillage, as at p. 39, and planting,	3	2	6
Plants,	2	5	0
Hoeing and digging two years,	4	3	0
Digging up,	11	0	0
Drying,	4	8	0
Rent, &c. at 20 s.	2	0	0
	26	18	6

APPENDIX. 485

	£.	s.	d.
Brought over—Product,	66	18	9
Expences,	26	18	6
Profit,	40	0	3
Or *per* acre *per ann.*	20	0	1½

Besides 75*l.* for 150,000 winter plants.

I shall in the next place draw all the experiments into one view, that a clear idea may be formed of them.

	£.	s.	d.
Expences, No. 1.	39	13	6
No. 2.	42	19	*6
No. 3.	43	17	6
No. 4.	43	17	6
No. 5.	26	18	6
Of five acres,	196	14	6
Average,	39	6	10

Product.	*Weight.*				*Value.*		
	T.	C.	Q.	lb.	l.	s.	d.
No. 1.	0	18	0	0	81	0	0
2.	1	7	1	0	122	12	6
3.	1	12	1	24	146	2	1
4.	1	12	1	24	146	2	1
5.	0	14	3	14	66	18	9
Of five acres,	6	5	0	13	562	15	5
Average,	1	5	0	2	112	11	1

	£.	s.	d.
Ditto *per* acre *per ann.* of the 4 first, being 3 years,	41	6	4
The fifth, being 2 years,	33	9	4

* 3 *l.* 6 *s.* added for drying 11 C. *wt.* the loss by 170,000 plants.

APPENDIX.

Profit.	Per acre.			Per ac. per ann.		
	l.	s.	d.	l.	s.	d.
No. 1.	41	6	6	13	15	6
2.	72	13	0	26	11	0
3.	102	4	7	34	1	6
4.	102	4	7	34	1	6
5.	40	0	3	20	0	1
Of five acres,	365	8	11	128	9	7
Average,	73	1	9	25	13	11

These are very considerable sums; 25 *l*. 13 *s*. an acre every year clear profit, from a crop that is kept perfectly clean by hand-hoeing, and which receives a digging of 11 *l*. an acre, is a degree of benefit that is uncommonly great, and should call on the possessors of extreme rich deep soils, to exert themselves in so profitable a culture. The rich black rotten mould of an old hop ground is undoubtedly the true soil for it; but Mr. *Crowe*'s trial on a much poorer land shews; that such a degree of fertility is not absolutely necessary. That madder is an article, which bids fair for yielding immense advantage, we may easily gather from the increase of the culture; 12 acres being planted last *Michaelmas*, and 30 more ready for this spring, shew this in the clearest manner. The publick is not a little indebted to this spirited active farmer, for introducing the culture in a country so well adapted to it.

Vol. III. page 59.

Mr. *Taylor* favoured me with a drawing of his drill plough; but it did not come in time for inserting the description in the proper place:

APPENDIX.

the following are the references given by the person who drew it.

A plan and elevation of a three drill plough, made in 1770.

No. 1. Is a side view, to an inch scale, and so are all the rest; what are marked W. is wood, and I. iron; P. I. plate iron. No. 2. Is the plan (or flat) of the beam, foot handles, with the shuttle through the beam, and irons screwed through the foot, for the use of letting out the side beams, A. No. 3. Is an intire iron frame to fix in the three drills; the frame takes asunder for the use of putting the drills nearer, as you want the beams, A. The iron, B, of which there are two, one at each side of the foot, fixed on to the foot, in No. 1. No. 4. Is the drill open, side-ways, in which you see the rollers on the end, where the axle goes through square, and a spring, pliable on a pin at top, and a screw at bottom, to screw tighter the spring occasionally; but the spring is no wider than the middle division in No. 5. The corn goes only in the middle division; (one of those two divisions, made of plate iron, has a hole cut for the roller to go free) then fix in the plate F, to No. 5, in which there is a square plate the width of the middle division, and to lay over the middle of the roller X, in No. 4. There are on each side plate irons fixed to keep the furrows open, which may be set wider as occasion requires. The carriage of this plough has a long axle, the wheels to let out in proportion to the drill, and the wheels only two feet high; but the fore and hind boxes are of a size, on account of the wheels being more steady when let out.

A. A. The roller at large, which is of wood, two inches diameter; the middle part is hollowed out for the corn, as you see in the circle, and a piece of thin iron between every hollow, because the wood should not break away; the two ends of the roller are hooped to the hollow.

a, in No. 2. a small iron bar across the handles, to which is fixed the chain B, to support the frame of the plough when it turns at the end of the field.

‡ This is only turned down to see the mortise in the frame.

Vol. III. page 107.

After the word *labourers*.

At *Ash*, near *Sandwich*, Mr. *Legrand* has tried some very important experiments on carrots, for an account of which I am much obliged to him; I received it by letter since my Tour through *Kent*.

Carrots, this gentleman observes, are certainly excellent food for all sorts of cattle. For their culture he chuses a sandy loam worth 20 *s*. an acre, a very kindly soil for all crops, and good enough for *Windsor* beans, having no respect to the preceding crop: gives it a clean earth, about eight or nine inches deep, as soon after *Michaelmas* as possible. About *Christmas*, taking advantage of a frost or dry weather, he carries out the manure, which is a compost of well rotted dung, with about two thirds of mould, at the rate in the whole of 80 cart loads *per* acre. The total expence of which is 3 *l*. This is ploughed

APPENDIX. 489

ploughed in the first opportunity, about half the depth of the first earth.

The latter end of *March*, or the beginning of *April*, he prepares for sowing, first working it with a large harrow with triangular plates, and the common tines alternately ranged (something like plate XXIII. fig. 2.) which operates as deep as the plough, and is sharp business for six able horses; then dressing the surface as fine as possible with the roller, and common harrow, he strikes the field into furrows, equally distant 11 inches asunder, with a light two chip'd plough; 5*lb.* an acre of seed are then sown, and covered by drawing the comb of the furrows in carefully with planting hoes.

Generally speaking, the weeds will first discover themselves, and to check them Mr. *Legrand* hand-hoes the intervals before the carrots appear, being guided in that operation by the ridge made by the planting hoes. As soon as the crop is seen, the plants must be carefully separated, the distance depending on the strength of the soil, &c.

In respect to taking them up, they are fit when the tops begin to turn yellow and lose their freshness. He chuses to clear the ground as soon after *Michaelmas* as he can conveniently. They are laid up in a barn or stacked, covering them with straw for preservation from the weather.

As to the quantity of the product, Mr. *Legrand* has generally found it to rise from 20 to 30 tons, which latter product he has gained, considerable as it may appear. This year, 1770, his best acre does not exceed 23 tons; but the crop in general is not nearly equal to what he has before had.

In the application of the crop, he has tried various sorts of cattle with them, particularly cows, sheep, swine, and horses. To four horses he allows a ton weekly, and he finds that they do to admiration on them; so well that they are very dainty with all other food. One year he fatted 60 porkers on them, weighing each 5 or 6 score; and they turned out as delicate meat as ever known at *Ash*. Geese and turkies will fatten very quickly on them. Much of this year's crop is applied to fatting wether sheep, 50 being kept on them regularly, that were bought in on purpose for a trial; 20 out of these 50 are confined to a grass close of two acres, where they have the carrots and good hay regularly given them twice a day. The 20 wethers weekly consume one ton of carrots, and 4 *C. wt.* of hay; and Mr. *Legrand* has found from experience, that they take 20 weeks to fat in. The sheep were bought in at 25 *s.* and will rise when fat to 45 *s.* In discovering the value, he has an easy method, which from experience he has found to be more exact than the nicest hand; it is to weigh them alive, and half that weight is the dead marketable weight. This is a very important fact, and particularly useful to *gentlemen* farmers: *Ellis* asserted it, but his authority has not been satisfactory. The account *per* acre, this gentleman calculates as follows, supposing it to yield but 20 tons.

Expences.

	£	s	d
Rent,	1	0	0
Tythe,	0	5	0
Poor rates,	0	2	6
First ploughing,	0	7	0
Carry over,	1	14	6

	£.	s.	d.
Brought over,	1	14	6
Second ploughing,	0	6	0
Heavy harrowing,	0	8	0
Light ditto and rolling,	0	3	6
Seed,	0	3	9
Sowing,	0	1	0
Drawing furrows,	0	1	6
Drawing in ditto,	0	2	0
Hoeings,	1	10	0
Digging up, and cutting off the tops, &c.	1	10	0
Stacking,	0	15	0
Manuring,	3	0	0
	9	15	3
Twenty sheep,	25	0	0
Four tons of hay,	6	0	0
Total,	40	15	3

Produce.

	£.	s.	d.
Twenty sheep, weighing 30 *lb.* a quarter, at 4 *d.* ½ *per lb.*	45	0	0
Improvement of the grass land,	3	0	0
Total,	48	0	0
Expences,	40	15	3
Clear profit,	7	4	9

Respecting the 3 *l.* charged as product in the improvement of the grass land, where the carrots are consumed, Mr. *Legrand* is extremely clear in the estimate being *low*.

He has had carrots two years successively on the same ground, the second crop better than the first,

APPENDIX

Observations.

That nothing is here exaggerated, I think is very plain, particularly from two circumstances; first, the lowest product is taken as the average; the crops, rising from 20 to 30 tons: and secondly, the whole price of the manuring being charged to the first crop of the course, whereas it ought certainly to be divided as long as the benefit remains, for instance three or four years; in which case that charge would be much lower. These circumstances considered, must be sufficient to convince one, that this estimate is extremely moderate.

Several very important conclusions are to be drawn from it: that carrots will repay very heavy expences with considerable profit, cannot from hence be doubted. Manuring 3*l*. Tillage 1*l*. 8*s*. Hoeing 1*l*. 10*s*. These are articles that are so advantageous to the land, that no persons can suppose the benefit exhausted by the carrots; they must be esteemed as a very noble preparation for succeeding crops, both by enriching, and cleaning.

The circumstance in the culture attending the sowing in drills, of hoeing the chief part of the ground before the carrots appear, deserves particular attention; in the broad-cast method, they generally appear in such a thicket of weeds, that the expence of the first hoeing is very great, amounting sometimes to more than all Mr. *Legrand*'s operations of that sort; the seed lies so long in the ground before it comes to the hoe, that the weeds have time to get a-head; great advantage in hoeing before the crop appears has been found in the culture of potatoes.

Mr. *Legrand*'s trials are in another point very important,

important, which is the deciding the value of a given weight of carrots.

	£	s	d
Product of 20 tons, exclusive of dung,	45	0	0
Deduct for sheep and hay,	31	0	0
Remains the value of the carrots,	14	0	0
This is *per* ton,	0	14	0
And *per* bushel, of 56 *lb*.	0	0	4

Upon this very low value I must however be allowed to remark, that it is decisive in only one application, that of fattening sheep with the assistance of hay: and from the extreme lowness of the value, I apprehend that other applications of the crop would prove far more profitable, particularly the fattening hogs, or that of oxen *stall fed, with* hay; it is a fact well known, and very commonly experienced in the case of turnips, that the crop pays not near the same value consumed abroad, as if the beast is stalled. Fattening an animal to an high degree, and as quick as possible, is certainly a very different affair from keeping him in health, air, and exercise; the latter may often be gained by partly sacrificing the former; fattening a boar for brawn, and Mr. *Moody*'s beasts almost suffocated with heat, but gaining flesh speedily, are I apprehend decisive instances of this.

For these reasons, this valuation of carrots paying no more than 4 *d*. a bushel, must not be taken in general, but merely in *fattening* sheep.

Mr.

Mr. *Legrand* has carried the products much higher than any other person in the kingdom: 30 tons are more by five than any one else has produced.

It is very material to know, that four horses will in proper feeding eat one ton *per* week; also that 20 large wethers will do the same with 4 *C. wt.* of hay.

It is likewise extremely clear, that carrots will fat porkers, and not a single accidental one or so, but so large a number as 60.

Upon the whole, Mr. *Legrand*'s account of this culture is perfectly satisfactory; the particulars are accurately noted, and curious; and though the *profit* is not so high as it has been carried, yet is it considerable, and may in different applications of the crop turn out much higher.

Vol. III. page 184.

The references to the turnrest plough are incomplete; the following supply the deficiencies.

From					Feet	Inches
1	to	2	—	8	Feet 2	Inches.
1	to	3	—	1		11
3	to	4	—	0		7½
5	to	6	—	4		4
7	to	8	—	0		4
8	to	9	—	1		1
9	to	10	—	2		4
10	to	11	—	0		8
11	to	12	—	1		6
11	to	14	—	1		9

Ground Plan.

From	1	to	2	—	2 F.	4 In. the fhare.
	1	to	3	—	1	5
	3	to	4	—	1	8
	4	to	5	—	1	2
	4	to	7	—	0	11¼ the heel.
	5	to	6	—	1	5

(15.) All this is fhare from (11) to the mark. .(16.) An iron fixed, rifing 3 inches from body of plough, and extending acrofs it 12 inches, forming a very flight fegment of a circle, 2 inches wide. The beam has a flit in it, through which it turns. (13) Is a fcrew that fixes it at any part of the fegment. The beam turns on the iron pin (3,) and may confequently be fixed by this fcrew. The fhare at (10) is 4 inches wide; the beam, 4 inches by 3, refts on a carriage; 7 to 6 in ground plan, the fame as 8 to 9 in the view.

Vol. III. page 243.

The references of plate XXV. fig. 2. are erroneous; for Mr. *Mitford* has been fo obliging as to fend me a more correct drawing of it.

A to B 3 feet 8 inches, A to C 5 feet, A to D 14 feet 6 inches, E an iron pivot, on which, and a correfponding one on the other fide, the machine turns. a a. Valves, which open on the infide. There is another valve at the bottom, clofe to the end A B.

The following are the references to plate XXV. fig. 3. from another drawing, with which that gentleman favoured me.

A. A rough frame fixt on the ground, which fteddies the pump.

B. The truſſel-tree, a ſquare frame of timber which moves round on the top of the great cylinder, H. From A to B 7 feet 6 inches.

C. The croſs-tree, a block of timber, to which the ladder G is fixt by pivots at c c.

D. The crank, which works the ſucker of the pump, by means of the iron rod I. The bend of the crank, meaſured perpendicularly from a to b, is 7 inches. From B to C is 2 feet 6 inches, C to D 4 feet 6 inches.

E. A ſemicircular iron which ſteddies the top of the loggerhead. There is ſuch another on the other ſide, but, to avoid confuſion, not expreſſed.

F. Four ſpokes, to which the vanes are fixt. The vanes are 11 feet 6 inches long by four broad, and, as well as the ſails, exactly like thoſe of a common windmill.

G. A ladder, 5 feet wide at bottom.

H. An elmen cylinder, 18 inches diameter at top. The other wood-work is oak.

To ſet the pump a working, a man takes the bottom of the ladder G from the ground, and with it eaſily turns the whole frame B E, called the loggerhead, ſo that the vanes may face the wind. To ſtop it, he in the ſame manner turns the vanes from the wind. Wherever the iron runs, as at K, it is in caſt braſs. The ſmall cylinder L is fixt to the great one H, and does not turn with the loggerhead.

The wind-pump is of that kind, called by the ſalternmen a clearing-mill, its uſe being to raiſe the brine, made by the ſun in the outworks, into a large wooden reſervoir, called a clearer, from whence it is let at pleaſure into the boiling-houſe. With a moderate wind, it

will

APPENDIX.   497

will difcharge twice the quantity of water that a common hand-pump will in the fame time.

It difcharges the water nearly at the top of the great cylinder H, into a pipe fixt clofe to that cylinder, which carries it down into the well again, and from thence under ground to under the clearer, into which the pipe rifes. It feemed needlefs to exprefs this pipe in the draught.

The other machine is called a laving-gun. Its ufe in the falterns is, where there cannot be a regular defcent from the feeding-pond through all the outworks, to raife the brine into thofe which lie nearest to the boiling-houfe. One man can with this cheap and fimple machine raife water fast enough to turn an over-fhot mill; but the work is violent, and requires two men to relieve one another. They have in fome of the great falterns near *Lymington*, wind-pumps, which they call drawing-mills, to ferve inftead of thefe laving-guns. Thefe are conftructed upon the fame principle with thofe above defcribed; but as they are required to raife the water but from 2 to 4 feet, inftead of 20 or upwards, their bore is from 12 to 15 inches diameter. It may be eafily conceived, that the difcharge of water by a pump of 15 inches bore, worked by any thing of a brifk wind, muft be very great. The faltern work requires no exactnefs in this particular, and therefore no exact calculations have been made of the power of thefe machines. The price of the wind-pumps is from 15l. to 22l. or 23l. according to the fort and fize.

In a letter I received lately from Mr. *Mitford*, concerning plantations, he writes me as follows on the growth of firs.

"There is one thing concerning fir trees, material to be known, and I believe fcarcely well known

known at present: and that is, to what size the different sorts will come in this country. As far as I can judge, by observing my own, I imagine the silver will grow to a greater height than the *Scotch*. A very flourishing silver fir was blown down last spring in my garden grove: it measured 50 feet 6 inches in length. The last year's shoot was 20 inches, and the four last years shoots together 6 feet 6 inches: this is at the rate of 16 feet in 10 years. There is scarcely any saying to what height a tree of that size, so flourishing, might not grow. I have many silver firs much taller than this, and which appear equally flourishing; but there is no measuring their upper shoots, or their exact length, as they stand."

Vol. III. page 303.

Since this work was written, an anonymous publication has appeared, entitled, *The Complete English Farmer*, 8vo. in which some expressions and calculations of mine, in my *Northern Tour*, are mentioned, as having been rather too free in suppositions of profit. The work has real merit; and therefore I am desirous, that writers of moderation, and apparently of practice, should not in these proportions think me chimerical. I am led into this observation by the following passage, page 137. " Fertile fields,
" loaded with corn, and giving food to nume-
" rous herds of cattle, ought, says the writer of
" the *Northern Tour*, to be the prospect in those
" tracts, not whins, fern, ling, and other trum-
" pery." "In proof of his opinion, he instances the little garden of the turnpike-keeper, in the road from *Bowes* to *Brough* in *Yorkshire*, which
is

APPENDIX. 499

is taken from the waste, and produces "excel-
"lent potatoes, good garden beans, and ad-
"mirable turnips." But from such little spots highly improved, it is not always safe to found an opinion of whole tracts. It is more reasonable to suppose, that if improvements were so easy on these immense heaths, as this writer imagines, they would not have been so long neglected. But the certain expence of building houses and barns, and other buildings, notwithstanding the almost incredible cheapness of buildings in that part of the country, and of inclosing and fencing, which is confessedly great, opposed to the uncertain event of improvements upon these wilds, ill watered, and worse roaded as they are, deters the land owners from hazarding their fortunes in projects of this kind, which Sir *Digby Legard* has candidly acknowledged to be much less profitable than the author of the *Northern Tour* would make us believe. I have myself made all the enquiry I could, concerning the supposed profit of the land owners on the wolds, or if you please, the extensive commons now inclosing on the *Broadway* hills, in *Gloucestershire*, &c. &c."

This writer is in general candid, and I am indebted to him for several genteel expressions, which I readily acknowledge; but I must on this passage remark, that through haste he has rather mistaken my meaning: my instancing the turnpike-keeper's garden was but as a small collateral proof of a fact, which wanted it not; for the appearance of the soil was enough without it; and I am since informed, that the proprietors have at last thought the same; for they are now engaged in procuring an act for the inclosure, having been for several large tracts offered

APPENDIX

15 s. an acre. This is information received in conversation; but I can readily assure this author, that the soil is richly worth it.

But he makes me give this as an instance of the immense heaths in general; whereas it was of that tract in particular; surely Mr. *Scrcop*'s improvements, Mr. *Danby*'s, and those by the fall of *Tees*, would have been more to the purpose, being facts really executed that *have* answered, in the degree I mention.

As to the heaths not remaining waste, if it would answer to cultivate them; I reply that all the modern improvements in the *North* speak the contrary: why were they not done before? Mr. *Elliot* of *Fremington*'s *Improvement* (vol. II. p. 192.) pays some hundreds *per cent.* and yet none of his neighbours follow his example. The whole range of husbandry improvements are but one aggregate proof of the sleepy folly, or term it prudence, if you will, of mankind. A thing not being universally done, a proof that it cannot be done: this is now the reasoning of those farmers, who will not hoe their turnips, nor sow clover, because their grandfathers did not.

But here are other circumstances, which convince me this author confounds all wastes together, *ill watered*, and *worse roaded:* I never yet viewed *a moor* without plenty of streams, and do not recollect any tracts upon the whole better, if so well watered. As to roads, some are bad enough; but as many on turnpikes, and admirable ones too. In that Tour I travelled, I suppose, an hundred miles on excellent roads, through the uncultivated moors I speak of.

But Sir *Digby Legard*.—Here again the writer jumbles two soils together; Sir *Digby Legard*'s

APPENDIX. 501

is *wold* land, which is as different from *moors*, as light from darkness: that gentleman cannot candidly acknowledge any such matter: for throughout the *Northern Tour* I give no calculations of that soil, which is a thin loam on lime stone or grit-stone; but the better part of the moors are deep black soils, or sandy loams; some sandy gravels, which are bad; but the chief is the black peat soil, which I will venture to aver to be as good land *for grass* as any in *England*. The *Broadway* hills resemble the wolds, though not exactly; but the same reasoning must never be applied to these as to moors. *

---

* This writer, at page 242, says, speaking of my *Course of Experimental* AGRICULTURE, " but I own " I do not understand his calculations, as the ex- " pences throughout are, in my opinion, much un- " der rated."

What the author can mean by this, I cannot well conceive. A critic has founded no small abuse on that work, from the *height* of the expences: so little possible is it to please every one. The writer of the *Complete* ENGLISH FARMER, I apprehend, means the expences of tillage; but, if he will take the trouble to turn to the respective chapters of *Expences of Tillage*, *General Expences of Horses*, &c. he will surely find, that I charge the expences, not by way of *calculations*, but what they in reality came to.

I may observe, that all the writers on husbandry give the nominal price of hiring ploughs, &c. in their experiments; and I believe I am the first that has attempted to ascertain the real amount. Let the author of this work register but one fair experiment in debtor and creditor, and I will venture to shew, that he cannot be accurate, unless he knows what his team costs him.

A farmer says, The expence of ploughing an acre of land is 10 s. Why is it 10 s. ? Why is it not 20 s. ?

Vol. III. page 413.

Another course;
1. Turnips,
2. Wheat,
3. Barley,
4. Clover.

Ditto on sand land, at *West Buckland*, near *Wellington*.
1. Turnips.
2. Wheat and eddish turnips.
3. Barley.
4. Clover one or two years.

Ditto on clay.
1. Fallow.
2. Wheat.
3. Barley or oats.
4. Clover, one or two years. If one,
5. Wheat. If two years,
5. Fallow.
6. Wheat; they reckon two years clover leaves the ground too firm for wheat on one earth.

Why is it not 5 s.? He knows nothing of the matter. Suppose you keep ten horses, which in oats, hay, chaff, straw, farrier, and decline of value, cost you 200 *l*. Suppose these horses in a year plough you 800 acres, is it not very plain, that this part of tillage costs you 5 s. an acre? Now to this is to be added the expence of the ploughs, man, (and driver, if one is used) and the wear and tear of plough and harness, divided in like manner; and the total of all is the expence *per* acre of ploughing. If this author has a clearer way of coming at the truth, let him declare and explain it; for, as to the common hiring price, as well might the price in the moon be taken. A farmer, who buys or grows oats at 16 s. a quarter, hay at 30 s. a load, who goes through the year without loss in horse-flesh, and never sees the face of the farrier, tells me

APPENDIX.

About *Curry Mallot*, on lime stone in the inclosures.
1. Fallow, ploughed with six or eight oxen.
2. Wheat.
3. Pease or oats.
4. If the latter, clover.

In the open field;
1. Fallow,
2. Wheat,
3. Pease or oats.

Vol. III. page 481.

January 18th, 1771, Mr. *Anderdon* weighed square perches of brown boorcole, *Scotch* cabbage, and turnips, for comparison.

	T.	C.	Q.	lb.
Boorcole, 34 plants weighed 3 quarters 5 *lb*. or *per* acre,	6	7	0	16
Scotch cabbage, 34 plants 3 quarters 12¼ *lb*. or *per* acre,	6	17	3	0
Turnips, 64 plants, 1 C. *wt.* 1 quarter 24 *lb*. or *per* acre,	11	14	0	0

All planted in *July*.

---

me his expence of ploughing is 10*s*. an acre. Another year, in which oats are 20*s*. hay 50*s*. the farrier's bill long, and two horses dead, I ask him the same question, and still the answer is 10*s*. Now is it possible, that the same price can be true in both? If it is said, that he takes 10*s*. as an average, I reply, then it is a conjectural average of conjectural sums, for the truth of not one is known.

For this reason I should not be discredited, because I give not the prices of the country, since in rejecting them I adhere to plain facts; but in part of *Suffolk*, and all *Norfolk*, the price of ploughing is below my rates,

Mr. *Anderdon* has further favoured me with the following account of his most approved method of making cyder.

"I should first tell you my orchards are on a clay, which circumstance, I think, conduces much to the strength and goodness of the liquor. I will be short in my practical account, making but few observations, and leave the curious to draw speculative reflections from it.

"I permit my fruit to remain on the trees till a great part of them fall by ripeness, then gently shaking the trees, take in the apples in dry weather, laying them in heaps, of equal ripeness, in a loft over the press. There they remain till they have perspired, and that perspiration ceases. As soon as convenient afterwards, I press out the juice. If it casts a pale colour, as the cackagee will, which is one of our best juices, I permit the pulp, after it has passed the mill, to remain in vats, trendles, or other convenient open receptacles, for about twenty four hours, which will heighten the colour of the juice. As soon as expressed, I pour it into vats through a sieve, or range, with high sides or hoops, where it remains about two days and a night, according to the nature of the apple, and the state of the weather, (the longest when a frost) till a thick head or scum rises on it; then I draw off a little

---

rates, though I lost not one horse, and had no expensive accidents, or decline in value.

This author appears a man of real knowledge, and no less candor; I therefore offer this note merely to undeceive him in a point, in which I apprehend he mistakes the ground, on which I state my expences.

little in a glafs, to fee if it is fine, and as foon as I catch it fo, I fail not without delay, to draw it off into other open receptacles, if I have them, if not into hogfheads, or other clofe ones. If the juice be put from the wring into veffels wider at top than bottom, and I draw it off as foon as fine, I need not take off the head firft; as in going downward it will not, in that cafe, break, and mix with the body of the liquor ; but if my veffels, in which it is, are of a different conftruction, or I have not been attentive to draw it off in the critical hour, I find I do better, before I begin to draw, to take off the head with a wooden fkimmer, and throw it away, and then fpeedily draw off the cyder. Whenever I find the brown head begins to open in the middle, or elfewhere, and a whitenefs appear at the opening, I am pretty certain it is high time to be bufy in drawing off. But I find from experience the fureft token is, to obferve its ftate by what is drawn off in a glafs, which is to be done by the help of a peg placed at a proper diftance from the bottom of the vat, and this method of obfervation fhould be clofely attended to ; for fince I had the pleafure of feeing you at *Henlade*, I have drawn a glafs of cyder out of a vat at eight o'clock foul, another at ten fine, almoft candlebright, without any appearance of the head's opening, as above obferved; at eleven, it was growing cloudy apace, without high winds, or any extraordinary event, as I could perceive, to occafion it ; and I found it abfolutely neceffary, not to lofe a moment in drawing it off. If then drawn off into other open veffels, a frefh head may arife in twenty four hours, or thereabouts, when it may be rackt into a clofe hogfhead, or other receiver, where it will begin to

ferment

ferment after a day or two, according to the weather, the nature of the fruit, and other circumstances. I then permit it to ferment four or five days generally, never exceeding a week for the hardest fruit, such as royal wildings, or cackagees. Then I fumigate a clean, sweet hogshead, or other close vessel, with a match or two made of coarse cloth, dipped into melted stone brimstone, and rack the cyder into it, as speedily as possible, racking it again in the same manner as often as it ferments, till I catch it very fine, when another such racking often turns out the final one. I cover the bung with a tile, or piece of thin wood only, during the season of racking; and when I put a bung cork into the hole in the spring, I leave a peg-hole open just by it. The fœces through the whole process are constantly removed.

I never seek to raise frequent fermentations, and often complete the business by two or three rackings; but have had very good cyder, which has been so prone to ferment, that I have been obliged to stop it by racking into fumigated vessels, ten and even upwards of a dozen times.

Many other, probably much better methods of stopping the fermentation, and bringing the cyder fine, I have heard of; but these are what I have in general hitherto used, and have the satisfaction of finding my cyder as good as most I meet with elsewhere; and though I am far from thinking my management unimprovable, I will answer for its turning out very well to those, who, being unacquainted with a better method, will attend to this,"

ADDENDA.

SINCE this work was printed off, I have read the minute of an experiment in Dr. *Hunter's Georgical Essays*, on fattening hogs with carrots. By *J. S. Morrit*, Esq.

In the preceding pages are several experiments on this use of carrots, which I apprehend will sufficiently clear me from any imputation of being so much prejudiced in their favour, as to publish successful experiments, and suppress unsuccessful ones; they will shew also, that I am not at all singular in the fact, that carrots will fatten hogs.

Mr. *Morrit*, rather angry I apprehend at being led into a losing trial by my book, gives his experiment as a commentary on one of mine; and from it ventures the bold assertion, *that carrots alone are of* NO VALUE *for fattening hogs*.

As I have (what I think) a very clear idea of the importance of carrots thus applied, it is necessary in my own defence, but more so in defence of a crop misrepresented, to make a few observations on that gentleman's experiment; from the particulars, he may look to other causes of his loss than the worthlessness of carrots.

Mr.

Mr. *Morrit* bought in 12 hogs, that weighed 177 ſtone 4 *lb*. (14 *lb*. *per* ſtone) which is more than 14 ſtone each. The 26th of *October* were put to fatting on boiled carrots. The 28th of *December* they were fat!

So hogs of 14 ſtone (14 *lb*.) will fatten on boiled carrots in two months. Such food being repreſented as worthleſs, is rather a contradiction. In Mr. *Burke*'s experiments, he could not get a hog to fatten on them at all; but Mr. *Morrit* does not hint ſuch an idea.

This gentleman condemns carrots, becauſe they were not profitable to him in the application of fattening hogs: will he condemn beans for the ſame reaſon? They are uſed in common throughout the kingdom: I beg leave to anſwer, that Mr. *Morrit* does not condemn them; but he moſt undoubtedly ought by the plain evidence of his own trial. Who would give 6 *l*. worth of bean meal to hogs for *no return?*

Twenty eight pounds worth of carrots are given to 12 hogs, the reſult, loſs: carrots are therefore condemned.

Six pounds worth of beans are given to 12 hogs; the reſult, loſs. Why not condemn the beans?

	£.	s.	d.
Prime coſt of 12 hogs,	22	9	6
Bean meal,	6	0	0
Total,	28	9	6
Hogs ſold for,	27	10	0
Loſs,	0	19	6

And theſe hogs *fatted* in two months on 574 buſhels of carrots beſides.

Mr.

Mr. *Morrit* adds 3 *l.* 12 *s.* for expence, and then strikes the balance, loss 4 *l.* 11 *s.* Now if this account proves any thing, surely it proves, that a man should not accept, gratis, 574 bushels of carrots, which in the same trial are proved to have the fattening quality. Is not this proving too much? Mr. *Morrit*'s conclusion that carrots are of no use in fatting hogs, might surely have been given to the beans with equal propriety.

The case is, Mr. *Morrit* is a man of fortune, who, it may be presumed, gives his orders, and leaves the execution to his servants: if they understood the attendance on fatting hogs no better than selling them, the mystery may be easily unravelled.

	Stone.
They produced in dry bacon,	104
Wasted in drying,	70
Total, profitable pork,	174

	£.	s.	d.
This was sold for, cheeks excluded,	26	0	0
Which is *per* stone,	0	2	11
And *per lb.*	0	0	2¼

So carrots are to be depreciated, because a gentleman chuses to give away his pork at 2¼ *d.* a pound.

But we are told, the excellence of the quality made up in some degree for the loss of weight. Note, it was sold dry at 4 *d. per lb.* which is under the price of common pork without any drying at all.

ADDENDA.

But what if I should attempt to persuade this gentleman, that he has so utterly mistaken the matter, that carrots are not only a good and profitable food for fattening hogs, but that they even proved so to him, and in the very experiment, from which he positively deduces the contrary, even in this trial, conducted by servants, who evidently were ignorant of the business:—and yet it will not be a difficult task. Two acres produced 20 tons, which at

	£	s.	d.
56 *lb.* are bushels, — — 800			
They cost, — —	8	13	0
Which is *per* bushel, —	0	0	$2\frac{1}{2}$
We find that the hogs weighed when fat 174 stone, this at 5s.* a stone is	43	10	0
Cheeks, — — —	1	10	0
Total, — —	45	0	0
Prime cost, beans and attendance,	32	1	0
Remains for carrots, —	12	19	0
574 bushels, coming to that sum, are *per* bushel, — —	0	0	$5\frac{1}{2}$
They cost, — —	0	0	$2\frac{1}{2}$
Clear profit on the carrots, besides the dung, — —	0	0	3
Clear profit *per* acre, —	5	0	0

* I think 5s. a stone, a fair price. In *Hertfordshire* we sell (not for the *London* market) at 5s. 6d. and 5s. 10d.; for if the whole hog is bought, the offal quarter is a great advantage to the buyer; I should not suppose the price at *York* in 1769-70, less than 5s.

This advantage is gained on hogs bought in very dear, for so I will venture to assert 1 *l*. 17 *s*. a head to be for Mr. *Morrit*'s; and under other disadvantages, besides the land producing but half a crop. Now if this does not prove carrots for fattening hogs to be a most important article of husbandry, I confess myself totally ignorant of the matter; and readily subscribe to the positive assertion (drawn from the experiment in question) that " carrots alone are of no " value for fattening hogs;" an assertion rather too hasty.

* * *
* *
*

I am rather unfortunate in the criticisms and observations that have been made on my works; as I have now replied to a gentleman who forms an unjust idea of my trials, from mistaken experience of his own, I shall take the same opportunity of answering a criticism which never was the effect of any experience, unless that of propagating scandal.

To let the world know in what manner books are reviewed by professed critics, I beg leave slightly to examine the remarks of the Monthly Reviewers on my *Course of Experimental Agriculture*, which will be sufficient to shew, that while a man employs his time, money, attention, health, and strength, in what he thinks the service of his country; while he endeavours by every method in his power to do what good he is able in an humble sphere, still there are men who will take equal pains to render his aims ridiculous, to laugh at his employment, and to endeavour with all their might to counteract his purposes, by persuading

perſuading their readers that his works are worthleſs and his views mere profit.

The Reviewers have criticiſed about a fifteenth part of the above-mentioned work, but they have done enough for me to make two aſſertions. *Firſt*, That they know nothing of huſbandry. *Second*, That they are quite uncandid. Here follows the proof.

1. They condemn my obſervations on *Blythe*'s crops of oats worth 6*l.* an acre on land abſolutely good for nothing; and add, *Such ground* frequently yields ſuch quantities of oats *at the firſt crop, if pared and burned*; that is, 6 *quarters*, at 20 *s.* a quarter.

I will not aſſert that oats never were ſown the firſt crop on pared and burnt land, but I will venture to aſſert, that the man who could quote ſuch management, cannot know his right hand from his left in farming; to get that work done early enough for ſowing oats with expectation of a great crop, it muſt be performed in the froſts and ſnows of winter. They ſhould have known that turnips are the crops for pared and burnt lands.—Nor do I think they will find that oats were 20 *s.* a quarter in *Blythe*'s time.

2. They explain *Adam Speed*'s nonſenſe of making 2000 *l.* a year by rabbits, by telling us, it muſt be *by the dung moſt likely.*——Two thouſand pounds a year profit by rabbit dung, which in theſe days that manures ſell at four times their former price, is had at 1 *s.* 2 *d.* a ſack! This truly is *agriculture de cabinet!*

3. I condemn *Bradley* for ſaying, in general, that no dung ſhould be uſed till it is like earth, and that the dung of pigeons and poultry ſhould be ſteeped in water; upon this they ſay, *there are*

ADDENDA.

are many *skilful farmers who will think the same*; *though we* PERHAPS *hold neither of these opinions.* Would they not be more explicit if they had an opinion?

4. They condemn me for drawing an average of the expences of all the experiments on wheat in the common method, because such expences are various. *How different acreable expences*, say they, *are* 5*l.* 10*s.* 10*d.* and 2*l.* 0*s.* 4*d.* ¼! *Is it not most evident, that in real regular culture upon one regular plan, there can never be such a difference in expences, and that therefore the knowledge of this average is absolutely of* NO USE?

I do not understand what *real regular culture upon one regular plan* is, and I will venture to assert that there is no such monster of regularity in the kingdom. Practical farmers will laugh at such regular plans as exclude great variations in the expences. Nothing but total ignorance of the subject could have produced this assertion. The wheat in one round of a course is manured; in another unmanured: turnips, in one round, manured with purchased dung; in another with yard dung: in one round carted off; in another fed on the land: wheat in one round sown on clover; in another on a fallow with two years rent and expences: clover fed in one round; in another mown once for hay and once for seed: What great variations in the expences are here in common crops, and in common hands: a difference of 5*l.* an acre will often be found among common farmers.

I ask such to inform me of the average of their expences. Who but these Reviewers will assert that such an average is useless, because the sums from which it is drawn are various? It will be no difficult task to shew that there would be something in it besides *mere amusement.*

I think these instances are sufficient to shew the knowledge on which these people found their abusive criticisms.

II. They are uncandid. Can I give a better proof than shewing that they praise me one month for what they abuse me the next?

1. At page 167, they say, *We entirely approve Mr. Young's stating the* REAL, *not* NATIONAL *prices of the products; especially as we believe that the latter can scarce possibly be stated with accuracy.*

But now turn to p. 306, and there you will find the matter quite changed. These are their words. *Mr. Young states what he calls the prices of the products in the five years under question, and makes the average price* 1 l. 18 s. 2 d.; *but surely to this average many objections may justly be made. In order to make an average useful, it* SHOULD BE GENERAL. *Our reader wishes to know what is the average price of wheat for five years, that is, what is the medium price of corn, neither* VERY GOOD *nor* VERY BAD, *in those years, upon the whole. Mr. Young's experiments produce some very bad corn, which sells for* 10 s. 6 d. per *quarter, when corn in general sells for a good price. Now it is most evident that this point must alone make a great lowering of the price of the year* 1763, *and consequently of the average price of the five years. We could give other instances; but this suffices.*

Relative to this utter want of candor, nothing more is necessary than to bring these curious passages face to face; but the latter is a fresh proof of the extreme ignorance of these people who pretend to criticise others.

I give

ADDENDA.

I give averages of the expences, products, profit and loss, and prices of the products. Now is it not sufficiently clear that the quality of the corn, that is, *the price of it*, depends on the culture. Insufficient tillage, or improper manure, produces bad corn that sells below the market price; of what use to reject the real value, in order to use the national, or the market average? It would lead to nothing but error and falshood. One part of the experiment, the quality of the corn, is regulated by another part, the culture; change this connection, and what good will attend your trial?

I draw an average price of the wheat produced by a given average of expence and other circumstances; the one is regulated by the other; what would national prices have to do here, any more than prices in the moon! Those who want the average of our markets, should turn to national accounts, not expect them in particular ones. Where therefore is the use of that wise remark, *In order to make an average useful it should be general*; as if the average of the nation, or even that of the county, had any thing to do with the experiments minuted!

2. In the Review for *February*, they say, *Mr. Young now proceeds to remarks on the chief writers on agriculture; a review of his account of whom will make a very agreeable part of our task, and we hope prove no less so to our readers.* From hence it was expected that the account given of those writers would have met with approbation, as these critics have more than once pretended that *the agreeable part of their task* is to *praise*, not *condemn*. But this case is changed too; for in the Review for *March* they give 10 pages on my account of

authors, of which nine and three quarters are filled with abusing me. A more illiberal criticism is not to be found in the whole range of their dirty annals.

3. In the article *Beati*, I remark that he mentions rape crops, which, he says, *cannot produce less than five or six quarters an acre.* I put the word *cannot* in italics, to mark the exaggeration of *fact* not *language*. But th' Reviewers add, *We are sorry to be thus obliged to review Mr. Y. as a critic in stile*. The truth is, they were very *glad* of this miserable opportunity for a field to exert those good-natured talents which husbandry did not offer so well.

4. I give the following character of a writer. "*Mortimer*, in one respect, is by no means a bad writer; he is every where practical, never hunts after new ideas, and had no vanity of shining as the founder of a system, or as an author; he pretends to no more than collecting and methodizing the commonly received ideas of good husbandry; and this he executed in a plain and judicious manner." — One would apprehend this passage as unexceptionable as could have fallen from the pen of any writer: but see the candor of verbal criticism; they change the words " as the founder of a system," to the barbarous term, *as a systematiser*, which they print in italics to make it appear a creature of mine; and immediately add, *As Mr. Y. has assumed to be the critic in language, we must conclude,* &c. No wonder they wanted me so much in the character of a *critic*, while they make such woeful work with that of a *farmer!*

5. They say, *Before we can reasonably depend on an* EXPERIMENTER, *we must know the* MAN *as well as his* NAME, &c. *Till we are acquainted with*

ADDENDA.

with his UNDERSTANDING, ATTENTION, *and even* TEMPER *and* PRINCIPLES, *we can form no juſt idea of the credit to be given to his experiments.*

This paſſage is thrown in merely to inſinuate that *myſelf, temper, principles,* &c. are ſuch as deſtroy my credit. If it means any thing it muſt be this; for as to their proof of my credibility, it is very clear, the paſſage was not written with that view. Now theſe circumſtances operate as ſtrongly in one experiment or obſervation, as in another. The Reviewers in general attempt to ſhew that my experiments are uſeleſs, but ſome they admit to be uſeful. Why are they three or four months examining experiments, if the *temper*, &c. of the experimenter decide their merit? Pray how can one be bad, and the other good, if the principles of the man are the guide for judging? But the aſſertion is ſuch arrant ſtuff, that nothing but ignorance could propagate it. May we take the negative of the inſinuation, and conclude that if a *man*, his *temper, underſtanding, principles,* and ſo on, be as the Reviewers would wiſh, that *therefore* we ſhould give credit to his experiments? Not the leaſt. I could name the experiments of ſome writers now living, of whom I have in all thoſe particulars the greateſt opinion, and yet I think their experiments uſeleſs. Foreigners agree in their character of *M. de Chateauvieux*; and yet what farmer will be guided by his trials?

On the contrary, who will aſſert that a man cannot be a knave and villain, and yet the publiſher of uſeful and credible experiments? — But in all this nonſenſe, the Reviewers muſt certainly have ſacrificed their common ſenſe to their prejudice.

I ſhall conclude theſe remarks with obſerving, that although theſe critics *cannot comfort me with an aſſurance that the candid publick will accept an apology for the imperfection of experiments*, yet I shall continue in my opinion that the publication of such experiments as I have ventured to lay before the public, may be useful though imperfect. These people have, in several instances, literally abused me for *my own expression of imperfection*, witness the present case, and my terming my work an *imperfect sketch:* their own ignorance cannot find out the imperfection, but their want of candor is too great to let them own, that in my expressions of my own want of merit, lies all their ability of discovering that want.

But let them point out experiments more satisfactory than mine; while they are indulging their malignancy, let them name a book of agriculture, or a set of experiments more useful than mine; such I am very clear are to be found; let these Reviewers give their author, and their reasons for their opinion; I will presently undertake to shew the world, that others will be praised for what they condemn in me, and probably condemned, for what they praise in me.

Their opinion, at page 307, is not a bad instance, where they assure their readers that I am both *ingenuous* and *useful* for observations which are void of merit, but of that common place sort, which however, if the trial opens to, one must not pass over. I refer the reader to their observations, 9, 10, 11. The truth is, that however expert they may be in expressing some abuse, and insinuating more, yet it will ever be (in husbandry) where the author least deserves it; as they are sure to praise where he merits condemnation, or at least neglect.

Did any person who first convinced the world that he really practised and understood husbandry,

ADDENDA.

publish criticisms on my works, and point out my errors, I should hold myself indebted to him; but as to such accounts as these of the Monthly Reviewers, I will venture to assert they are as opposite to the genius of true criticism, or the spirit of candid enquiry, as the husbandry of an *Arbuthnot* is different from that of *the many skilful farmers* quoted in the Review. Let them shew as much knowledge of the subject, as appeared in 1755 in the review of the *Complete Body of Husbandry*, and *Aaron Hill*'s *New System of Agriculture*, and I will pay due attention to their opinions.

They have made but small advance in their criticism: I expect in future every exertion of petulant malice;———(for nothing but that of some secret enemy could have given rise to such injurious reflections as I have met with in their criticisms.) I expect an hundred miserable * remarks on petty circumstances, with a total neglect of those that are important. They will go through a criticism of 2000 trials, without going to the bottom of the *husbandry* of a single one; without analizing any piece of management sufficiently to convince their readers that they really understand farming; the most they will

---

* Such as at page 305, where they say, *Certainly 2 l. 8 s. is substituted for* 12 s. Certainly no such thing, Mr. Reviewer.—And page 306, Wheat sold at 10 s. 6 d. a quarter; this is another error; it was a guinea. And page 231, where they refer to an *anonymous*, but *excellent* contributor to the *Museum Rusticum*, for an account of the ancient *English* writers *De Re Rustica*, speaking of that letter as *an original*; when had they been pleased to have READ Mr. *Harte*'s *Essays on Husbandry* before they REVIEWED them, these accurate gentlemen would have found the letter they praise so much, mere extract from that work.

will dare beyond that line of criticism, which may as well be executed by one totally ignorant of agriculture, as by one skilled ever so well in it, is some such wise remarks as on Mr. *Weston*'s manures (p. 300.) " *We know* BY EXPERI-ENCE *that coal ashes will bring up the white as well as, or better than the red clover on some clays.*" This is a great exertion of their *experience* ; and yet I should be glad to know where they found that coal ashes brought the *red* clover ; and what *clays* are to be named for an effect in the *white*, which is common to *all* soils.—Such criticisms I look for. I expect all this, and I shall be well satisfied with all, provided they do not change their note, and give me that damnation in their praise, which their censures will never convey. *

---

* An honest linen-draper in the environs of *Newgate*, by name, *Joseph Wimpey*, run mad on account of the price of Bread, informs his readers very gravely, in a visionary pamphlet he published, that I live in a garret in *Field Lane*, and quotes the Monthly Review, chap. and verse, for his authority. Now the Reviewers are certainly such respectable gentlemen, that they have an undoubted right to pronounce a man the author of a book he never saw—and dub him a garretteer in a lane he never heard of. The progress of the criticism is droll enough ; and would make one believe that the linen-draper and the Reviewer are one and the same person ; for in the account given of the pamphlet, the Monthly critic requotes much of the abuse, *living by one's wits*, &c. &c. without any disapprobation, and gravely adds, that this poor harmless being *lays about him very severely* ; intimating that he is a most redoubted champion ; and in another place, the Reviewer says, he *shall leave the champions to fight it out.* But I beg to be excused from battles in which victory is unattended by honour. I thought the first pamphlet might impose on weak minds, and therefore refuted it ; in the *second*, the author is run *stark staring mad*, it is therefore the best antidote to the folly of the first ;

ADDENDA.
Vol. III. page 320.

Since the preceding papers have been printed, Mr. *Mawde* advises me by letter, that his potatoes yielded 296 bushels the acre.

The spot of ground under cabbages measures one acre and three quarters, wanting 4 perches. Many of them weighed 25 *lb.* some few more; but the average about 17 *lb.* As they were planted in squares of three feet, an acre of course yielded 36 tons 14 *C. wt.* Suppose we allow the odd weight for vacancies, 36 would then be the profitable crop. *Nov.* 23, they were began to be drawn, and given to two large milch cows in a close: the milk had no bad taste, and they improved in their flesh very much. *Dec.* 15, sixteen wethers were put to the cows. The 22d, two heifers of two years old and two calves. The 28th, seven cows more. All which stock continued on them until the 22d of *February:* with the cabbages they had a little hay given them every morning. The outside leaves were all given to pigs.

The account of the whole as follows.

Nov. 23. Two cows, 13 weeks, at 2 *s.* 6 *d.*	£. 3	5	0
Dec. 15. Sixteen wethers, 10 weeks, at 4 *d.*	2	13	4
Dec. 22. Two heifers, 9 weeks, at 1 *s.*	0	18	0
Two calves ditto, 6 *d.*	0	9	0
Dec. 28. Seven cows, at 2 *s.* 8 weeks,	5	4	0
Total,	12	9	4

Which is *per* acre 7 *l.* 2 *s.* 4 *d.* and as they produced 36 tons and a half, it is about 4 *s.* a ton.

ADDENDA.

Sixteen acres of turnips well hoed and very fine, kept 126 wethers from *Martinmas* to the 23d of *March*; also 120 from *January* 16 to *March* 23.

	£. s. d.
126 Wethers, 18 weeks, at 4*d*.	18 18 0
120 Ditto, 8 weeks, -	16 0 0
Total, -	34 18 0
Which is *per* acre, -	2 3 7

A View

ADDENDA.

A View of the DIMENSIONS of the SEATS of the NOBILITY, &c. throughout this TOUR.

ROOMS	Stow Len.	Stow Bre.	Radburn Len.	Radburn Bre.	Fornark Len.	Fornark Bre.	Keddleston Len.	Keddleston Bre.	Chatsworth Len.	Chatsworth Bre.	Wolterton Len.	Wolterton Bre.	Blickling Len.	Blickling Bre.	Crictoth Len.	Crictoth Bre.	Eaftbury Len.	Eaftbury Bre.	Came Len.	Came Bre.	Enmore Len.	Enmore Bre.
Hall,	36	26	37	30	52	26	67‖	42	60	27	30	27			30‡	30	60*	30	29	20	40	28
Ditto,	36	22	35	23	30	21	42†	42†							33	22						
Saloon,	36	25	25	20	30	20	36	24	50	30	36	30		26					34	24	44	30
Dining Room,	43	25	25	20	28	20	30	20	30	20			45	24	36§	24	26	22	30	20	41	22
Ditto,	30	25	22	20	21	21	44	§28	36	30	25	21	24		45‖	30	21	21	24	23	25	19
Drawing Room,																						
Ditto,					34	21																
Gallery,	70†	25	20	20	20	20	36	24	100	22			120	22	36‡	29			27	17	66	22
Library,			25	20	20	20	24	24													46	19
Mufic Room,	35	30	22	20	20	21	24	18			21	21	33	21	30	18	25	22	19	17		
Dreffing Room,							24	18			21	21	21	21	30	16			19	17		
D.tto,													25	21					22	14		
Ditto,													25	21								
Bed-Chamber,	50	25	12	15	20	20	30	22	22		25	22	27	21			30	25	29	16		
Ditto,							13	18	30		22	22	25	16					22	20		
Ditto,							22	18					27	22								
Anti-Room,					12	10	24	12	18				25	24	24	30						
Ditto,							18	18							24	20						
Ditto,							14	18														
Wardrobe,							22	18							28	22			21	19		
Breakfaft Room,																						
	336	203	178	326	148	256	436	160	445	773	328	294	476	181	210	394	184	429	692	263	323	574	251	263	431	168	165	268	123	470	303	773
	539																					

† And 22 high. ‖ And 40 high. § Twenty-eight ditto.
‡ A circle 54 feet high to the top of the dome, and 34 to the cornice.
†‡ And 25 high. ‡‖ And 20 high. ‡‡ Twenty high.
§‖ Eighteen high. * And 30 high.

F I N I S.

ADVERTISEMENT.

AS I have been mentioned in several periodical publications and newspapers, as the author of books which I never wrote: I desire leave to inform the public that I prefix my name to all my works, and therefore am not answerable for any anonymous ones.

ARTHUR YOUNG.

www.ingramcontent.com/pod-product-compliance
Lightning Source LLC
Chambersburg PA
CBHW031947290426
44108CB00011B/705